Likeable
BADASS

Likeable BADASS

HOW WOMEN GET THE SUCCESS THEY DESERVE

Alison Fragale, PhD

DOUBLEDAY
New York

Copyright © 2024 by Alison Fragale
Penguin Random House values and supports copyright.
Copyright fuels creativity, encourages diverse voices, promotes free speech, and creates a vibrant culture. Thank you for buying an authorized edition of this book and for complying with copyright laws by not reproducing, scanning, or distributing any part of it in any form without permission. You are supporting writers and allowing Penguin Random House to continue to publish books for every reader. Please note that no part of this book may be used or reproduced in any manner for the purpose of training artificial intelligence technologies or systems.

All rights reserved. Published in the United States by Doubleday, a division of Penguin Random House LLC, New York, and distributed in Canada by Penguin Random House Canada Limited, Toronto.

www.doubleday.com

DOUBLEDAY and the portrayal of an anchor with a dolphin are registered trademarks of Penguin Random House LLC.

Book design by Cassandra J. Pappas
Jacket design by Emily Mahon

Library of Congress Cataloging-in-Publication Data
Names: Fragale, Alison, author.
Title: Likeable badass : how women get the success they deserve / Alison Fragale.
Description: First edition. | New York : Doubleday, [2024] | Includes bibliographical references and index.
Identifiers: LCCN 2024003443 (print) | LCCN 2024003444 (ebook) | ISBN 9780385549141 (hardcover) | ISBN 9780385549172 (ebook)
Subjects: LCSH: Women—Vocational guidance. | Career development. | Work-life balance. | Success in business.
Classification: LCC HF5382.6 .F73 2024 (print) | LCC HF5382.6 (ebook) | DDC 650.1082—dc23/eng/20240131
LC record available at https://lccn.loc.gov/2024003443
LC ebook record available at https://lccn.loc.gov/2024003444

MANUFACTURED IN THE UNITED STATES OF AMERICA

First Edition

*For my family, Team P.A.J.A.M.A.
Thanks for making life a "Party."*

likeable badass:
[lī-kə-bəl bAd-as] **noun**

A person who gets credit for their greatness, consistently perceived by others as Assertive *and* Warm.

"Her superpower was being a likeable badass."

Contents

PART I ★ Understand the Game

1. Ladies, We Have a Status Problem — 3
2. The Likeable Badass Solution — 19
3. Get Your Head in the Game — 46

PART II ★ Master the Plays

4. Tell Your Story — 65
5. Recruit an Army of Other-Promoters — 97
6. Get What You Want (and Make Them Love You for It) — 127
7. Start with the End — 154

PART III ★ Coach Others

8. Teach and Learn — 175
   Conclusion — 199

   Alison's Book Recommendations — 203
   Acknowledgments — 205
   Notes — 211
   Index — 227

Part I

Understand the Game

CHAPTER 1

Ladies, We Have a Status Problem

"We want it to be solution-focused."

Until I heard those six words, I was only half listening. This was pre-Zoom, back when all meetings were in person. I couldn't multitask by internet shopping, so I was taking a mental inventory of the dinner options in my refrigerator. My business school colleagues were talking with representatives of a national bank about a leadership program for the bank's up-and-comers. I was one of the faculty scheduled to teach in the program, and my role in this meeting was limited: I introduced myself, cracked a joke to reassure the client that I had the stage presence to handle their hard-charging, type-A, take-no-prisoners audience, nodded as my colleagues spoke, and waited to see if anyone had questions about my session. I've taken this type of meeting countless times over the years: Sit, nod, joke, repeat.

Then came the sentence that snapped me back to attention. Solution-focused? It was a line I had never heard cross a client's lips. In most ways, this leadership program was the same as many others that had come before it. But in one very important way, it was a first—this leadership program was solely for *women*. Until that point in my career, I would occasionally work with a corporate audience that was 50 percent women, but just as often I was the only woman in the room. Rare was the client that had enough women to fill a room and was invested enough in their development to create a program just for them.

"Solution" struck me because it implied that these women had a problem. I was equally struck that I immediately understood what they meant. They didn't want me to gather these top-performing women so they could complain about how difficult it was working in the "old boys' club" of financial services. Rather, they wanted me to offer specific, practical advice about "succeeding while female." Still, their tone was defeatist, as if they were asking for solutions they didn't think existed. Surely, women's problems were so numerous, so enduring, and so rooted in systemic bias, they seemed to be saying, there was little I could do to solve them in three hours. Despite investing significant time and money developing this program, I got the sense they didn't think it could deliver results.

At this point, I spoke up. Yes, women play an unfair game, I said, and they probably always will. But that doesn't mean they can't win. They can, and I was just the person to show them how.

IT'S TIME TO CHANGE THE GAME

I love nothing more than translating the science of my field—organizational psychology—into actionable advice that helps people, especially women, live and work better. Although it feels like women face a million sources of disadvantage relative to men, they face only two: a lack of *power* and a lack of *status*. These are big challenges, no doubt. But, having studied power and status for over twenty years, I assure you that women can triumph in the face of these problems—if we focus on the right one. Spoiler alert: It's not the one you think it is.

Your *power* is your control over resources—like money, authority, and a seat at the table where decisions are made. Despite decades of attention to closing the gaps, women continue to lag men on all these dimensions. I could cite depressing power statistics for days, but here are a few of my favorites:

- At the current rate of progress, the global gender pay gap will persist for 169 more years, even though women in many countries are more educated than their male peers* and are consistently rated as equal or better leaders.
- When transgender people transition from male to female, their pay drops about one-third. In contrast, those who transition from female to male continue to earn as much or more after transition as they did before.
- Women are significantly less likely than men to be promoted from entry-level to first-time manager, a finding known as the "broken rung." For every 100 men promoted to manager in 2023, only 87 women were promoted. For Black women, that number dropped to 54 promotions per 100 male counterparts.

Your *status*, on the other hand, is the way others see you—specifically, how much you're respected, admired, and valued.† Women are disadvantaged here, too. We are disproportionately denied opportunities to have our ideas and contributions presented, acknowledged, and rewarded. Take interruptions, as just one example. When you're interrupted, you're literally silenced. Interruptions deny the speaker an opportunity for influence and are a subtle, important way that we communicate how much we value others' contributions. When Tonja Jacobi and Dylan Schweers studied eleven years of conversations in a nine-person workgroup, they found that the women were disproportionately silenced. A quarter of the group members were women, and they did 25 percent of the talking, but accounted for a third of the interruptions. Only three individuals in the group were interrupted more than a hundred times, and all three were women. What makes these findings particularly noteworthy is the prestige of the specific

---

* For example, in 2018 women in the United States earned 57 percent of the bachelor's degrees, 60 percent of the master's degrees, and 54 percent of the doctorates.
† Another meaning of the term *status* is an "official position in a group," such as when we refer to someone's social status, socioeconomic status, marital status, employment status, and the like. This is not the definition of status I'm discussing. From here on out, every time you see the word *status*, I'm referring to how much a person is respected and regarded by others.

workgroup in question: the United States Supreme Court. Despite their credentials and objective success, Justices Ruth Bader Ginsburg, Sonia Sotomayor, and Elena Kagan were all interrupted significantly more than their male colleagues.* As the brilliant Stanford sociologist Cecilia Ridgeway eloquently stated, even "powerful women are disadvantaged by gender status beliefs compared to their . . . powerful male peers." And women's status woes aren't limited to losing the mic. When we're not fending off microaggressions, we're hepeated,† mansplained, undervalued, and overlooked: all ways the status problem rears its ugly head.

We need to solve both problems, of course. Power and status are two of only a few "fundamental human needs." Like our needs for social interaction and intellectual challenge, our desires to "have control" and "be respected" are universal motivators that drive us and define our quality of life. When our aspirations for power and status are thwarted, the negative consequences are far-reaching, impacting everything from our mental health to our reproductive success. Both physically and psychologically, lacking control and feeling disrespected are just as damaging as living a life without friends.

Despite their equal importance to our life satisfaction, however, there's one glaring difference between them. Both as individuals and as a society, we have primarily focused—perhaps overfocused—on increasing women's power, while neglecting their status.

In their groundbreaking book *The Power Code*, acclaimed journalists Katty Kay and Claire Shipman acknowledge the importance of status for women, but astutely label it one of *"power's underrated cousins."* We see evidence of this everywhere we turn. I chuckled when this post from digital health strategist Lauren Howard crossed my LinkedIn feed:

---

* According to the authors, this analysis excludes interruptions between Justices Scalia and Breyer, who would frequently talk over each other (specifically, Scalia interrupting Breyer).

† Possibly the greatest word invented in the twenty-first century. Credit goes to astronomy professor Nicole Gugliucci, who tweeted in 2017, "My friends coined a word: hepeated. For when a woman suggests an idea and it's ignored, but then a guy says the same thing, and everyone loves it."

Women really only want three things:
1. Equal pay.
2. Respect.
3. Pockets.

I agreed with the general sentiment but found the order telling. Although they both make the cut, power is #1 and status is #2.*

I get the logic: Respect and regard are nice to have, but they don't pay the bills. Like mine, I'm sure your daily to-do list is never-ending and when you know you can't accomplish everything, you triage your efforts to achieve your top priorities. We've traditionally made the same calculation with power and status. Forget respect, just pay me (and promote me while you're at it).

Consider the advice published by two of the most influential sources for personal and professional wisdom today: *Harvard Business Review* and TED. I searched both for power and status content related to women or gender and the results were stark. In every format, we devote significantly more attention to power than status:

	SEARCH TERMS	
	Women/Gender and Power	Women/Gender and Respect/Status
Harvard Business Review		
Books	43	3
Case Studies	158	44
Digital Articles	118	66
Magazine Articles	41	6
Magazine Issues	12	0
TED		
Talks	608	388
Playlists	14	3
Blog Posts	397	226
TEDx Events	144	55

* For what it's worth, I also think "comfortable shoes" deserves to be on the list.

We keep the focus on power in other ways as well, such as acknowledging annual milestones like "equal pay day," the day into the current calendar year that the average woman must work to earn what the average man earned the year before.* And many organizations have been created to increase women's power in the workforce. For example, 81cents, a nonprofit founded by Jordan Sale, matches women with expert volunteer coaches to help them negotiate their job offers, and First Women's Bank in Chicago was created to address the gender disparity in business funding, with a mission to get more capital into the hands of female entrepreneurs. Many volunteers lend their time and talent to supporting these organizations, including me; I sit on the advisory board of First Women's Bank. In contrast, I know of no organizations created with the mission of helping women get more respect, and no holidays to bring global awareness to the issue.

The problem with this "power first, status second" mentality is that it contradicts the science. Research shows that power is awarded *based on* status. Technically, you can obtain power by force, but few among us are dictators. If a person has power, it's almost always because someone else has given it to them—the title, the authority, the budget, the autonomy, the paycheck. If you were going to grant someone control over you, perhaps by accepting a job as their subordinate or electing them to be the captain of your sports team or the president of your neighborhood association, what kind of person would you pick? You would pick someone you *respected*, someone you *admired*, someone you thought would use their power responsibly and for good. That is, you would pick someone you judged to have high *status*. When we look at the research, we see evidence that this is what everyone does. In short, *resources follow respect*.

When we bring status into the equation, women's long-standing struggles to achieve the power they deserve, while still infuriating, start to make sense.

---

* The specific dates vary each calendar year. In 2024, the average across all women was March 12. Segmented by race and ethnicity, the dates were April 3 for Asian American, Native Hawaiian, and Pacific Islander women; July 9 for Black women; October 3 for Latinas; and November 21 for Native American women.

Power is based on status + Women have lower status = Women have less power

I see this dynamic play out all the time in my work. For years, I've taught and coached people—either in my MBA classes at the University of North Carolina or in corporate leadership programs—to improve their negotiation skills. Although negotiation skills can be used to solve any type of problem, women are most often interested in negotiating more effectively to increase their power—their pay, promotions, and perks. However, women often don't find as much success with these strategies as men. A 2018 study of 4,600 employees across 840 Australian companies found that men and women were equally likely to ask for a pay raise, and a survey of students from a top United States MBA program between 2015 and 2019 found that significantly *more* women (54 percent) reported negotiating job offers than men (44 percent). Unfortunately, both studies found that, despite asking, women are still less likely to get the raise—women in the Australian study were 25 percent less likely to be successful in their negotiations than their male colleagues, and the female MBA alumnae reported 22 percent lower salaries than the male alumni. These findings mirror countless conversations I've had with women over the years. Invariably, after every class, people approach me at the podium to ask advice on a failed negotiation—most commonly about pay or promotion—that they felt too vulnerable to discuss in front of the entire room. These struggles almost always stem from status problems; women fail in their attempts to acquire more power not because they lack negotiation skills or qualifications, but because the person they're negotiating with doesn't recognize or value their contributions. *How do I negotiate successfully,* the women wonder, *with someone who doesn't hold me in very high regard?*

My answer has always been the same: If you change the way the person on the other side of the conversation sees you, you'll have a much easier time getting what you want. When people don't respect and value your contributions, it's easy to justify (often unconsciously) not paying you more or promoting you, no matter how well you negotiate or what accolades are listed on your résumé. It's hard to solve your power problem without solving your status problem first.

If you think for a minute, you can undoubtedly come up with a time when you experienced something similar. When I explained "resources follow respect" to one of my friends, she immediately said, "Oh, like the time I was a forty-one-year-old graduate student and none of the other [younger] students wanted me on their project teams." Since many assignments were completed collectively, team members had the power to impact others' grades. Initially, her classmates treated her like she had little to contribute—until the day that she was randomly placed in a group for a class competition, and she discovered the key piece of information that led her team to win. That earned her status and then everyone wanted her on their team.

This is why I'm evangelical about managing status first, rather than focusing only on power. When we get others to respect our value—which we can all do, regardless of our gender or any other characteristic—we have a much easier time getting what we want, including power. Even if you don't want to be promoted or paid more, you still benefit from power. Maybe you want to work from anywhere or set your own work hours, maybe you want to spend your budget or make hiring decisions without approval, maybe you want to have your ideas be the ones implemented, maybe you want to control the distribution of information. These are all different forms of power, giving you control over how you use your resources. And your power doesn't just benefit you. The resources you control can help others, too—you can use your authority to hire the woman returning to the workforce after caring for her family, your money to pay the babysitter what she's worth, and your flexible work schedule to make time to volunteer for a cause that matters. There are countless ways to use your power for good—once you have the status.

As Mark Twain allegedly quipped, "If it's your job to eat a frog, it's best to do it first thing in the morning. And if it's your job to eat two frogs, it's best to eat the biggest one first." Well, ladies, we've been handed two frogs. And status is the biggest one.

LET'S PLAY TO WIN

Deep down, women understand the importance of status. In a clever series of experiments, organizational psychologist Nicholas Hays showed that when men and women were given hypothetical choices about work groups they could join that differed in both power (authority to delegate work, make decisions, and evaluate others) and status (respect and admiration from others, deference to your opinions), women prioritized joining groups with high status, whereas men gravitated to high-power groups. When given a choice, women choose—smartly—to improve their status first.

But how should they go about it? As a professor immersed in this research, with a Rolodex* of fellow experts who are colleagues and friends, I can see the path we need to walk. But so far, too little of our academic knowledge is widely shared. Take "mansplaining," for example. If you search the internet to find advice on how to deal with this common frustration, you'll find countless articles defining the issue. I got lost for over an hour reading hundreds of hilarious and cringeworthy examples (men regularly explain childbirth to women, I learned). There were also several articles offering advice, but the few tips I found all focused on how to address mansplaining *after* it had already happened (use humor, point out the transgression, etc.). Notably absent was any explanation about *why* it occurs in the first place, or any advice about what to do to *prevent* it. When it comes to women's status, we've been coached to play defense when it would be easier and more effective to mount a strong offense. It's time to change that.

The good news, even great news, is that everyone's status is malleable. You can change yours. The key to managing your status—and reaping all the benefits that come with it—is showing up as a *likeable badass,* getting others to see you as both *Assertive* and *Warm.* While that may sound like an impossible task—it's hard to find a woman who

---

* Even my middle-aged self is too young to have actually used a Rolodex, and my kids have never even seen one. Yet, I'm still not aware of a better term to describe a list of contacts. If there's a catchy term for the digital equivalent, please tell me!

hasn't walked the tightrope between competence and likeability—I assure you that it's not.

The proof is all around us. We all know women, lots of them, whom we consider likeable badasses, highly respected by us and everyone else who knows them. And, after interviewing hundreds, if not thousands, of women in my work, I know what sets these high-status women apart. It isn't intellect or achievements or charisma—on paper, the likeable badasses look just like everyone else. They aren't better *people*. They are simply better *salespeople*.

What you need to remember about status is that it exists only in others' minds, so you only get as much as they are willing to give. In this sense, managing your status isn't much different than selling vacuum cleaners. You can't force another person to respect you any more than you can force a customer to buy a vacuum. If selling vacuum cleaners was your job, you wouldn't assume the customer knew why yours was best; you would show them. And, even then, you would expect that some customers wouldn't be convinced right away. You'd understand that overcoming resistance is part of the process. You'd try different sales tactics until you found one that worked, which might be different than the one that worked with yesterday's customer. There's no way to sugarcoat it: Women will always encounter customers who "just don't get it." But if we have enough strategies at our disposal, we can always find a way to make the sale.

Likeable badasses are simply women who have found effective, authentic strategies to shape how their "customers" see them. Sometimes, they don't even realize what they're doing or why it works. That's where I can help. I'm trained to see the world through a status lens—to think about my own status and how I can influence it, and to look at another person's behavior and explain the science of why it's effective (or not).

Take Stacy Brown-Philpot. After graduating from both the University of Pennsylvania and Stanford University Graduate School of Business, Stacy climbed the ranks at Google for close to a decade, ultimately serving as the head of Google's Hyderabad, India, office, before she served as the CEO of TaskRabbit from 2016 to 2020.* In 2015 she ranked on *Fortune*'s influential "40 Under 40" list, and in 2016 the *Financial Times* recognized her as a "rare example of a Black, female chief executive in the tech industry." Stacy now sits on the boards of StockX, Noom, HP Inc., and Nordstrom. Even with that résumé, Stacy recalled being taken aback the first time she was called an "OG" (short for Original Gangster), a "term of affection for someone who is well respected in the Black community." "I don't want to be the OG," she remembers thinking. "I'm not that old!" She knew she was highly accomplished, but also knew that this didn't necessarily equate with status: "You can't demand somebody to call you an OG. You can't fill out an application, you can't complete a checklist." As more people used the term to describe her, she warmed to it, but was still a bit puzzled: "It feels good to have it, but how did I get chosen versus somebody else? It feels so amorphous and hard to control."

As Stacy astutely recognized, status is based on perception, not achievement. No amount of objective power or success—no degree, title, award, or paycheck—will necessarily raise your status unless it also affects how much other people respect and regard you. The challenge is we never know for sure what others are thinking, so when we look only at our own experience it can be very hard to know what we did right or wrong to manage their impressions of us. When we look across lots of women, though, as I have, clear patterns emerge.

As I told Stacy, the people who respected her didn't come to that decision randomly. Stacy influenced her status. She may not have done it intentionally or known what she was doing, but the way she showed up and interacted with people contributed to their impression of her. And her status was not only built through big gestures; more often it was built in small moments—moments that may not have been that significant to her but made an impact on her audience. When I pushed Stacy to identify some of those moments, it didn't take her long. "I've never forgotten to help people." She recalled her relationship with

---

* If you're not familiar with TaskRabbit, the online labor marketplace, you must check it out. It will change your life.

a former subordinate at Google, one of the people who always calls Stacy an OG. She realized she earned his respect through her kind and direct mentorship. "I told him, 'I want you to have my job one day, but it's not going to happen unless you do the following things right.' I don't think anyone in his career had ever had that conversation with him. But I didn't walk away after that conversation and say 'Good luck, go do it.' I continued to support him, through the personal things in his life as well as the professional." And thanks in part to Stacy's mentorship, he eventually did get her job! As I reflected her actions back to her in my own words, Stacy acknowledged that she had done a lot of things to deserve the OG moniker, including mentoring others. She had always been showing up as a likeable badass, she just hadn't tried to articulate it before.

By coupling stories like Stacy's with decades of status research, my goal is to help you see the connections between how you show up and what others perceive, so that you can take ownership of your value. Only then can you repeat what's working, ditch what isn't, and teach others to follow in your footsteps. And because status is based on perception, you don't need to work harder or achieve more. You just need to act intentionally to get maximum credit for the greatness you've already achieved.

Together, we will get "solution-focused" on the status problem. While we didn't cause it and we don't deserve it, the best solutions are, happily, within our individual control. In the words of famed Peloton head instructor and vice president of fitness programming Robin Arzón, a queen doesn't wait for anyone to save her. "The queen saves herself."

MASTERING THE PLAYS

This is a *playbook* for winning the status game—taking ownership of how others see you, respect you, and value you from the get-go. Like any good playbook, there are many plays to choose from. The objective of the game is always the same, but no two games are identical, and no two games use exactly the same plays. My goal is to present more strategies than you need, so you always have one to use when an obstacle arises.

The strategies I offer are based on a combination of science and stories. The science comes from my research, and the work of many others in my field. The stories recount the triumphs of countless likeable badasses I've been privileged to meet and coach throughout my career. Some names you'll recognize, but most you won't. The world is full of nonfamous women, of all backgrounds, who are just as likeable and badass as your favorite celebrity. If they can do it, we can do it. Our playbook hinges on the wisdom of the everyday women all around us.

My reference to status as a game is deliberate and important. I don't mean that pursuing status is frivolous, or for entertainment value only. A game is simply a "problem-solving activity approached with a playful attitude." By this definition, Monopoly is a game, but so is getting into college, asking someone out on a date, and managing your status. Although the status challenges that women have long endured are stressful, frustrating, and sometimes outright painful, the solutions don't need to be. Games are meant to be fun, and I truly believe that showing up as a likeable badass is fun. I navigate my own status with a "playful attitude"—full of enjoyment and authenticity—and I can help you do the same.

I also think that the game label is apt here because games aren't always fair. Sometimes referees make bad calls. Sometimes other players cheat or knock you down. Sometimes you just end up with a bad outcome through no fault of your own, twisting an ankle or losing a turn in Candyland. There's no doubt that women have been asked to play games with unfair rules since the dawn of time, and the rules for women who aren't white, cisgender, or heterosexual are ridiculously unreasonable. The rules of the game need to be changed. You know it and I know it. Unfortunately, when you're in the middle of a game, rewriting the rules can't happen fast enough to level the playing field. Instead, I recommend playing the best game you can, given the rules as they stand right now. But just because I coach you on how to play an unfair game doesn't mean I'm endorsing the rules. I'm not.

Importantly, "winning" the status game is different than winning at chess or pickleball. With status, we're not trying to beat other people (most certainly not other women), and our wins don't need to come at others' expense. In our context, to *win* means to *overcome*. Gender can be a source of status disadvantage, but it doesn't have to be. When we know the science and use it to enact strategies that remove gender as a barrier, we've won. And while we're winning, the women around us can win, too.

I've written this playbook for women. But it's not exclusively for women. One of the most flattering questions I was asked by men who read this book early on was "Why didn't you write this book for me? I could benefit by following these strategies, too." I wrote this book for women because it's an audience I know, and care about deeply. I know that viewing women's age-old struggles through the new lens of status provides an actionable path forward, and I want other women to feel optimistic, fierce, and inspired in that knowledge. And, in writing for women, I hope to use my expertise to help them score every ounce of advantage they can get. We sure as hell deserve it.

That said, the advice in this book is science-based best practice for everyone. Although gender is a determinant of one's status, it's not the only determinant—far from it. Some status characteristics are "ascribed," which means they're usually determined by birth or lineage—such as race, age, caste, appearance (e.g., height and weight), ethnicity, religion, and sexual orientation, to name just a few. Other status characteristics are classified as "achieved"—such as credentials, awards, occupations, and educational degrees. Because so many variables influence status, everyone experiences higher status in some situations and lower status in others. Managing status is a fact of life for everyone.

I also hope that many people will come to this book as allies. Although it doesn't always feel this way, women aren't the only people who care about women. Several years ago, I developed a new MBA course focused on gender and negotiation to create a safe space for women to discuss negotiation challenges that I thought only they worried about. The first time I taught it, I was surprised that half of the students in the class were men. I didn't dare ask why they were there because I was convinced they would just get up and leave. However, at the end of the semester, one of the men emailed me that he enrolled in the class because he had daughters. He wanted to see the world "through their eyes," and help them enter a workforce where their gender wouldn't hold them back. I was so touched I almost cried. I soon realized he wasn't alone. Once I got up the nerve to ask them, I found that almost all the men in my class told a similar story—they cared about women's experiences, were committed to their advancement, and wanted to do their part. Like my courses, this book is designed for all who enter—women, their allies, and anyone else who's curious enough to invest the time.

And, while I often compare women's status challenges to men's, based on the research that has been done so far, I recognize that this binary comparison fails to capture the full spectrum of gender and identity. When I refer to men and women, I'm really making a distinction between people who typically have more status and those who have less. Despite using gender terms that are sometimes inaccurate and insufficient, my intent—and most sincere hope—is to create a community of inclusion and belonging for everyone in these pages.

★

Our playbook is organized in three parts: (1) understand the game, (2) master the plays, and (3) coach others. As you read, you'll likely identify ways that you're already managing your status very well, and others that you'd like to improve. For your growth areas, I encourage you to embrace the idea of *practice*. Ask any athlete, from novice to elite, how they improve their skills, and they'll give you the same answer: practice, practice, practice. Professional golfers, for example, have played hundreds, if not thousands, of rounds of golf, but that's not all they do. To get to that level, they've spent untold hours on the driving range, in sand traps, and on the putting green practicing the same shot over, and over, and over again. Managing status is as much a learned skill as playing golf—the more we practice, the better we become.

Options for practice are endless. To spark your thinking, I offer some suggestions at the end of each chapter, which range in "heat level" from

🔥 (very low risk) to 🔥🔥🔥 (requires some courage). By no means do you need to limit yourself to these ideas. My intent is simply to inspire you to find a way to practice that feels fun. That doesn't mean you'll have instant success. Any worthwhile practice should challenge you at first; if it doesn't, you're wasting your time. But if it never gets easier or you despise it, you're better off abandoning that effort and finding a new way to practice. No two people are likeable and badass in the exact same ways. Keep experimenting until you find ways to manage your status that you truly love. When you do, you'll see that showing up as a likeable badass is doable, enjoyable, and the key to winning the status game.

CHAPTER 2

The Likeable Badass Solution

Often the women I find most brilliant at managing their status aren't the most senior women in the room. Many experienced women in high-ranking positions have a lot of status, but there are lots of young women in lower-level positions who have just as much. This was the case with Kate, a woman I met when I spoke at her company's annual women's conference. As my guide for the day, Kate met me at the hotel, showed me to our meeting room, and helped me transition from meeting to meeting. As I walked alongside her, I noticed that all the senior (male) leaders knew who she was and would stop to talk as they passed her in the hallway, as though they were talking with an executive peer and not a mid-level employee twenty years their junior. What's more, they weren't just stopping to discuss the weather, they were asking her advice or giving her important updates. I could see they respected her.

As we talked, I learned that her status in the organization was helping her gain power faster than her peers. She had joined the company as an analyst after earning her undergraduate degree and had already been promoted twice in less than four years, which she acknowledged was unusual. She was later promoted again, this time to a vice president role, a two-level jump, to take on a new position created for her—chief of staff to the CEO. Three promotions, a senior title, and daily interaction with the CEO, all while Kate was still in her twenties.

Eventually, a few years into knowing Kate, I asked what she had done to achieve such success. Her answer was as simple as it was brilliant—a true likeable badass move. From her first day in the company, she said, she was intentional about adding value to as many people as possible, especially senior leaders. Or, as Kate puts it, "I made shit happen. I got shit done."

On one of her first days at work her boss pulled her aside and said, "Your job is to make my life easier." Although Kate thought his delivery was rough, she took the idea to heart. Without even knowing the term, her boss's comment made her think about managing her status: How did other people view her? Did they think she was making their life easier? This mentality shaped the way she behaved at work. She was proactive at offering help, and whenever someone had a request, she would say yes. Some of the things she did were poor uses of her time—like the time her boss called to tell her that his hotel had bedbugs and asked her to research fumigators in New Jersey. "I learned a lot of weird facts about bedbugs," Kate remembers. But she didn't give up on the idea of being helpful. Instead, she kept experimenting with helping different people in different ways, and as she did, she got more savvy about what kinds of help to offer, and to whom. One day, when a senior leader mentioned that she needed to make a PowerPoint presentation, Kate jumped in to help without being asked. It wasn't officially her job (the company had a graphics department), but Kate felt it was a skill she could contribute. The slide decks weren't sexy (mainly compliance training documents), but they would end up on the desk of the deputy chief operations officer (her boss's boss). Soon after, when the COO—three levels up from Kate—needed someone to help on a high-visibility presentation, the deputy COO suggested, "Kate's good at making PowerPoints. Why don't you ask her?"

Although she initially accepted these presentation requests just to make other people's lives easier, Kate soon realized that she added unique value—she was very good at storytelling and understood how to make an argument compelling to someone in a different group. She had enough business knowledge to tell the story well and was also willing to do the mundane task of turning the story into charts and graphs. It didn't take her long to realize that, unlike researching fumigators, this type of assistance was both noticed and valued by powerful people. "I started getting more and more exposure to senior leaders," Kate said. Soon, every senior leader in the company knew Kate's name, and most had asked her directly for assistance making executive-level presentations. Because of this, she developed a reputation as a problem solver, and earned widespread respect as a result.

Of course, humble and grounded, Kate told me the story with a shrug of her shoulders, as if to say, "No big deal, anyone could have done it." That's true. Anyone can do what she did, but not everyone does. As I heard her story, I could immediately pick out the critical, yet easily replicable, actions that led to Kate's early rise in both status and power. She may not have known exactly why it worked, but I did. In short, *status is the problem, and being a likeable badass is the solution.*

LIKEABLE BADASS, DEFINED

When you hear the term *likeable badass,* you get it. It's more than a catchy term of endearment, though. It has a specific meaning, rooted in psychology, that is central to our discussion of status.

To understand the definition, we need to begin with the science of how people judge other people. Every time you observe, or even hear a story about, another person, you draw conclusions about their underlying personality, abilities, and traits. Other people do the same to you. You might think that because no two people are the same, our judgments of them are likely to be just as varied. That's not the case. Our perceptions of people are organized around two fundamental dimensions: Warm-Cold and Assertive-Submissive.

Warm-Cold (Likeable)

When we observe other people, one thing we try to figure out is how they'll treat us—will they care about us, will they help us, will they be pleasant? This is the Warm-Cold dimension of person perception, and it captures our *social functioning*—how well we get along with others. A person at the Warm end of the continuum is one we perceive to be very concerned about others and who interacts well with them. There are a lot of different ways that a person could convey Warmth, such as being agreeable, charitable, respectful, or cooperative. A person at the Cold end of the spectrum would be perceived as the opposite: impolite, uncivil, quarrelsome, and uncooperative.

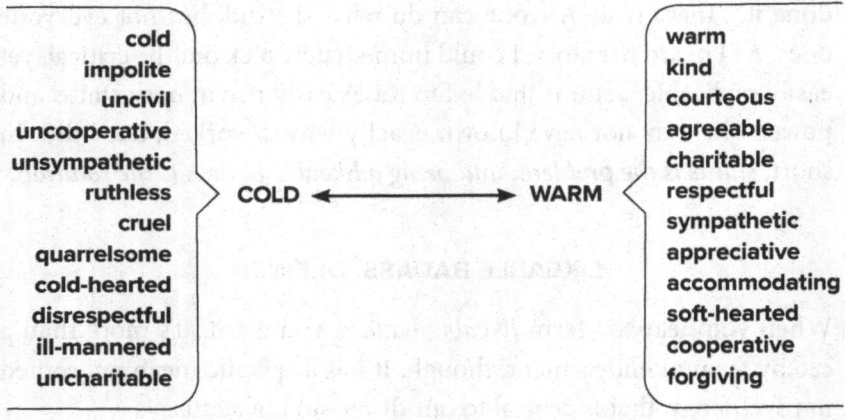

Assertive-Submissive (Badass)

The other thing we try to figure out about people is how capable they are—will they work hard, will they avoid mistakes, will they produce good work? This is the Assertive-Submissive dimension of person perception, and it captures our *task functioning*—how well we can complete tasks, achieve goals, and get things done. An Assertive person is one we perceive to be very capable of succeeding at whatever is asked of them. We would describe this person using adjectives like competent, organized, self-confident, ambitious, and persistent. A Submissive person, on the other hand, is perceived as incapable of accomplish-

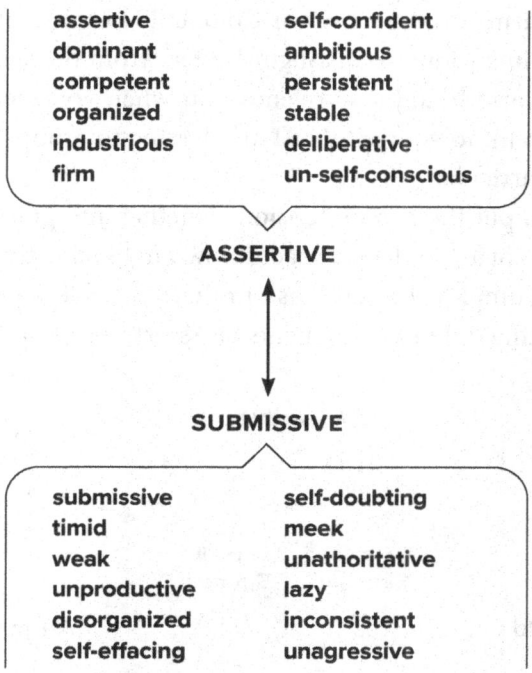

ing tasks successfully, characterized by descriptors like timid, self-doubting, meek, lazy, and unproductive.

As the illustrations suggest, each dimension is a continuum, so a person can fall anywhere along a given line. And each dimension comprises multiple traits (even more than I've listed here). To be perceived as very Warm, for example, you don't necessarily need to check every box on the list. You just need to do something that leads people to conclude that you play well with others. Being agreeable is different than being charitable, but they're both signals of Warmth. Similarly, persistence and self-confidence both signal Assertiveness, even though they are different qualities. This is an important point to remember as we explore the relevance of these dimensions for status—how you show up matters a lot, but there are lots of different ways to get there.

For simplicity, I'll usually refer to these dimensions as Warm and Assertive (or Warmth and Assertiveness), while occasionally referring to the other endpoints (Cold and Submissive). And as you can see, I capitalize Warm and Assertive (or Cold and Submissive) when referring to the dimensions, to distinguish them from the specific characteristics of warmth and assertiveness. So when you see these words capitalized, remind yourself that I'm referring to groups of traits, not any one in particular.

When you put the two dimensions together and graph them, they form the axes of a 360-degree space known in psychology as the interpersonal circumplex. Perceptions of others can fall anywhere in this circle, reflecting different judgments of Assertiveness and Warmth.

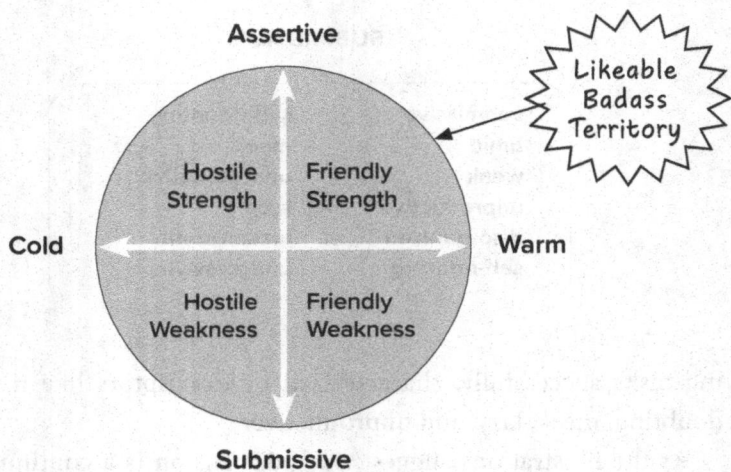

For our purposes, it's helpful to think of this circle in four quadrants. Moving counterclockwise from the top left, we have the following:

Hostile Strength: A person perceived as Cold and Assertive. They can get things done, but no one enjoys them. If the person is a woman, they may be labeled "aggressive" or "a bitch" and told they are "too much."

Hostile Weakness: A person perceived as Cold and Submissive. This person is both ineffective and uncaring.

Friendly Weakness: A person perceived as Warm and Submissive. This person is sweet and harmless, but not very capable. If the person is a woman, they may be told they lack "confidence" or "presence" and told they are "not enough."

Friendly Strength: A person perceived as Assertive and Warm. This person can both get along and get things done. This is likeable badass territory.

WE ALL WANT TO BE LIKEABLE BADASSES

The interpersonal circumplex is foundational in psychology research, including my own, and is central to our understanding of status. Importantly, the interpersonal circumplex is essentially a reputational map. When we refer to people as having a "good reputation," what does this mean? Looking at the circumplex, we see the answer. If you could choose how others perceived you, which quadrant would you want to be in? If you chose Friendly Strength, congratulations, you're just like everyone else. Assertive is more positive than Submissive, and Warm is more positive than Cold. A "good reputation," then, isn't idiosyncratic: We all aspire to the Assertive-Warm quadrant of this reputational space. We all want to be seen as capable and caring.

As an academic, I've known this for a long time. Still, writing this book gave me a new opportunity to experience this truth through others' eyes. No matter whom I spoke with, I found that simply sharing the title elicited a common, effusive reaction: "*Likeable Badass*. YES! That's exactly what I'm going for." Perhaps you experienced this yourself if the title of the book enticed you to pick it up. Most people have never heard of the interpersonal circumplex, but we spend our entire lives trying to navigate it—all hoping to end up in the exact same spot.

LIKEABLE BADASSES GAIN STATUS

Not only is a likeable badass reputation desirable in its own right, it's also our path to status. We award status to those that we see as both Assertive and Warm.

Remember that a person's status is the extent to which others respect and regard them. Our brains (usually nonconsciously) decide how much to respect someone by making inferences about how much *value* they contribute—past, present, and future—based on what we observe. The more we expect someone to have useful skills and knowledge to offer, the more respect and regard we have for them. This is why demographic characteristics, like gender, age, and race, affect status—they (unjustly) influence our perceptions of a person's potential contributions based on cultural biases.

However, demographics and group memberships aren't the only observable signals of value. More generally, to be seen as a valuable contributor, people need to believe you have the conviction and ability to perform tasks effectively and efficiently, *and* you care enough about other people to use your talents to benefit them, not just yourself. In other words, the more you show up as Assertive and Warm, the more people assume you have value to offer. And fortunately for our purposes, conveying Assertiveness and Warmth through your behavior has been shown to have a greater effect on your status than your group memberships (e.g., occupation, gender). *Showing up as a likeable badass is the most effective and controllable way to gain status.*

Evidence for this comes from a robust line of research on *task cues*, which are behaviors that signal how good a person might be at a task.* Task cues indicate that a person is Assertive (e.g., confident, competent, knowledgeable, persuasive), Warm (e.g., likeable, pleasant, reasonable, and other-oriented), or both. Because task cues imply ability and competence, we award status to those who display them. To give you a flavor of the diverse types of task cues that have been linked to status, here are a few examples:

Speech Rate, Response Time, and Airtime

The faster we talk, the more status we get. A faster speech rate is associated with greater perceptions of confidence and competence, as is shorter response latency—the length of time that passes between when

---

* Task cues can be distinguished from dominance cues, which signal intimidation and threat (e.g., shouting, glaring, intruding on someone's personal space). Although both task and dominance cues convey Assertiveness in different ways, dominance cues don't signal competence or care for others, which are important for determining one's potential contributions to a group. For this reason, dominance cues are less effective for gaining status than task cues, and I don't recommend them. Ridgeway (1987) examined all-female groups and found that women gained more status when displaying task cues but did not when displaying dominance cues.

another person stops speaking and you begin. The quicker you enter a conversation and the faster you talk, the more confident and knowledgeable you're perceived to be. Both fast talking and quick responding also enable you to get (more than) your share of airtime, and your overall level of verbal participation in a group (holding the content or value of that participation constant) positively affects your status. The more you talk, the more you're seen as having the potential for meaningful contribution, and the more status you're granted.*

Speech Style

Traditionally, people—particularly women—have been counseled against the use of "powerless speech"—a tentative style of speaking characterized by hedges (I *think*, it *might*), disclaimers (*This might be a bad idea*, but . . .), and tag questions (Let's meet at noon, *OK*?). Instead, we have been advised to use "powerful speech"—the Assertive alternative that eliminates these signs of hesitation. In reality, some of my earliest research in this area demonstrated that both powerless and powerful speech are valuable task cues. Whereas powerful speech conveys Assertiveness, powerless speech conveys Warmth.

In general, status is granted to people who are both Assertive and Warm. If you can signal to others that you're both capable and caring, then your potential value is beyond reproach. But there are some circumstances where one dimension is weighted more heavily than the other. Specifically, I found that when people expected to work closely with someone, they valued that person's Warmth more than their Assertiveness, and awarded the person more status when they used powerless speech. However, when people didn't expect a future interaction, powerful speech was more status-enhancing, as Assertiveness was valued more than Warmth. From this work we see that (a) speech styles influence status and (b) powerless speech isn't universally inferior to powerful speech; they each have their own advantage.

---

* If you've ever wondered why the person who rambles on in every meeting never saying anything that really matters is always so influential, this is why. The conscious brain rewards the quality of one's contributions, but the nonconscious brain also rewards quantity.

Eye Contact

Making and sustaining eye contact conveys Assertiveness, whereas looking away conveys the opposite. Eye contact also boosts perceptions of Warmth—those who look at us are judged as more likeable, trustworthy, and relationship-building than those who avert their eyes. However, it's awkward and uncomfortable to sustain eye contact for too long, so most people will break off eye contact at some point. The person who holds eye contact longer is considered to have "outglanced" the other person, and in a group of multiple people it's possible to measure an eye-contact hierarchy: If A outglances B, and B outglances C, then A is at the top of the eye-contact hierarchy. In three-person groups of strangers, researchers found that one's position in the eye-contact hierarchy in the first minute of interaction was predictive of the person's ultimate status in the group after working together for thirty minutes. That one minute of eye contact was an even bigger predictor of status than a person's overall participation rate in the group.

Choosing Your Seat

Have you ever walked into a conference room and debated where to sit—at the head of the table, along the side, or perhaps in those random chairs that are pushed up against the wall? In one study, researchers explored whether choosing to sit at the head of the table could help a person with a minority opinion influence the decision of a majority. They assembled small groups of strangers and varied whether individuals selected their own seat or were assigned seats. They found the person who held a minority opinion from the rest of the group was more influential when they were seated at the head of the table (rather than on the side), but only when that person was seen choosing their own seat! That is, it wasn't the act of being seated in any one chair that mattered, but the act of selecting it. Choosing to sit at the head of the table conveyed more confidence and consistency, two elements of Assertiveness, compared to being assigned the head seat. And, as a result, the person's ideas were held in higher regard.

Humor

There is a strong relationship between humor and status. People who have high status engage in more humor: Men use humor more than women, high participators and frequent interrupters use more successful humor in groups, and being the subject of frequent interruptions—a mark of low status—makes individuals less likely to attempt humor. Just as status leads to humor, humor also leads to status. Individuals who engage in successful humor are awarded more status, in both new and existing relationships, so long as the humor is seen as appropriate. Why? You can probably guess by now: The use of humor signals Assertiveness. And successful humor leads to positive emotions and interpersonal cohesion, boosting perceptions of the joke teller's Warmth.

Offering Help

Status also comes from being a generous exchange partner—giving more help, advice, and support to others than you receive in turn. Offering wisdom demonstrates Assertiveness, and when it's done to help others, it also signals Warmth. Helping others is what earned Kate her reputation as a likeable badass. In her case, the help she offered was in the context of her job, and she spent a lot of time on it. But there are many ways to offer valuable help that take mere minutes (if that) and could be done for anyone—giving someone directions, recommending a restaurant, making an introduction. As my friend Scott Tillema, FBI-trained hostage negotiator, says: "If it doesn't cost you much, always be generous." Not only is it the kind thing to do, it's also a great way to boost your status.

PUBLIC SERVICE ANNOUNCEMENT:
YOU DO YOU, STRATEGICALLY

As you can probably tell, I love the science of task cues. What fascinates me is how powerful they are—in initial interactions between strangers, we judge others' Assertiveness and Warmth in minutes, if not seconds, based on subtle (and sometimes meaningless) behaviors people exhibit. Yes, it's true that we're all under a microscope. People are always watching us and drawing conclusions about us, just as we are watching and judging them. And, of course, those conclusions aren't always correct, which is frustrating when you're the one being misjudged. However, as an advocate for women, and all others who are undervalued, I find the research on task cues very encouraging. It's proof that we can exert a *lot* of control over how others perceive us, and therefore our status.

Maybe this all sounds like great news. Look people in the eye, speak faster, sit at the head of the table, and do a few favors for good measure—*yes, I can do these things!* Or maybe this idea irks you—*these behaviors are so "not me."* Fear not. We see from this research that there isn't only one way to be a likeable badass. You can signal Assertiveness and Warmth through lower-effort behaviors, such as being aware of your verbal and nonverbal signals, higher-effort behaviors, like Kate's executive team presentations, and all kinds of strategies in between. Each tactic is simply one play out of many in our playbook. This means that everyone can find plays that work for them and ignore any that don't.

For example, I've given up on smiling. I admire a very successful female colleague who is widely beloved as a likeable badass and is always smiling—literally always. I can only conclude that she was born with her face that way, because no one else I know smiles that much. After observing her for years, I've concluded that she's no Warmer than I am, but she's often perceived that way—and I attribute this to her perma-smile. It has occurred to me more than once that I should smile more to convey more Warmth, but, alas, I cannot. Since I was a child, people—even strangers—have asked me, "What's wrong?" When I respond, "Nothing, why?" I always get the same answer: "You have that look on your face." Years later, one of my research collaborators emailed me an article discussing the newly coined term "resting bitch face." There was no text in the body of the email, only the article. I read it and reread it, confused about why he had sent it to me, and then suddenly I understood. In that moment, decades of strange conversations about "that look on my face" finally made sense—I'm the poster child for resting bitch face. I can smile, but it requires a lot of conscious effort, and leaves me no brain space to think about much else. This means that smiling, which has been the signature likeable badass move for my colleague, is near useless for me. So I've let it go. I don't need it. I have my own ways to convey Warmth. I'm hilarious and I'll rely on my humor to get me through.

You, too, may have observed a likeable badass in your life who manages their status in a way that won't work for you. Sometimes, like with smiling, you don't want to mimic them simply because their approach doesn't feel authentic to you. Other times, you may feel that you wouldn't get the same result with their strategy. For example, when I asked Stacy Brown-Philpot, the former CEO of TaskRabbit, if she had ever seen a highly respected white woman manage her status in a way that Stacy couldn't, her answer hit close to home: "I am hesitant to use foul language, particularly when making a strong point or giving negative feedback." Aware of the "angry Black woman" stereotype (in which a Black woman's anger is seen as an indicator of her aggressive personality, rather than a justifiable response to an inciting circumstance), she had learned to be very tempered at work. She acknowledged that although many people she worked with, including women, would swear freely, she wasn't sure that she, a "Black woman with dreadlocks, even one who went to Penn and Stanford," would benefit from the same approach. I was struck by this because I swear constantly—even in front of other people's children. Until Stacy's comment, I had only thought of my foul language as a bad habit, but I realized in that moment it was more functional than that. It was one of the ways I learned to manage my status in rooms full of men. I had sensed, especially when I was younger, that my presence often made the (older) men in the room uncomfortable because they were worried about saying or doing something that would offend me. When I swore, which would happen within the first thirty seconds of meeting them, I could see the visible relief on their faces—they were free to be themselves. They would let out a few expletives in response, and we would then have something in common (which builds a sense of Warmth). It was only by talking with Stacy that I became consciously aware of how I was conditioned to use profanity as a status-management strategy—and that my ability to do so could be a mark of my privilege as a white woman.

What I want you to take from these stories is this: There are many benefits that come from high status, and many ways to achieve it, without making it a complicated, time-consuming endeavor. Just be your likeable badass self—in the most effective, strategic way possible. In every interaction, ask yourself: *What can I do to show up as both Assertive and Warm?* Then, do it. By showing up as Assertive and Warm, as often as you can, to as many people as you can, you're doing the most effective thing to manage your status. You may not do it the same way your friend does, and That. Is. Okay. You do you, as long as you do it Assertively and Warmly.

CONQUERING THE "COMPETENCE-LIKEABILITY BIND"

Showing up as a likeable badass is very doable. However, women aren't crazy when we lament how difficult it is to get credit for being capable and caring at the same time. It *is* more challenging. Fortunately, the interpersonal circumplex also helps us understand why this is the case. And once we understand the science, we're better equipped to overcome this infuriating double standard.

What I've found in my work (alongside my two likeable badass collaborators, Margaret [Maggie] Neale and Jennifer Overbeck) is that there is a reciprocal relationship between high status and perceptions of Assertiveness and Warmth. When you're perceived as Assertive and Warm, others grant you status. *And* when you're perceived as high status, because of your gender, occupation, or any other reason, others assume you're both Assertive and Warm—without ever seeing you, and regardless of how much power you have. High-status people are assumed to be likeable badasses from the start of a relationship.

However, those with lower status aren't as fortunate. How we judge lower-status people depends on how much power they have. If we think someone lacks status *and* they also have *low power,* they're assumed to be Warm and Submissive (a stereotype of friendly weakness). If a low-status person has *high power,* though, we assume them to be Assertive and Cold (a stereotype of hostile strength).

Spelled out like this, the perplexing competence-likeability bind for women suddenly makes sense. Anyone judged as lower status—which women often are, in the absence of other information—is at risk to be seen as Assertive or Warm, based on their level of power, but not both. This is why women often mistakenly think they need to choose between Assertiveness and Warmth—for many, that is their lived experience, repeatedly bouncing between allegations of friendly weakness and hostile strength.

What's more, these initial judgments of Assertiveness and Warmth function like any other kind of stereotype: our brains use them to fill in missing details. In one of our studies, we asked people to write about an anticipated interaction with an individual named L. We told participants almost nothing about L—only that L had a job where they did/didn't control a lot of resources (power) and were/weren't highly respected in that role (status). These two pieces of information alone were enough for participants to fill in a wide array of specifics about what it would be like to interact with L, consistent with the stereotypes depicted above.

When L had high status, regardless of L's level of power, people assumed L would show up as a likeable badass. As one participant wrote:

> L is very agreeable and pleasant to hang out with. She[*] always takes my opinion into account and always shares her own insightful opinion. She's always humble and friendly. She makes me feel fine about myself and pleased with the interaction.

[*] We did not specify L's gender. We found that participants tended to assume that L was the same gender they were.

When L had low status and low power, people anticipated a Warm, Submissive person, exemplified by this sample response:

> L would be polite, maybe to the point but possibly chatty if I chatted with him because he doesn't have much interaction with a lot of people in the organization. If I showed him caring and kindness, I think he would show the same. It would be important for me to be on good terms with him if I was going to feel good about my workplace.

And individuals imagining an interaction with a low-status powerholder expected someone Cold and Assertive, best illustrated by this participant's vivid imagery:

> He'd probably be smarmy and ooze with disrespect and be completely unaware of how disrespectful he is. I could see him making offensive jokes and eating with his mouth open. He'd probably take forever answering whatever question I'd asked him and would always emphasize his position of authority. He's not very helpful either. He just wants to boast. I would probably despise my interactions with him.

My colleagues and I predicted these results, but even we were surprised by the specificity of these stories, given how little participants knew about L. Imagine meeting a new person who has seen only your business card and therefore knows almost nothing about you, except for your job title and your assumed gender based on your name. That information alone may be enough for them to draw conclusions about your power and status, make inferences about your Assertiveness and Warmth, and enter the interaction with vivid assumptions about you, from the jokes you'll tell to how you'll chew your food!

Importantly, these findings solve three maddening, head-scratching mysteries for women. These mysteries are why many women believe that a likeable badass reputation is impossible to achieve. But once I pull back the curtain, we can see our path forward.

Why Your Male Colleague Gets More Credit for the Same Behavior

As we've established, when people meet you for the first time (or even hear about you), your reputation isn't a blank canvas. People have already drawn conclusions about you based on the few status- and power-related details they know (such as your demographics and occupation). Then, confirmation bias kicks in. Confirmation bias, one of the most well-documented judgment errors in all of psychology, is the tendency to interpret new information in a way that is consistent with, thus confirming, beliefs we already hold. Imagine, for example, you see someone raising their voice. What story would you tell yourself? If you held a prior belief that this person was helpful, sincere, agreeable, confident, and competent, you might conclude that the person was reacting justifiably to some negative event or provocation. But what if you saw the same frustration emanating from a person you believed to be quarrelsome, unsympathetic, dominant, and controlling? *Here they go again*, you might think, *acting like an aggressive bitch and unfit to lead*. Or consider someone speaking up in a meeting with a new idea. If you saw the person as sweet and friendly, yet timid and unassured, you may dismiss their idea. Surely they have nothing of value to add. But what if that same idea came from someone kind, thoughtful, confident, and knowledgeable? Now you're all ears, of course.

Differences in initial reputations, combined with confirmation bias, explain why we can behave just like the guy in the next office and get wildly different results. The high status inherent in being a man, specifically a white man, leads to a default reputation that's more favorable than either of the default reputations that befall lower-status individuals, like women: sweet and submissive, or dominant and bitchy. These reputations serve as the prior beliefs through which future behavior is viewed.

Annoyingly, this means that cultivating a likeable badass reputation *is* more work for some people than others. Those who are handed high status simply need to *maintain* their reputation—which isn't very hard, thanks to confirmation bias. Those who begin with low status are forced to *change* their reputation, which takes some strategy. As a case in point, consider the experience of Joan Roughgarden. Joan transitioned from male to female during her tenure as a biology professor at Stanford University. When Roughgarden's colleagues perceived her as a man, they took her competence as a given. After her transition, though, Joan found she had "to establish competence to an extent that men never have to. [Men are] assumed to be competent until proven otherwise, whereas a woman is assumed to be incompetent until she proves otherwise," she recalled. "I remember going on a drive with a man. He assumed I couldn't read a map."

Why Things Can Get Worse as You Advance, Not Better

It's also perplexing to see women experience *more* mistreatment, not less, as they advance in their careers. As a case in point, Jennifer Chatman and colleagues conducted a brilliant (and depressing) study examining fifteen years of teaching evaluations for male and female business school professors at one U.S. university. For female professors only, they found middle-aged professors received lower student ratings than younger professors. At first glance this is surprising, as you would expect a professor to improve with experience, and to see this reflected in student opinions. This happened for the men, but not for the women.

However, this finding is very predictable when we consider women's status and power over the life cycle of their career. Remember that people who lack both status and power are seen as Warm, but Submissive. This isn't as advantageous as a likeable badass reputation, but it's not terrible. People don't see you as very competent or capable, but they still like you. However, the low-status, high-power reputation—Assertive and Cold—is a recipe for misery. We've found in our work that this reputation for hostile strength is the worst one to have. People perceived as Assertive and Cold are the most likely to experience *incivility*—low-intensity harms of ambiguous intent.[*] Examples of incivility include subtle rudeness (e.g., ignoring another's input;

---

[*] If you're wondering, incivility and microaggressions are generally the same thing, though the latter term is usually reserved for when the target of the mistreatment is a member of any marginalized group, implying a specific charge to the interaction.

neglecting to say "please" or "thank you"), withholding information that could make someone's job easier, using a condescending tone in conversation, interrupting someone, and devaluing their performance.

Lacking status makes it harder to get power, but if we somehow defy the odds and snag the title or the paycheck, we assume life will be peachy. Sadly, the opposite is true. As soon as we're seen as a low-status powerholder, we're typecast as Assertive and Cold—and then others' claws come out. This is what happened with the professors. The female professors who were fortunate enough to advance in their careers gained power. As they did, they experienced a shift in how they were perceived, for the worse. When we're young and powerless, we're seen as sweet and harmless, even if we also have low status. However, if our status remains unchanged and our power increases, we may awaken one day surprised that others are suddenly judging us more harshly, and treating us worse, than they ever did before.

This pattern is not limited to academia. In 2021, record numbers of female senior leaders left their corporate roles, relative to their male peers. For every woman who was promoted to director level in her organization, on average two female directors quit. One of the top reasons cited: greater instances of incivility at these ranks, such as having their judgment questioned or others implying they weren't qualified for their jobs. And these microaggressions were even more frequent for Black women leaders.

These results are particularly troubling given what we know about the impact of incivility. While the behaviors are less overt than bullying or aggression, the psychological effects of incivility can be just as severe. Recipients of incivility experience greater emotional exhaustion, depression, stress, and lower life satisfaction. At work, those subject to uncivil treatment are more likely to engage in workplace deviance, be less helpful, exhibit worse task performance, feel less engaged and satisfied with their work, and experience greater psychological withdrawal, as well as higher turnover. In sum, incivility is psychological torture. When we subject our top talent to this torment, namely senior women, it's hardly surprising that they sprint for the exits.

Why You're Revered One Moment, and Reviled the Next

For anyone who has been a low-status powerholder at some point, these results may hit very close to home. They also explain why our identical self can be horribly mistreated in one environment and beloved in a different one. Take, for example, retired professional poker player turned cognitive psychologist Annie Duke. Before earning her PhD from the University of Pennsylvania and authoring multiple bestselling books on decision making under uncertain conditions, Duke was one of the winningest female poker players in World Series of Poker history. As of 2023, she still ranked among the top five female all-time money winners, over ten years after her retirement. When Annie and I became members of the same book authors' group, I was starstruck. Annie had long been a likeable badass in my eyes—as a lover of poker, gambling, and all things Las Vegas (I even got married there), I spent way too many hours in graduate school watching televised professional poker events. My initially high opinion of her was reinforced after listening to her brilliant advice meeting after meeting. However, when I reached out to her for likeable badass tips, she confessed that she didn't think she fit the moniker because "lots of people in poker didn't like" her. Only about 5 percent of the World Series poker players are women, and Annie—an Ivy League graduate (times two) and a mother of four—was unique even among the female minority. Many fellow players resented the disproportionate media attention Annie received, and let it be known, even though she was the first to admit that her unusual profile led to increased exposure. Her power in the sport increased further as she won more money and titles. This success improved her relationship with fans, like me, but not with fellow players, who seemed to dislike her more with each victory. When she started speaking to companies about making smart decisions amidst uncertainty (a skill she had honed, in part, through poker), she was struck by how "nice" everyone was to her. Ultimately, the contrast between how she was treated in poker and how she was treated as a speaker prompted her to change professions and become an educator through speaking and writing.

For Annie, these disparate reactions were frustrating and perplexing. After all, she was the "same person" in both situations. However, as we discussed her experiences, I pointed out that one very important thing about her did change across audiences—her status. Among poker fans and corporate leaders, being a successful professional poker player is a mark of high status, regardless of gender. However, among other professional players (most of whom are men), being a *female* poker player is a low-status role, no matter how much you win. The more successful she became in poker, the more power she attained—particularly her ability to control a coveted resource, media coverage—and the more she was treated as a low-status powerholder. The business leaders in her audience were no more or less nice *in general* than her poker competition, but they were nicer to *her* because they saw her status differently.

You may not see much reason for optimism in Annie's story, but I do. Her experience is consistent with the science: Some studies have found that women experience more incivility than men, whereas others have found that gender has no effect. Although gender *can* affect one's status, and subsequently how one is treated, it doesn't always. It's possible—very possible—for women to become *high-status* powerholders. To do this, though, you need to get your audience to pay less attention to your gender and more attention to your amazing qualities. Sometimes, this may mean finding a new audience where your contributions are more valued, as Annie did. Other times, this may mean staying where you are, but making some tweaks to how you show up. The likeable badasses all around us are proof this is possible—if we adhere to two principles.

ADD, DON'T SUBTRACT

The harder the game, the more strategy matters. Given women's challenges, we need to find every advantage we can to achieve the likeable badass reputation we deserve and avoid any mistakes. One critical mistake is what researchers term "compensatory impression management," our tendency to make ourselves look worse on one dimension of the interpersonal circumplex to make ourselves look better on the other. That is, when people want to be seen as Warm, they downplay their Assertiveness. When people want to be seen as Assertive, they downplay their Warmth. This practice is very common, but problematic—particularly for those who start out with lower status.

To help you understand how compensatory impression management works in practice, let's look at a study. Participants imagined that they had just joined a book club and had to send an email describing the current book to other members of the club. They were asked to choose from a list of twenty-four adjectives to describe the book, and these adjectives varied in how Warm or Assertive the person using them would appear. Positive words conveyed the author's Warmth, and words that were considered "sophisticated vocabulary" conveyed the author's Assertiveness (specifically competence). This led to six words in each of the following categories:

High Warmth/High Assertiveness (e.g., euphoric)
High Warmth/Low Assertiveness (e.g., happy)
Low Warmth/High Assertiveness (e.g., melancholy)
Low Warmth/Low Assertiveness (e.g., sad)

Before selecting twelve words to use in the email, participants were given different impression management goals. Some participants were told that the book club valued those who were warm, friendly, and personable. Others were told that the club valued members who were smart, intelligent, and competent. These goals affected the words that participants chose for their emails. Specifically, when tasked with appearing Warm, participants chose simpler words that made them look less Assertive (e.g., "great" instead of "unprecedented"). Participants who wanted to appear Assertive chose more negative words that made them look less Warm (e.g., "mediocre" instead of "commendable"). This tendency to make oneself look worse on one dimension to showcase the other is noteworthy given that participants didn't need to make this choice. They could have selected at least six words—half of their required list—to showcase both Assertiveness and Warmth.

Given an opportunity to show up as a likeable badass, most people didn't take it.

Everyone does this, and some evidence suggests that men do it even more than women. But I'm not a fan of this strategy—particularly for women. We saw that when people judge us as low status, they're likely to typecast us as either Assertive or Warm, but not both. The last thing we want to do is to reinforce these judgments through our own actions. Because compensating is such a common impression management strategy, we may not realize we're behaving in ways that hold us back from the likeable badass reputation we deserve. Then we conclude, falsely, that it's just not possible to be a likeable badass.

I see this play out in real life all the time. I recall a friend telling me how her use of compensatory impression management with a client almost cost her the sale. Like many women, she had received feedback throughout her career that she was "too intense," and she was fearful of conveying that impression during this first meeting with a potential client. Instead, she vowed to show up as friendly and likeable. She did so, however, by attempting to downplay her Assertiveness. She sat politely in her chair, with her legs crossed at the ankles and her hands in her lap, to take up as little space as possible. She listened more than she spoke and smiled a lot. She tried not to "oversell" her accomplishments. Midway through the meeting, the client commented that he didn't think she had the qualifications for the job. She was shocked and frustrated. When she displayed confidence, she was told she was "too much," and when she held back, she was told she was "not enough."

When I heard the story, I thought it was both predictable and preventable. My friend wanted to be liked and attempted to do so by showing up as less Assertive than she normally would. Then, the client saw her as less Assertive. It was a perfectly executed strategy! The only problem was it didn't get her the outcome she wanted. Fortunately, once the client pointed this out, she was able to correct his misimpression, change her behavior in the rest of the meeting, and ultimately make the sale. Still, I offered her advice should this situation ever arise again: *Add, don't subtract.* Start by being yourself, and then find ways to add Assertiveness or Warmth to the situation, as needed.

For example, given my work on speech styles, I'm often asked if women should speak more directly, or if they should embrace less assertive speech. My answer is the same for speech styles as it is for any other behavior: You don't have to change it, but you should be aware of it. If you have a very direct communication style, recognize that others will see you as more Assertive because of it. If that feels comfortable, great—keep it. Then find an authentic way to signal Warmth. Conversely, if your natural speech style is more tentative, realize that's a signal of Warmth and look for another way to showcase your Assertiveness. In the case of my friend, I suggested that she could have showcased her accomplishments unapologetically, as she was inclined to do, and added behaviors that revealed her friendly nature, perhaps by complimenting the client on what his organization was doing well or telling a humorous story at an appropriate point in the meeting. This small tweak—from "either/or" to "both"—is a common theme that underlies many likeable badass strategies.

This also explains why Kate's efforts paid off so beautifully. Solving someone else's problem is one of the most surefire ways to get people to see you as both Assertive and Warm. As she reflected, "Being likeable is important, and when you solve other people's problems, they like you. Solving problems also makes you useful, and that gets you exposure [to powerful people]."

PLAY OFFENSE, NOT DEFENSE

Equally important to Kate's success was that she acted quickly. For women, or anyone else who has inherited a reputation that's neither desirable nor accurate, the key is to take action *as soon as possible*. The more time people have spent thinking of you in a particular way, the harder it will be to change their minds. So, you don't want to marinate in an unfavorable reputation one second longer than necessary. Fortunately, if you act quickly enough, you can shape how you're perceived from the outset of a relationship, without ever spending a moment saddled with a reputation you don't want. This was exactly what Kate did. Since she was a new, entry-level employee, her senior colleagues barely knew who she was or paid her any attention. The first time they became aware of her existence was when she was identified as the person who had the skills and willingness to solve their problem—she entered their consciousness as a likeable badass, and once she was there, confirmation bias made it easy for her to stay there.

Kate's story exemplifies the value of offense over defense—building your reputation is easier and more fun than fixing your reputation. Rather than waiting until she received feedback suggesting she had a status problem, Kate took action early in her relationships to elevate her status from the beginning. Unfortunately, I have many conversations with equally talented women who are passive—until they realize they are saddled with undesirable reputations they want to change. Only then do they look for solutions, and I'm tasked with being the bearer of bad news. Changing how you're viewed is possible but takes much more time and effort.

As an example, consider Victoria Pelletier's reputation turn-around. If you met Victoria today, it would take you less than five seconds to sense what a likeable badass she is. In addition to holding multiple C-suite roles through her career, she's also an author, speaker, mentor, fierce diversity and inclusion advocate, parent, and philanthropist. Like Kate, she embodies excellence in service to others. However, Victoria is the first to admit that she had to rehabilitate her reputation to get to this point. At age twenty-four, she became chief operating officer for a large multinational organization. It was a stretch role for her. She was managing more people than she ever had. Added to that, she was a queer woman, the only woman in the C-suite, and twenty years younger than her peers. Her uniqueness, intersectionality, and lack of experience made her feel conspicuous and insecure, and she "wasn't really sure she belonged there." So she showed up the way she thought she should—she hid her emotions and empathy, fearing they made her seem vulnerable, and leaned into her no-nonsense, all-business, take-no-prisoners style.

For example, over the course of her career, Victoria has been involved in twenty post-merger integrations, which often involve layoffs. In her early years, she would never let on—to those she had to let go, or to those who remained—how emotionally difficult this was for her, and how much sympathy she felt for those whose livelihoods were affected. Unfortunately, years later she learned that this approach had earned her a regrettable nickname among those who worked with her: the Iron Maiden. That was a wake-up call. She vowed to turn her reputation around. She realized that she needed to add, not subtract, by showing her true Warmth while maintaining her signature ambitious, driven, results-oriented approach. She found that simple things made a big difference, such as allowing time at the beginning of meetings for people to chit-chat and get to know each other, or acknowledging and labeling another person's hurt when making decisions that impacted others, like mergers, restructurings, or layoffs. It was doable, but it took time and effort. As she admits, "To undo the damage of the Iron Maiden era, I had to be incredibly intentional and consistent about being the kind of person I'd want to work for, not the one that was followed out of fear." But even with consistency and intention, confirmation bias made it difficult for those who knew her as the Iron Maiden to see her differently. When I asked Victoria how she was finally able to ditch that image, her answer was telling: "I transitioned to a new organization." Building a likeable badass reputation from the get-go with new people proved to be the easiest path forward.

PLAYS TO PRACTICE

🔥 This week, bring task cues to your conscious awareness. Pay attention to others' behaviors, and how Assertive and Warm you perceive them as a result. Pay attention to your own behavior. How do you typically signal Assertiveness and Warmth?

🔥🔥 Which is your bigger strength, conveying Warmth or conveying Assertiveness? Find one way to add a behavior on the weaker dimension. If you're naturally very Warm, commit to signaling more Assertiveness by talking more in your next meeting, for example. If you're naturally very Assertive, look for an opportunity to showcase Warmth, perhaps through a friendly greeting or offering some help.

🔥🔥🔥 Kick a bad habit. Think of a natural behavior that is either Cold or Submissive. Maybe you're seen as rude when you talk over people, or uncaring when you are repeatedly delinquent in responding to emails. Or, like me, maybe you're bad at eye contact, which makes you seem timid. Identify the behavior and try to correct it. Don't panic if it doesn't work. There's always another way to signal that you're a likeable badass, but you should at least try to eliminate all the counterproductive behaviors you can.

CHAPTER 3

Get Your Head in the Game

Managing your status well is like sticking to an exercise routine. You can't do it twice a year and expect good results; you need to make it a daily habit. But on any given day you can always find a good reason to put it off. That's what happened with Felecia Carty.

Felecia sent me a message after she heard me on a podcast—partly to confess, partly for advice. After a fourteen-year career in retail management, working for five different retailers including Macy's and Ralph Lauren, Felecia wanted to pursue a different path, working in customer success for a technology firm. In retail, she excelled at building rapport with her teams and always knew she was well respected. However, she moved companies and locations frequently as she advanced and would often lose touch with her prior teams. Two years after her last retail position, as she searched for technology jobs, she discovered that some of her former colleagues were now working in the tech industry. "Dang," she thought each time, "I should have kept in touch with that person." She desperately wanted help in her job search—information, referrals, and recommendations—but she was reluctant to reach out to them; it felt icky to ask a favor from a person she hadn't spoken to in years.

Ultimately, Felecia was concerned about her status. Because they'd fallen out of touch, she wasn't sure her colleagues would still value her like they did when they worked together. What would they think of her if she showed up, out of the blue, wanting assistance in her job search? Did they respect her enough to even write her back, let alone use their time or connections to help her get a job? I encouraged Felecia to reach out anyway. It was hard to predict how much could be gained by contacting them now, but she had very little to lose. When I met Felecia virtually a few months later, she confessed that she did contact a few old colleagues, but she could have reached out to more of them. She found it easier to ask for help from someone she had never met than someone she knew but hadn't spoken to in years.

If the story stopped there, you might think that Felecia just wasn't that strategic about managing her career. Nothing could be further from the truth. I'd challenge you to find a person alive who approaches their career with more forethought and tenacity than Felecia. When she set her sights on a career in customer success, she immediately attacked this goal from all angles. She enlisted help to refine her résumé. She earned three customer success certifications. She joined multiple industry groups. She spent her days on LinkedIn making connections with people in the industry and scheduled "coffee chats" with more than forty of them. She had a bulging notebook full of information related to the job search—notes from every coffee chat, multiple versions of her "elevator pitch," advice she received, key learnings from her certification programs, customer journey mapping, and more. To stay motivated, she filled the inside cover of the notebook with inspirational quotes: *Do it scared; Simplify your message; Done is better than perfect; What's meant for you won't miss you; and* (ironically) *Your network is your net worth.* Even more impressive than her preparation was her persistence. Ultimately, she applied to 104 jobs, which resulted in 11 callbacks, 7 second-round interviews, 3 final-round interviews, and one offer—the 89th one she had applied for.

Felecia's fierce determination and commitment to excellence blew me away. But the stark contrast between how she managed her job search and how she managed her status was noteworthy. She was investing hundreds, if not thousands, of hours setting herself up for a successful career change but hadn't spent the mere minutes it would have taken over the years to maintain her status with people who already valued her. I empathized with Felecia because I've been in this situation myself many times—wanting something from a person I haven't spoken with in ages. If you've ever started a call or email with "You may not remember me, but . . ." you've found yourself in this predicament, too.*

We're not alone. I have at least one conversation a week with a woman seeking advice on an upcoming interpersonal challenge: an impending performance review, a salary negotiation, a critical meeting with a colleague or client, etc. No matter the specifics, the person seeking advice is always worried about their status—are they valued enough by their audience to get the outcome they want? Ninety-eight percent of the time (perhaps an underestimate), I'm contacted less than forty-eight hours before the discussion in question, and the tone of the message is usually frantic—generally some version of *"Sorry for the short notice, but is there any way we can chat TONIGHT?"* When we talk, I can hear the stress in their voices, so I usually don't say what I'm thinking: *Why are you only strategizing about this now? What were you doing a year ago, six months ago, or even a week ago, to set yourself up for success in this conversation?* We often don't think about managing our status until we need to rely on it. But by then, it's too late. Like Felecia, these are strategic and forward-thinking women in all other aspects of their lives. Why not with their status?

By far the easiest, and most enjoyable, time to build your status with another person is when you don't need anything from them. The chal-

---

* By the way, don't ever do this again. Yes, the fact that you feel the need to start your message with this disclaimer means you have failed to manage the relationship properly, but no need to call attention to it. Instead, start your message with an anecdote that will jog their memory—ideally one that acknowledges their status (because everyone loves flattery) or reminds them of why you are a likeable badass. For example, "Since we've last talked, I've been promoted twice, and the great advice you gave me about advocating for myself helped me succeed in both negotiations with my manager. You were the voice in my head through the entire process, and I can't thank you enough."

lenge is that, like Felecia, you don't always know *whose* assistance you will need in the future. What you *do* know, however, is that you will *always* depend on other people—for information, introductions, recommendations, raises, rides to the airport, and more. The more others respect and value you, the more comfortable you'll be asking for what you want, and the more likely they will be to say yes. The most foolproof strategy, therefore, is to build your status broadly, long before you need it, so you always have one or more people you can rely on for support no matter what need arises.

FIVE LIMITING MINDSETS (AND WHY WE SHOULD DITCH THEM)

There are several convenient excuses we tell ourselves to avoid some of the status-building behaviors we know we should be doing, like networking and self-promoting, but would rather not. When we fail to build our status before we need it, it's usually because we've allowed one or more of these excuses to get in our way. Ditching these *limiting mindsets* and replacing them with what I call the *likeable badass mindset* is the first thing we can do to manage our status better.

I'm an imposter.
Let's get this one out of the way first, because it's a big obstacle. One reason we may not invest in getting *others* to respect us is because we don't respect ourselves. This is more generally known as imposter syndrome—doubting our skills and talents, living in fear of being exposed as a fraud. Imposter syndrome is a psychological pandemic, and no one is immune. The list of well-known, successful women who have publicly confessed to imposter syndrome is long and distinguished: Tina Fey, Associate Justice Sonia Sotomayor, Lupita Nyong'o, Maya Angelou, Arianna Huffington, Amy Schumer, Padma Lakshmi, and Joyce Roché, to name just a few, have all gone public with their occasional (or frequent) feelings of inadequacy. Perhaps being in the company of these talented women is enough to ease your insecurities. But I have even better news for you: The only people who never feel

like imposters are the imposters. *Occasionally feeling like an imposter is the best evidence that you're not one.*

I recognize you may need some convincing on this point, so let me offer data from an unexpected source: one of my favorite negotiation studies. Participants were assigned to play either a job candidate or a job recruiter negotiating the dollar value of the candidate's signing bonus. The recruiter was authorized to pay the candidate up to $20,000 in signing bonus, but was told to pay less if possible, around $5,000. The candidate was told to accept no less than a $10,000 bonus, but their stretch goal was $30,000. Based on these numbers, the range of possible outcomes in the simulated negotiation looked like this:

Least Candidate Would Accept $10,000 ←——→ **Most Recruiter Would Pay** $20,000

Those in the job candidate role were further split into two subgroups. Half of the job candidates were told to keep their worst acceptable outcome in the front of their mind, focusing on getting at least $10,000. The other half were told to focus on their ideal outcome, getting as close to $30,000 as they could. Essentially, this was a mindset manipulation: mentally focus on either your bottom line or your goal.

Recruiters and candidates were then paired to negotiate. As you probably guessed, the candidates who focused on their ideal outcome of $30,000 did much better. The more ambitious the goal, the better the performance.

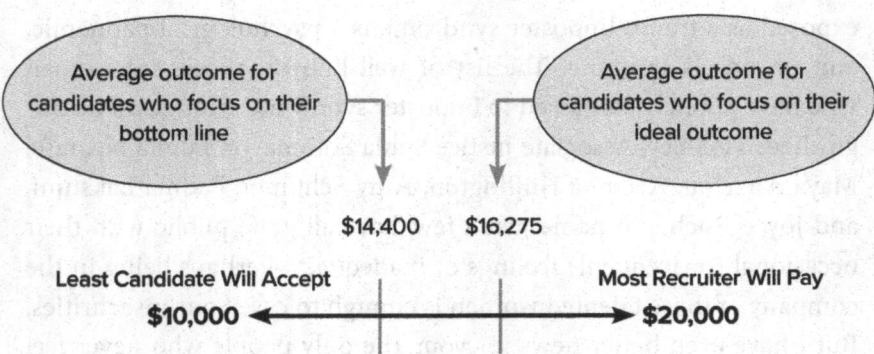

But here's where it got really interesting: At the end of the negotiation, the researchers asked each job candidate how satisfied they were with their outcome, on a scale of 1 (not at all) to 7 (very). Surprisingly, the candidates who focused on their bottom line, and negotiated *less* money, were *more* satisfied. Why? Because each negotiator evaluated their outcome relative to their *expectations*. If they hoped for at least $10,000 and got $14,400, they happily exceeded their goal. But if they hoped for $30,000 and only got $16,275, they fell short. It wasn't objective success that drove negotiator satisfaction, but how that success compared to their expectations. Paradoxically, we see from this study that setting ambitious goals leads us to *do better* but *feel worse*.

This study is one of my favorites for a few reasons. For one, it demonstrates the benefit of setting Big Hairy Audacious Goals (BHAGs). We won't get more than 100 percent of what we aspire to, so we should all aim high.

I also love this research because it helps us think about imposter syndrome in a new, more productive way. When we feel like imposters, we often think it's because our talents and achievements are inferior in comparison to others. Feeling unworthy of others' respect is terrible, but it's doubly problematic when it causes us to retreat and hide from the world. What's worse, the conclusion that feeling like an imposter means we're flawed or lacking in some way isn't even true! What this study shows us is that we can be objectively more successful than those around us, and still feel like the biggest failures in the room. The more we aspire to, the more we achieve—and the more we're left unsatisfied that we fell short of all we had hoped for.

Many accomplished women echo the notion that imposter syndrome increases, rather than decreases, with success. Take, for example, Emma Watson, who skyrocketed to international fame as Hermione Granger in the *Harry Potter* movie series, and Lupita Nyong'o, who won an Academy Award for best supporting actress in the movie *12 Years a Slave*. Both Watson and Nyong'o are superstars with acting résumés beyond compare. I'd trade places with either of them any day—but apparently, I'd still feel like a fraud. As Watson reflected:

It's almost like the better I do, the more my feeling of inadequacy actually increases.... It's weird—sometimes [success] can be incredibly validating, but sometimes it can be incredibly unnerving and throw your balance off a bit, because you're trying to reconcile how you feel about yourself with how the rest of the world perceives you.

And Nyong'o expressed a similar feeling:

I go through [acute impostor syndrome] with every role. I think winning an Oscar may in fact have made it worse. Now I've achieved this, what am I going to do next? What do I strive for?

Imposter syndrome doesn't come from our accomplishments; it comes from the *gap* between our achievements and our aspirations. This is why I say that the only people who never feel like imposters are the imposters. Like the negotiators in the study, if you set your expectations low enough, you're guaranteed to exceed them. You won't achieve as much, but you'll feel great about it. It's only the true likeable badasses among us, the ones who continuously set ambitious goals and achieve great outcomes as a result, who will feel the pain of imposter syndrome. So the next time you feel like an imposter, reassure yourself: *I only feel this way because I have high aspirations, not because I have low achievements.*

Being respected at all times by all people is definitely a BHAG, which means some level of imposter syndrome is inevitable. Rather than trying to make our imposter syndrome go away, let's accept it as unavoidable and reframe what it's telling us. If we see imposter syndrome for what it is, a byproduct of setting really high goals, then we don't feel like frauds. And if we respect our own value, it's much easier to take action to make sure others respect us, too.

LIKEABLE BADASS MINDSET: *I love my inner imposter— as long as she's with me, I know I'm reaching for the stars.*

★

I don't want to be a "status-seeker."

A male colleague once offered to ask faculty and students to nominate me for a prestigious and lucrative teaching award. I was flattered, but aghast: "Absolutely not!" I would have been honored to receive the award, and certainly felt I deserved it, but I wanted to win because my students spontaneously professed their love for me in numerous, glowing recommendations, not because I executed some covert nomination strategy. I believed that if I simply continued to do great work, I would eventually be rewarded. Well, I never did win that award, and I later learned that I was one of the few who subscribed to these (incorrect) beliefs of meritocracy. Most of the winners won, it turned out, because they asked others to nominate them.

For many women, the idea of influencing how others see you feels just as inauthentic and sleazy as the award-nominating process did to me. But remember, our definition of status is being respected and valued by others, not chasing recognition or prestige. Managing your status means having your contributions and talents appreciated for their worth, rather than devalued. It means having other people see you as a person they respect and trust. It doesn't mean you are seeking the spotlight.

This reflexive reaction to managing status is similar to how many people, especially women, feel about "office politics." By definition, office politics is nothing more than managing relationships at work to gain influence, yet the term has generally become synonymous with manipulative, undesirable behavior, like backstabbing and information hoarding. You don't want to be associated with those unsavory traits, so you proudly proclaim, "I don't play office politics." What you mean is "I don't play office politics *that way.*" I'm here to convince you that (a) a little bit of status strategy will provide tremendous payoff, and (b) you can do it in a way that feels true to who you are and who you want to be. *Authentic and strategic aren't opposites. You can, and should, be both.*

On this point, renowned psychologist Bob Cialdini has a great metaphor for how to be authentically strategic (or strategically authentic).

Cialdini is arguably the world's expert on the science of influence. He has effectively given us the tools to get other people to do what we want them to do. As a result, he's often asked about the ethics of his work. By teaching people to be more influential, many wonder, is he helping them manipulate or con others? I love his response, and I find it very applicable to our discussion of status. There are three types of influencers in the world, he says—bunglers, smugglers, and sleuths. *Bunglers* are poor influencers because they fail to apply effective influence tactics (such as a person whose "Tips for a Healthy Heart" article is rejected for newspaper publication because they failed to mention that they're a cardiologist). Bunglers are authentic, but not strategic. Conversely, *smugglers* rely on dishonest or unethical tactics (claiming your product reduces hair loss by 50 percent when you know it doesn't), making them strategic but not authentic. *Sleuths* are effective like smugglers, but they influence through honorable means (making shoppers aware that the sale ends tomorrow when in fact it does). That is, sleuths are both authentic and strategic in their influence attempts.

We know we don't want to be smugglers. This is also why imposter syndrome feels so terrible—it makes us feel like we're smugglers, fooling everyone into thinking we're something we're not. Yet we don't aspire to be bunglers, either—a life spent sitting politely by, letting other people undervalue us, doesn't sound particularly appealing. So, by process of elimination, we should be sleuths!

I explained the concept of sleuthing to Felecia as she reflected on her relationships that had fallen by the wayside. Now that she needed help, she regretted not staying in touch with past colleagues. At the same time, she felt that staying connected to them just in case she needed a favor one day was a smuggler's move. If she disliked her co-workers and kept in contact only to take advantage of them one day, that would be true. But that wasn't the case. These were colleagues with whom she had built a genuine relationship of mutual liking and respect, based on years of reciprocity (a fundamental basis of influence, according to Cialdini). I asked her if they had ever popped into her mind over the years, and if she ever missed talking with them. Yes and yes, she said. I challenged her: What would have been disingenuous about reaching out at those times with a simple "thought of you today and hope you are well" message? And, by staying in touch, might there have been opportunities over the years when *you* could have helped *them*? Staying connected to people from your past is *strategic*—it's easier to ask for a favor when you need one. But it's also *authentic*—these are people you enjoy in your life and want to help. Framed this way, caring for relationships that you've worked hard to build is a form of sleuthing, not smuggling.

On this note, let me offer an important disclaimer: What is sleuthing to one person or in one context may be smuggling to another person or in another context. If you're given advice, in this book or elsewhere, that feels like smuggling to you, DON'T FOLLOW IT. I promise you there's another way to achieve the same ends through sleuthing. For example, I have asked many people to write recommendation letters for me over the years. Each time, I strategized about whom to ask (whose credentials would be most impressive to the readers, which recommenders had the most glowing things to say about me), and I also strategized about how to ask (in person or via email, how to word the request). Through all this planning, I never felt one bit of guilt or discomfort—I was simply being a sleuth. Yet, when my colleague suggested asking others to recommend me for a teaching award, I recoiled. Technically, there was nothing dishonest about this approach; he wasn't suggesting we falsify recommendations, merely that we ask people who already thought highly of me to write them. He and many others saw it as sleuthing, and it wasn't fundamentally different than the sleuthing I had done to secure recommendations over the years. But for me, in this context, it made me feel like a smuggler, so I wanted no part of it.

This isn't because I'm more ethical than the average person. In other situations, I proudly use tactics that others reject. Case in point, I lie to my children for at least three months every year. Starting each October, I respond to every one of their purchase requests with "You should ask Santa for that." And every misdeed leads me to say, "I wonder what Santa will think when he hears what you did." For some of my dearest friends, these tactics constitute parental smuggling, especially if they have chosen to raise their kids without the Santa narrative. I understand their perspective. Yet I consider my strong Santa game some of the best sleuthing I do, and I employ it unapologetically.

This is why I present more tips and tactics for managing status than any one person needs—so you can find plays that make you feel like a sleuth and disregard any that don't feel true to who you are. Again, growth may require some momentary discomfort as you practice new strategies, but never to the point of feeling like a smuggler.

LIKEABLE BADASS MINDSET: *I'm not a smuggler or a bungler. I'm a sleuth—authentic AND strategic.*

*

I don't care what other people think of me.

When I lost my eleventh-grade election for student body vice president, my mother tried to console me. "You can't let it get you down," she said. "There will always be those who don't see your worth. Don't worry about what other people think of you." It wasn't the first, or last, time she offered this advice. And when I find myself reflexively saying similar things to my kids, I cringe because I think it's terrible guidance.[*]

Technically, this wisdom is sound. It's not useful to sit around just *worrying* about what other people think. My problem with this well-intentioned statement is that it's often misconstrued in a few different ways, and these false interpretations serve as convenient excuses for avoiding status-building behaviors. One misleading narrative is "What other people think of you doesn't *matter*." This is false. Your status, one of the biggest determinants of your quality of life, is entirely defined in the minds of others.

Another misinterpretation is "I can't control what others think of me." Again, technically correct. At the end of the day, you don't get

---

[*] Don't judge me, at least not for this. This is nowhere near my biggest failure as a parent.

to decide whether someone else respects you. That decision rests with them. But this doesn't mean that you don't play a role—a huge role—in shaping how others see you. As sixteenth-century English playwright Christopher Marlowe allegedly said, "We control fifty percent of a relationship. We influence one hundred percent of it." The opportunity to influence how others see you is invaluable, and you shouldn't squander it.

The third false variant of this advice is "It's cool not to care what other people think of you." That is, disregarding the opinions of others is seen as a mark of high status. For example, *goblin mode*—doing what you want, without regard for social expectations—sprang to popularity in 2022, so much so that it won the Oxford Languages Word of the Year. If, like me, you had never heard of this term, just imagine Instagram posts of people eating vats of ice cream in bed or shuffling to the store in their pajamas. Although I don't pass judgment on anyone for how they dress or what they eat, I find the allure of goblin mode problematic. Its social media rise is rooted in the idea that ignoring the expectations of others is a path to status, but that's not true. High-status people, by definition, already have the respect and regard of others. This gives them the freedom not to care, or at least pretend not to care, what other people think. But the converse is not at all true—not caring what other people think isn't an effective strategy for gaining status. Once everyone in the world sees us as likeable badasses—the BHAG we'll set for ourselves—we can live in goblin mode if we choose. But until that point, this strategy doesn't serve us well. We should replace the pride of indifference with the pride of effectiveness: "It's cool to get others to see me as I truly am, a serious likeable badass."

LIKEABLE BADASS MINDSET: *I DON'T need to obsess or ruminate over how others see me, but I DO need to shape how others see me.*

★

I'm just one of the guys.

"Stop thinking about the fact that you're a woman. . . . If a woman wants her gender to be irrelevant [to others], then she shouldn't consider it relevant or really, consider it at all."

This is the advice of Amy Trask, who served as CEO of the Oakland Raiders professional football team from 1997 to 2013, and remains, to date, the highest-ranking woman in NFL history. In recognition of her tremendous impact on football, in 2019 she was named one of the "NFL 100 Greatest" Game Changers in history. While most women have been in majority-male groups at some point in their lives, Trask's experience was extreme. Often, she was the only woman in the room. Despite this, Trask maintains that gender isn't salient or important to her and encourages others to adopt a similar mindset. As she reflected on walking into meetings full of men, "I hope that they won't be thinking about my gender. For me to be thinking about my gender, it just doesn't make sense."

In one sense, thinking that you're "just one of the guys" can work to your advantage. When you aren't worried about whether you lack status, it's easier to walk into any room and take up the space you deserve, believing that you have every right to be there. This confident mindset will affect how you show up and how others see you, for the better. It's maddening for women when they're told to "be more confident," but there's truth to this advice (even if the statement is motivated by unconscious bias). Confident people speak more, with a factual tone of voice and a calm, relaxed demeanor. As a result, confident people are perceived as highly competent, and are granted high status.

At the same time, the "just one of the guys" mindset can work against you if it makes you think that managing your status is unnecessary. If the guys don't need to do it, then why should I? I understand the allure of this logic, but it's faulty. First, the guys *do* need to do it. Everyone benefits from high status, including men. Second, the fact that *you* aren't focused on your gender doesn't mean that others won't take notice. For example, Stacy Brown-Philpot, before she became CEO of TaskRabbit, was caught off guard when she moved to India to run Google's office there. No matter where she went, people assumed that some man next to her was in charge, even if that person was her driver. As a Black woman in the United States, she had dealt with plenty of discrimination, but she noticed that the relative importance of gender and race were essentially reversed in India. "My color didn't really matter there," she noticed, "but there was a much stronger assumption that high-status people were men than there was in San Francisco." Similarly, Amy Trask recounted a time that she was blocked from greeting the head of the players' union by a member of the union staff, who said, *"Whose secretary are you?"* I feel confident that Trask wouldn't have been physically intercepted and assumed to be anyone's secretary had she been male.

Despite our collective hope that others won't judge us by our gender, that decision is—unfortunately—not ours to make. We know, both from decades of research and our own lived experiences, that people notice gender. Consider the well-documented gender bias in job recommendation letters. Even in fields like academia, science, and medicine, where applicants are highly educated and accomplished, men are more likely to be described with *standout adjectives,* like "exceptional" or "remarkable." In contrast, letters for women are more likely to contain *doubt raisers,* short phrases that are designed to plant uncertainty in the minds of employers, such as "Even though she doesn't have a lot of experience . . ." Notably, these findings persist even after controlling for the quality of the applicant, and both male and female letter writers exhibit this bias. As the job applicant, you may not be thinking about your gender. But your letter writers might be, and this could have a real impact on whether you get the job.

So, if you rock a mean "I can do anything men can do, but better" swagger, I'm here for it! To the extent it boosts your confidence, you'll show up better for it. But don't let this confidence make you complacent. Build your status before you need it.

LIKEABLE BADASS MINDSET: *I'm not defined by my gender, but I am vigilant about it.*

★

I don't have the time for this.

Of all the mental obstacles to managing our status, I'm most sympathetic to this one. We all have way too much on our plates. I get up earlier each day to get a "head start" on the day's to-dos, only to end each day depressed that my list seems to have grown. I'm always looking for ways to multitask or items I can cut. I play "to-do list dodgeball," ducking and weaving to avoid being hit by new tasks. And on more than one occasion I've pondered the maximum number of days a respectable adult can go without a shower. So, trust me, I understand the belief that you simply do not have time to add "manage status" to your list.

Of course, as you've come to expect by this point, I have a rebuttal. If you need to make more time in your schedule, you should cut practically everything else before you skimp on building your status. In their brilliant book *The No Club: Putting a Stop to Women's Dead-End Work,* scholars Linda Babcock, Brenda Peyser, Lise Vesterlund, and Laurie Weingart provide evidence that nonpromotable tasks—work that helps others but doesn't advance your own interests—overwhelms women's to-do lists, more so than men's. By this definition, though, managing status is the opposite of a nonpromotable task. The sole purpose of building status is to advance your *own* interests—to get the power you deserve, making it easier to get what you want and live the life you want to live. Investing in your status is a gift to yourself, akin to putting on your own oxygen mask before assisting others.

But wait, there's more. I've saved the best news for last. Managing status shouldn't cost you much, if any, additional time. Yes, you should still get those nonpromotable tasks off your list, but you can use that reclaimed time to binge Netflix (or take a long-overdue shower). Showing up as a likeable badass isn't about doing more than you already are. In some cases, it's about doing what you're already doing, just a bit differently. In other cases, it's about eliminating ineffective behaviors, enabling you to get more credit for your greatness in less time.

LIKEABLE BADASS MINDSET: *If I have time to play Wordle, I have time to get credit for my awesomeness.*

PLAYS TO PRACTICE

Once you ditch these limiting mindsets, it's much easier to see yourself as someone who is worthy of status, and willing to go after it. This makes it much easier to act in ways that build your status. Of course, I recognize that this is easier said than done. Controlling our thoughts is so straightforward in concept, but often hard in practice. If you struggle with mindset, like I do, here are a few places to start:

🔥 Become aware of your narrative. Listen to your inner monologue today and notice if any of these limiting mindsets arise. Which ones, and when? Try to replace them with likeable badass mindsets.

🔥🔥 Think of someone you know who exemplifies the "likeable badass mindset." Invite them to lunch or coffee, tell them that you admire them, and ask them how they squash their limiting beliefs. Commit to practicing one of their strategies and see how it works for you.

🔥🔥🔥 Do it scared, as Felecia wrote on the inside cover of her job search notebook for encouragement. Build your status before you need it by identifying one person that you want to think highly of you and one thing you can do to increase their respect for you (even if it's already high). Commit to doing the thing, no matter how many excuses you find to avoid it.

Part II

Master the Plays

CHAPTER 4

Tell Your Story

Showing up as a likeable badass starts with telling your *story*. Most of what people know *about* you comes *from* you—how you talk and write about yourself, how they see you behave. You are the biggest source of your own press, so you need to make that press as positive as possible. I learned this lesson early in my career—in a very frustrating way.

After college, I took a job as a management consultant for McKinsey & Company because influential people in my life told me I should—it was a prestigious firm, they said, one that purported to hire only the best and brightest. On my first project, I was assigned to work alongside a slightly-more-senior colleague—let's call him M—who was widely regarded as a rising star. M had joined the firm about a year before I did, after earning his MBA. "He's a rockstar, definitely on a path to make partner," everyone told me.

Imagine my surprise and dismay, then, when I discovered that M was *not* the likeable badass everyone proclaimed him to be. He was neither competent nor kind. I still vividly recall the day when M gave me a set of hastily drawn charts and tasked me with turning them into digital presentation slides. Just like Kate, I knew this wasn't officially in my job description, but being young, new, and eager to contribute in any way I could, I said yes. As I created the slides, I also corrected the misspellings and grammatical errors in M's original documents. I returned the finished product to him, mentioning that I had caught a few errors in the hope that I would get some likeable badass credit in his eyes. That hope, unfortunately, was misguided. He was enraged. *Who do you think you are?* he shrieked. *If I wanted you to think, I would have told you to think.*[*] I yelled back: *I was a math major, not an English major, but even I know the difference between "there" and "their."*[†] The argument continued, and it didn't end with us hugging it out.

As I endured the three-month project, I was subjected to countless examples of M's incompetence and incivility. My suffering was made even harder to bear as I continued to hear others praise him. Interestingly, though, I soon realized that the people praising M had never actually worked with him. Perplexed and angered, I worked up the courage to share my experiences with another teammate, J. J was a true likeable badass, but he didn't have nearly the positive reputation of M. To my great relief, J agreed with me on all counts: Yes, M had a stellar reputation at the firm, and no, it wasn't deserved.

Months later, after my hellish project had ended, J came to my office with a *Eureka!* expression. "I've discovered the source of M's great press," he exclaimed. Every time J heard something positive about M, he would ask the messenger, "Where did you hear that?" Many times, the trail would go cold; the person didn't remember. Sometimes, though, the person named the source. J would then go to that source and ask the same question. He eventually traced M's story to a few people who remembered that they heard it from—wait for it—M himself! M would brag to them about how his clients and colleagues loved him and the great work he was doing. Never having worked with M, they took his self-praise at face value, and then passed this information on to other colleagues, who then passed it on to even more people.

---

[*] Yes, that is an almost-exact quote, as best I can remember it over twenty-five years later.
[†] When I err, it's almost always on the side of too Assertive, rather than not Assertive enough.

Thanks to a game of office-gossip telephone, M had self-promoted his way to a likeable badass reputation. Accordingly, he was praised, paid, and promoted at levels and rates above his peers.

Even with the mystery solved, I was angry about the whole experience; my only solace came from planning my eventual escape. It wasn't until years later, when I was immersed in the science of organizational psychology, that I heard the saying "People don't leave companies, they leave managers." I immediately understood the truth of that statement and flashed back to how my experience with M had been pivotal in my decision to leave McKinsey.

I realize that hearing this story will likely trigger some serious imposter fears. *This is why I don't like the idea of managing my status,* you protest, *because others will gossip about what a fraud I am. The last thing I want is to be like M.* However, my objective in retelling this (still) painful story is to make the opposite point: We should *all* be more like M.

Obviously, you don't aspire to be overconfident, undercompetent, and cruel. But what I learned from M, a lesson that still benefits me to this day, is that how you talk about yourself matters—a *lot*. Fortunately, unlike M, you have the goods, so you can use his strategy without fear of being exposed as a fraud—because you're not.

★

Your *story* is any information about *you* that originates with *you:* Things you say to people in conversation, your emails, your social media profile and posts, your bio, your résumé, and more. The goal is to use every opportunity to share information about yourself in ways that convey both Assertiveness and Warmth, so your audience respects you more as a result. To be clear, this is self-promotion. Like it or not, self-promotion is critical to building status. If you don't tell a good story about yourself, no one else will either.

When I meet women who have advanced more quickly than their peers, particularly at a young age, I often find that it's because they learned early in their careers, usually the hard way, to tell strong stories about themselves. This is what happened to Meghana Dhar. After graduating with her MBA from Harvard Business School at age twenty-nine, she was hired by Instagram as the head of partnerships for Instagram Shopping. As the first hire on this new team, it was a coveted role with a lot of responsibility. A few months into the role, she went into her first performance review "guns blazing" because she had "crushed it"—working night and day, she knew she had delivered results. She was excited to hear the praise her manager was sure to offer. Instead, he said that other teams had complained about her and her lackluster performance. Meghana was confused and devastated. However, even though she didn't get the review she wanted, her manager believed in her and wanted her to succeed. He offered her a piece of advice: "Look at what Walt[*] is doing." Walt was Meghana's same-age peer who was widely considered a rockstar performer. It took Meghana only a moment of observation to see the difference between them. Walt was sharing his accomplishments widely—on the internal messaging network, in weekly update meetings, in a newsletter he created, and more. Meghana had an epiphany—Walt's "wins" were just conversations he was having as part of his job. "I was having ten of those a day," she realized, "but Walt had done all the work to give everyone around him the narrative." Walt was telling a better story.

Meghana started "beating the drum," but in her own way. She began sending out a weekly email update and hosting one cross-functional meeting every other week where she would showcase the great work of the people on her team. She also would ask members of her division to lead the meetings, which gave them an opportunity to shine while also supporting her story. Within one quarter, her boss gave her an "exceeds" performance rating, the highest possible mark, and shortly after that she was promoted. She also realized that she was reaping more rewards with less effort. Doing 90 percent of the work *with* self-promotion was better than doing 150 percent of the work *without* it. This realization was a turning point for Meghana: "I had never talked about my wins before then. It felt improper." But once she saw the payoff, it became "muscle memory" for her and set the foundation for her entire career. "I became

---

[*] Name change.

a player in the game," she recalls. When she took a new job at Snap Inc. (formerly Snapchat) as the global head of brand partnerships, she made storytelling her top priority from day one.

Snap's culture differed from Instagram's, so Meghana adapted her self-promotion to the new environment. Without an internal messaging network like Instagram's, there was less information sharing at Snap, so Meghana had to adjust both her channels and her frequency. She built a newsletter and continued her practice of regular update meetings, but she reduced the frequency to monthly instead of biweekly. This allowed her to control her narrative from the beginning, while also honoring the norms of Snap's culture. Now, starting her own business, a social and e-commerce consultancy, she's finding a way to tell her story to potential clients in her authentic style. While she has observed men being more outright "salesy," Meghana is a social media wizard and has found great success promoting herself in a less direct way, through her social media posts. There, she can frame her accomplishments around lessons learned and mentorship for others, while making it known to a large audience that she is open for business.*

As Meghana's experience demonstrates, telling a strong story is (a) critical for building our status, and (b) nowhere near as risky as it sounds. We've learned to dislike self-promotion because it triggers fears of the likeability bind: *If I talk about myself in ways that showcase my confidence, ambition, and competence, people will see me as boastful and like me less.* If you're a bungler, this might happen. But sleuths have lots of ways to self-promote that garner credit for both Assertiveness and Warmth, without appearing boastful. In Meghana's case, sending "shout out" emails to recognize the good work of others, giving subordinates opportunities to shine by leading meetings, and offering advice to help others succeed on social media are all ways she showcases Warmth while advertising her wins.

Meghana's storytelling strategies were relatively low effort for her, especially once they became part of her weekly routine. You can also

---

* Those social media posts are how I first met Meghana. A friend of mine, Meghana's former colleague, saw the posts and texted me—the gist was "Meghana is a total likeable badass, you need to know her." Correct on both counts!

find ways to tell your story that are even lower effort, taking mere seconds. One of my favorite examples comes from a very telling interview with Stacey Abrams, American politician, lawyer, bestselling author, and voting rights activist. Abrams, a graduate of Yale Law School, served for ten years in the Georgia House of Representatives before twice running for Georgia governor (in 2018 and 2022)—making her the first Black woman to be a major-party gubernatorial nominee in the United States. As a result, Abrams gained fame and prominence as a rising star in the Democratic Party.

On *CBS Sunday Morning,* in 2021, interviewer Erin Moriarty asked Abrams a pointed question: *Did she aspire to be the president of the United States?* This was a tricky situation for Abrams. She had narrowly lost her bid for governor in 2018 (as she would again in 2022), so setting her sights on the presidency may have seemed too ambitious—if not to her, at least to her audience. To further complicate matters, research has shown that when Black people attempt to overcome the stereotype of low competence through self-promotion, it often backfires—Black people who self-promote are seen as less Assertive *and* less Warm than Asian, Latinx, or white people who engage in the same behavior. This leaves Black people, and especially Black women, in a horrible bind. Say nothing and let people assume you're not competent or tell a strong story and take a hit on both competence and likeability. Even though this maddening finding hadn't been published at the time of Abrams's interview, she probably understood her conundrum all too well.

Fortunately, what Abrams also likely understood is that *how* you tell your story matters. Not all stories are created equal.* Abrams is clearly a sleuth, and her answer was a textbook example of how a likeable badass gets it done. Without missing a beat, she responded:

> Do I hold it as an ambition? Absolutely. And even more importantly, when someone asks me if that's my ambition, I have a responsibility to say yes, for every young woman, every person of color, every

---

* In the above-mentioned research, investigators did not examine differences in how individuals self-promoted. Subjects in the study simply self-reported whether they had engaged in self-promotion or not.

young person of color, who sees me and decides what they're capable of based on what I think I am capable of.

This is a brilliant response. A master class in how to talk about yourself. Faced with this question, many of us would downplay our ambition, fearful of killing our likeability by coming across as overconfident or boastful. I've done this myself more times than I want to admit. In contrast, Abrams proudly confessed her goals, which is Assertive. The truly genius move, though, is the addition of the second sentence. Highlighting that she feels a responsibility as a Black woman to be a good role model shows that she cares about helping others, one of the best ways to convey Warmth. This sentence is what changes her story from badass to likeable badass. Reread her response and think about how you would feel about her if she stopped speaking after the word "Absolutely." Not a terrible answer, but not nearly as good as the full response, in which she comes across as both very giving and a total boss.

It's also important to note that Abrams wasn't running through the streets screaming, "I want to be president!" She didn't even lead the interview with this information. Instead, she waited until she was asked a direct question. When asked, though, she didn't deflect. A door opened and she strutted through, seizing the chance to tell her story. Telling a stronger story doesn't mean you need to overshare details of your résumé with people you meet at the grocery store. It's perfectly OK, sometimes even preferable, to wait for a natural opportunity to arise, if you're willing to take it when it comes. To borrow one of the most memorable lines of the musical sensation *Hamilton*, let's not throw away our shot.

THE STACEY ABRAMS STRATEGY
When you have an opportunity to reveal your accomplishments or confess your ambition, do it! Then add a concluding statement focused on benefiting others.

Even if you're never interviewed on national TV, this technique is one everyone can add to their toolkit. For example, when it's your turn to give an update on your work in the weekly team meeting, you could offer up something like this:

"We should finalize the sale to customer X next week. I'm very excited because we're on track to hit our division's annual sales goal for the year."

Or

"I attended our industry conference last week and was honored to receive an award for my service to the event. I put a lot of effort into that conference because I think it's one of the best ways to showcase our company, which helps us recruit top talent."

Telling a strong story doesn't need to be a complicated, time-consuming process. It can be as simple as a well-crafted, two-sentence response to a question.

TWO BAD HABITS THAT WEAKEN YOUR STORY

Stacey Abrams's response is a great one not just for what she said, but also for what she *didn't* say. By far, the easiest way to tell a strong story is to avoid telling a weak one. Unfortunately, two counterproductive tendencies hurt our stories. Before we adopt more storytelling "dos," we first need to eliminate these "don'ts."

Bad storytelling habit #1 is hiding our successes—intentionally withholding or downplaying positive information about ourselves. Bad habit #2 is advertising our failures—inventing, exaggerating, or voluntarily confessing our shortcomings. We don't do these things because we're weak, stupid, or unable to change. We do these things because we *think* that they will protect our status, especially our Warmth. However, the research proves us wrong: These habits backfire, threatening our status rather than building it. Based on the science, there are better choices we can make instead.

HIDING SUCCESS

Concealing Achievements

What we do: Keep our accomplishments to ourselves. In one survey, more than 80 percent of adults reported concealing an achievement—like receiving a promotion, a school acceptance, or an award—from others at some point in their life.

Why we do it: We worry that sharing our success will come across as boastful and will make others feel inferior. By withholding information that showcases our competence, ambition, and effort, we hope to preserve our Warmth, but we forgo an opportunity to boost Assertiveness.

Why it backfires: Concealing success damages our status and relationships, especially if it's later discovered. The science shows that when people find out we kept quiet (often after they hear the news from someone else, which they eventually will), they conclude we didn't tell them because we didn't want them to feel sad or envious.[*] This insults them, because it reflects a negative assumption about their character and resilience (that they're too fragile or self-centered to be happy for us). As a result, the relationship deteriorates. In comparison to people who talk about their successes, we feel less close to those who stay quiet, especially if we eventually hear their good news from someone else. We also trust them less and are less interested in socializing and cooperating with them.[†]

What to do instead: Shout our good news from the rooftops! This

---

[*] If you're curious, psychologists refer to this as a paternalistic motive.
[†] These reputational consequences are the same if you share your news in a public forum (like Facebook) or a private conversation, and if the person you're sharing with is a close or distant acquaintance. Concealing success in response to a direct question (e.g., "Heard any news on the promotion?") is worse than with an indirect question (e.g., "How are things?"), but both are still insulting.

research also indicates that when we tell others about our success we're seen as more Assertive and Warmer than when our success remains unknown. That is, one of the easiest ways to get likeable badass credit is by simply talking about our wins.

Humblebragging

What we do: Mask our achievements in a complaint or humility (e.g., *"I hate watching myself on TV"*). Humblebrags are annoyingly common, particularly on social media! In one survey, when asked to recall a humblebrag they heard from others, more than 70 percent of people were able to remember an example.

Why we do it: The rationale is that bragging and complaining at the same time makes you appear both accomplished and humble, thereby increasing both Assertiveness and Warmth.

Why it backfires: Again, the evidence pokes holes in this logic. Humblebraggers are seen as insincere, and therefore *less* competent and likeable compared to those who simply brag.

What to do instead: Opt for a straight-up brag. If you worry that doing so will hurt your Warmth, you can employ the Stacey Abrams Strategy and add a concluding comment focused on benefiting others. Using the example above, you could say, *"I was interviewed on TV this morning. It was rewarding to share my advice with a wider audience."*

If it fits your style, another effective option is a "humorbrag," a self-promoting statement that is combined with self-enhancing humor. For example, *"I was on TV this morning. Their makeup artist made me look so good I offered to tattoo her name on my arm."* This approach has been shown to increase perceptions of both Assertiveness, by highlighting your skills, and Warmth, by signaling that you are pleasant and entertaining.

Rejecting Compliments or Gratitude

What we do: Downplay or counterargue the kind words of others. For example:

"Thank you for this wonderful dinner. You're such a good cook!"

"Not really. I just follow recipes. It's like paint-by-number but with food."*

Or

"You clearly haven't been talking to my kids."†

Most of us, between 70 and 95 percent, have deflected or rejected praise at some point, according to the research of Chris Littlefield, an expert in employee recognition.‡

Why we do it: Praise makes us feel embarrassed and uncomfortable for a variety of reasons. Sometimes we worry that accepting the comment "raises the stakes," and we'll let people down if we fail to sustain that level of performance. Other times we don't see ourselves as exceptional, and the kind words embarrass us. Or we may worry that accepting praise is boastful and think that minimizing it will make us seem Warmer.

Why it backfires: As Littlefield astutely points out, when someone offers you a compliment, they're stating the effect your behavior had on them. They're not asking you whether you agree. By offering *your* opinion on *their* opinion, you risk losing both Warmth and Assertiveness.

A compliment or thank-you is a gift, and rejecting it is no less rude than handing a beautifully wrapped package back to the giver and saying, "*Nah, you keep it.*" That doesn't build our Warmth, it kills it. The other person feels a sting of rejection and sees us as *less* kind and appreciative, if only in their nonconscious brain.

Rejecting appreciation also threatens our Assertiveness. When we respond with some version of "*No, I'm really not as good as you think I*

---

* If you're thinking no one would ever say such a dumb thing, you're wrong. I said that.
† Yep, I also said this.
‡ Littlefield is the founder of Beyond Thank You, a training company specializing in employee recognition and appreciation. He spent about a year interviewing over four hundred people on commuter trains in Boston, Massachusetts. Published reports of his early findings reported 70 percent of people expressing discomfort with praise. However, Littlefield says this is an underestimate. By the time he finished his interviews, the number was higher, closer to 95 percent.

am," or "*All of the credit for that belongs to someone else*," people believe us! As we saw with M's success, we're the ultimate experts about ourselves. People take what we say at face value. That's good news when we talk ourselves up, but bad news when we talk ourselves down. Littlefield experienced this firsthand, while sitting in the dentist chair. He complimented his dentist and her assistant on their ability to communicate without talking. The dentist replied, "We screw up all the time." Littlefield left the office and never went back.

What to do instead: All we need to do to show up as Assertive and Warm in the face of a compliment is to respond with a simple "*Thank you!*" When we want to take it to the next level, we can add that second sentence focused on building Warmth, such as

> "Thank you! I take a lot of pride in my cooking. It's my favorite way to show love to my family and friends."

Or

> "Thank you! You just made my week!"

Or

> "Thank you! That means a lot coming from a master chef like you."

ADVERTISING FAILURE

Self-Deprecation

What we do: Put ourselves down and highlight our faults. Sometimes we do this as a strategy for deflecting a compliment, but other times we do it outright, without provocation.

Why we do it: One reason we put ourselves down is to be funny (e.g., "*The only abs I have are abnormalities*"). Other times, we self-deprecate to manage others' feelings when we've outperformed them (e.g., "*The only reason I won the 'manager of the year' trip to Florida is because my* *colleagues wanted a break from me*"). In these situations, we use self-deprecation to showcase our humility and preserve our Warmth.

Why it backfires: Although certain forms of humor, like humorbragging, can be very effective for gaining status, self-deprecating humor is likely to incur reputational costs. Like other things we say about ourselves, self-deprecation is also taken at face value—when people mock their own intelligence, others see them as less intelligent; when people joke about their physical appearance, others see them as less attractive. When we downplay our Assertiveness or Warmth, we are seen as less Assertive or less Warm, even if it gets us a laugh.

Self-deprecation also fails when we use it to convey modesty about our successful performance. When "winners"—those who have outperformed others—attempt to appease those with lesser performance through self-deprecation, the winner is no more liked than if they said nothing, and their performance is attributed less to skill. Self-deprecation to those worse off reduces your perceived Assertiveness and doesn't increase your perceived Warmth.

What to do instead: Regardless of your motivation, putting yourself down has few upsides and many risks. Instead, we're much better served following a modified version of Mom's advice: If you don't have something nice to say—about yourself—don't say anything at all.

Unnecessary Apologies

What we do: Create the perception of failure by apologizing for tiny or imaginary transgressions, such as a ten-minute delay in responding to an email, a long-winded response to a question, or an interruption. I still vividly remember saying, *"Sorry I missed your call,"* to a colleague who had left me a voicemail around 8 p.m., while I was in the hospital delivering my second child. I felt compelled to apologize when I returned the call even though only twelve hours had passed since my son was born.

It's well publicized that women apologize more than men. In one diary study, women and men were asked to keep track of wrongdoings and apologies for twelve days, either as transgressors or as victims. When people thought they had done something wrong, men and women reported apologizing at equal rates, about 80 percent of the time. But women offered more apologies than men overall. Why? Because women have a lower threshold for what constitutes an apology-worthy event. Compared to men, women see the identical offense (e.g., snapping at a friend) as more severe, and therefore find the victim more deserving of an apology. Because of these different standards, women feel that they're wronged more often, and that they commit more wrongdoings. This is what leads to the gender difference in frequency of apologies.

Why we do it: We apologize to preserve or restore our Assertiveness, such as when our performance is substandard, or our Warmth, when we have been selfish or unkind.

Why it backfires: When you have transgressed, it's usually wise to apologize.* It's the right thing to do, and myriad studies have documented how apologies repair both your reputation and the relationship. The challenge comes when we constantly apologize for insignificant or imagined failures. Because we've done nothing wrong, there's no reputation to repair, so the apology has no upside. There is, however, a downside: We risk damaging our Assertiveness. Apology words are markers of powerless speech. Powerless speech, as we've discussed, is viewed as Warm but Submissive. If you've done nothing wrong, then you're probably perceived as Warm already. You don't need yet another behavior that signals Warmth, especially if that behavior might threaten your Assertiveness. This is the rationale behind the frequently offered advice to replace apologies with equally polite but more Assertive alternatives, like *"Thank you for your patience."*

However, there's another, less obvious, benefit of reducing your apologies. Refusing to apologize has been shown to increase your self-esteem, and your sense of power, strength, courage, and control. Choosing not to apologize makes you *feel* more Assertive. The more Assertive your mindset, the more Assertive you'll be.

---

* Although beyond the scope of this book, there are circumstances where apologies can hurt your reputation. Specifically, if you commit an integrity-based failure, you are better off denying the wrongdoing than apologizing for it. I'm not advocating for this approach, just reporting the science.

What to do instead: If you're committed to reducing unnecessary apologies in your writing, technology can help! Download the Google Chrome extension Just Not Sorry, which scans your emails for powerless speech words, including apology words, and underlines them. Unfortunately, there's no analogous AI tool—yet—to help us reduce our spoken apologies, but I'm sure it's only a matter of time.

If unnecessary apologies are in your DNA, consider swapping some of your usuals for *superfluous apologies*—expressions of regret for undesirable circumstances outside of your control (e.g., *"Sorry about the weather"*). Research has shown that superfluous apologies build Warmth. They convey that you can see another person's perspective and have empathy for their situation. As a result, you're more liked and trusted. And, because it's clear to the receiver that you're not at fault, these types of apologies don't reduce perceptions of your Assertiveness.

CONDUCT A STORYTELLING AUDIT

I intentionally refer to hiding success and advertising failure as "habits." These behaviors have been practiced for so long that we do them without thinking. If I asked you how many cups of coffee you had yesterday, you could probably give me a fairly accurate answer. But if I asked you how many times you self-deprecated yesterday, would you have any idea? Probably not. This suggests that your storytelling is on autopilot. You're putting information about yourself out into the world without being fully aware of what that information is. To tell a stronger story, you need to replace *habits* with *choices*. The difference between a habit and a choice is *conscious awareness*. Only when you become aware of your behavior can you decide whether you want to keep it or change it.

The best way to become aware of your current story is to conduct a *storytelling audit*, in which you track details of the story you're telling about yourself. I'm a huge fan of this exercise because it's simple to execute and very eye-opening. All you need to do is observe your verbal and nonverbal behaviors for a week, paying attention to both one-on-one interactions (conversations and emails) and one-to-many interactions (presentations, bios, social media). By the end, you'll be able to answer several important questions:

- What typical opportunities do you have to tell your story (e.g., work emails, introductions, lunches with friends, social media)?
- Who is hearing your story? Is it generally people who already know you, or people you're meeting for the first time?
- In which situations are you telling a strong story, conveying both Assertiveness and Warmth?
- In which situations do bad habits weaken your story?

I never advise anyone to do something that I haven't done myself, so I will explain the process using my own audit as an example.

1. Decide how you want to take notes about yourself. I found a small notebook and tossed it in my purse, and I also set up a notes page on my phone. I used whichever was convenient at a given moment.
2. Write down a short description of every storytelling success, no matter how big or small. A success is any time you feel confident that you conveyed both Assertiveness and Warmth to your audience. Note just enough information about what happened so you can remember the details later. Again, many aspects of your story will be conveyed through words, but also note any relevant nonverbal behaviors. In my case, I observed these types of successes:
   - Gave advice to a friend.
   - Accepted a compliment with a smile and a "Thank you."
   - Introduced myself with a firm handshake, eye contact, and a smile.
   - Nailed both the facts and the jokes during a presentation.
   - Posted on social media about one of my accomplishments.
3. Track your bad habits. Jot down a note every time your *first instinct* is to hide success or advertise failure. By first instinct, I mean that this is the first thought that pops into your mind,

even if you don't follow through with it. For example, if you catch yourself wanting to start an email with "Sorry for my delayed reply," as I did often, make a note of it, even if this exercise leads you to consciously choose a different opening line.
4. Summarize your notes into a table like the one on the following page. I would either enter my tally and notes at the end of each day, or after a few days if I was pressed for time. At the end of the week, I sat down with my coffee to review and reflect.

I had a decent number of wins—15 times where I thought I did a good job showing up as a likeable badass, which equated to about twice a day. But I had more than twice that number of potential fails. There were 38 instances where I was on the verge of speaking about myself in ways that reduced my Assertiveness or Warmth. Assuming this was a typical week, that would add up to nearly 2,000 instances in a year. That's 2,000 missed opportunities to show up as a likeable badass. And, as a woman who thinks about these behaviors for a living, I'm confident that my numbers are lower than average.

As I became more aware of my storytelling, I became more deliberate. I started to ask myself the critical question: *Given my goals in this situation, how can I show up as both Assertive and Warm?* In some cases, but not all, the answer led me to change how I tell my story. Specifically:

I have found new ways to be funny. Making people laugh is one of my superpowers. But I realized a *lot* of my humor is at my own expense. By comedic standards, my self-deprecation is very successful. But as a likeable badass, my self-deprecation undermines my status. Now that I'm aware of how much I put myself down, I'm better able to self-correct. Before I speak, I think about my goal. If I want to empathize with someone who's feeling down or enlist someone's advice or support, then I'll continue with my self-deprecating story. If I'm simply trying to be funny, I'll look for another way to convey humor, such as humorbragging or telling an amusing story about one of my kids.

Behavior	Tally (Number of Times)	Notes and Examples
STRONG STORYTELLING		
Showing up to your audience as both Assertive and Warm	15	◉ I tell my strongest stories on social media, or when interacting one-on-one with people I already know.
WEAK STORYTELLING (BAD HABITS)		
Concealing achievements	6	◉ Didn't mention I attended Stanford when introducing myself onstage.
Humblebragging	0	◉ This never once occurred to me. However, I did notice that I had a lot of complaints (without the brags).
Rejecting compliments or gratitude	4	◉ Caught myself a few times, but was usually able to correct myself before I responded. However, I did laugh in response to one, and could see on the person's face that my reaction had hurt their feelings. ◉ I found compliments from strangers (like people in the airport taking note of my shoes) made me more uncomfortable than compliments from colleagues, friends, and clients.
Self-deprecating	12	◉ "I suck at making PowerPoint slides." ◉ Lots of self-deprecating attempts at humor.
Unnecessary apologies	16	◉ "Sorry if I wasn't clear." ◉ "Apologies for the long message." ◉ Most apologies happening over email.

I now mention where I went to school. I'm privileged to hold a bachelor's degree from Dartmouth College and a PhD from Stanford University. I'm grateful and proud of these experiences, but I've never been able to say "I went to Stanford" without feeling like a total snob. I choke on the words every time. Instead, I'll say dumb, vague things like "I went to school in California." I'm not alone—research has shown that people who attended high-status schools often conceal this information when talking to others. But just because lots of people do it doesn't make it a good idea. When talking to people one-on-one, being cagey about my alma mater is concealing an achievement. If the person later finds out, which they can easily do by looking at my website or social media, I've likely hurt my status. Further, I teach and speak for a living. When I introduce myself to audiences meeting me for the first time, I have about thirty seconds to convince them that they should put down their phones and pay attention to me. Like it or not, letting people know that I'm a professor with a PhD from Stanford is one of the quickest ways I can signal competence, ambition, and confidence. Through the storytelling audit, I realized the solution wasn't to *subtract* information about my credentials from my introduction, but rather to *add* information that would showcase my Warmth. Now, I always mention my degrees and titles in my introductions, but also work in one or more attempts at Warmth—conveying humor through funny (but not self-deprecating) stories or sharing some personal details of my life to create feelings of similarity (e.g., I'm a mom of three, I'm scared of flying, I love coffee but hate all coffee-flavored foods).

I'm a serial apologizer, and I'm good with that: Sorry I missed your call. Excuse the delayed reply. Sorry I can't be of more help. As a result of the storytelling audit, I became more conscious of how often I do this.* However, upon reflection, I've decided to keep most of my apologies. For one, these apologies feel natural to me, and it felt like too much work to keep deleting these phrases (especially from my emails

---

* Ironic case in point, as I was writing this paragraph, I received a text from a former babysitter saying that my plumber had called her instead of me to confirm my upcoming appointment. "Sorry!" I texted back. "No need to apologize!" she responded. You can't make this stuff up.

and texts, where I use them a lot). I also know that I show up as very Assertive to most people, so I'm generally more at risk of conveying hostile strength than friendly weakness. In my case, some unnecessary apologies might be helpful for conveying Warmth. However, I have become more careful when interacting with someone who doesn't know me well, like a prospective client. Often, I'm younger than the people who hire me, and I have a very casual conversational style (for a professor, anyway)—both of which might cause me to be perceived as Submissive in a first interaction. In those cases, I'll delete the unnecessary apologies, and the exclamation points and emojis that I otherwise love to use. I'll still work to convey Warmth, but will do so in more Assertive ways, such as sharing a research article that's relevant to their work.

WHY SELF-PROMOTION ISN'T AS RISKY AS YOU THINK

Before we discuss more strategies for artful self-promotion, let me explain why you shouldn't be terrified of it.

As I said, my experience with M gnawed at me for years. Not only did it violate my sense of justice, but I also couldn't understand why his self-promotion was so effective. At the very least, his lack of humility should have killed his Warmth. Later, though, once I was a professor immersed in the science of human behavior, a theory about M's success started to take shape: I suspected that M's self-promoting message was effective because people weren't paying that much attention when he spoke, and therefore didn't remember he was the messenger.

If not for a steak dinner with Adam Grant, that theory might still be untested. Before he was a Wharton professor and author of multiple bestselling books, including *Give and Take*, *Think Again*, and *Hidden Potential*, Adam was a doctoral student interviewing for a faculty position in my department. As the most junior professor in my group at that time, it was often my role to take job applicants to dinner. While dining with Adam, I asked him the question I asked each candidate: *What is one research idea you've always wanted to test, but never have?* He answered, but then did something no applicant had ever done: He asked me the same question in return. Like water from a broken dam, the story of M, and my corresponding hypothesis, gushed forth. Forty-five minutes later I took my first breath, and Adam responded, "We should write that paper." So we did.

Multiple studies, including some that I have published, have demonstrated that our brains often forget or confuse the sources of our information (which is why so many good stories start with "I can't remember who told me, but . . ."). When people are only half listening, they'll remember *what* they heard (*M is excelling*) but forget *where* they heard it (*M told me this*). As a result, self-promoting to busy, distracted people is an effective tactic for building status: You'll be perceived as Assertive (by revealing your successes), without the risk of losing any Warmth (by appearing boastful). And the great news is that most people, especially the powerful ones—the exact people you want to promote to—aren't paying that much attention to you. They have their own lives to worry about.

To test this theory, Adam and I put participants in a common self-promotion context: applying for a job. Participants read a job applicant's cover letter and three recommendation letters from the applicant's former co-workers. We varied two things: how self-promoting the applicant was in his cover letter, and how busy and distracted the readers were.* As predicted, we found that when participants were distracted, the self-promoting job applicant was perceived as both Assertive and Warm. Busy participants were able to recall the positive information about the applicant but forgot where they read it (the applicant himself or his recommenders). The more confused they were about the source, the more effective the self-promotion was.

The moral of the story: Don't be afraid to self-promote, especially to busy, powerful people. Those are the people who can make good things happen for you, and because they're not hanging on your every word, all they'll remember is that they heard you're spectacular.

---

* In one study, the distracted readers had something else on their mind, a nine-digit number they needed to remember, and in the second study they were under time pressure.

STRATEGIES FOR TELLING A STRONGER STORY

When you're ready to lean into self-promotion, there are many ways to go about it. As Meghana found, you can start by observing someone who does it well, then modify their approach to fit your authentic style. For more inspiration, here are my favorite easy-to-implement strategies, based on what has worked for me and others. Don't limit yourself to only these suggestions, but instead use them to spark creativity and find new ways to tell your best story both easily and effectively.

I present these ideas roughly in increasing order of heat. As you gain experience and comfort telling your story, you'll master cooking at low temps and be ready to bring the fire.

Automate

For years, I never set an automatic out-of-office reply to my work emails. If I was working, I didn't feel that I needed one. If I wasn't working, I didn't want to advertise it. But I changed my strategy after meeting Rachel Sheerin, a wildly successful keynote speaker and emcee who headlines stages both in the United States and across the globe. Rachel is—hands down—the most masterful woman I've ever met when it comes to showing up as a likeable badass. One of the best storytelling hacks I learned from Rachel is the strategic use of the out-of-office message. Every time Rachel speaks at an event, she creates an automatic email reply, like this one:

Subject: Live on Stage! I'm Keynoting Today!

Aloha & thanks for your email!
  If you're getting this email, it means that I am currently rocking a keynote on stage today with the XXX Team! Streaming socially-distant style and delivering fun engagement, beautiful visuals, and an impressive virtual experience for clients, I love partnering with S, M and their team—check them out at [company url]. 🖤
  Since I'm 100% focused on serving my clients and attendees today (like I will be focused on you soon)—my replies will be slightly delayed.

If this is a time-sensitive matter (or you want to text me a cute picture of your dog!), please text me at xxx-xxx-xxxx—if not, I look forward to replying to your email within 36 hours!

Cheers + Warm Wishes,
Rachel

Totally awesome, right? Most of us privileged enough to have email either take it for granted or despise the never-ending to-do list it creates. Rather than see it as a nuisance, Rachel harnesses the power of technology and automation to build her status. Through her message, Rachel showcases that she's in demand with clients and confidently "rocking" the stage with a "fun" and "impressive" experience, all signals of Assertiveness. Her praise of her clients, her commitment to serving them (and you) fully, the sharing of her cell phone number, and her humorous reference to dog pictures[*] are all great ways to signal Warmth.

I had already come to love and respect Rachel by the time I read one of her automated messages. But I've also gotten similar emails from people I know less well and been able to observe how it improved my opinion of them. For example, Felena Hanson is the author of *Flight Club—Rebel, Reinvent, and Thrive: How to Launch Your Dream Business*, as well as the founder of Hera Hub, a spa-like co-working space catering to women entrepreneurs. When I first read about Felena and her work, she immediately struck me as someone I wanted to know. We exchanged a few emails, and through that interaction I received an automated email reply:

My response to email will be delayed as we are busy opening our 7th location in Chicago.

Thank you,
Felena

---

[*] In case you're curious, I asked Rachel how many dog pictures she's received over the years. Her response: "Probably 500. I have everything from a 2-legged dog named HOPS in Portland to a distinguished white terrier named Mister Bucklesberry who lives in CT—who wasn't even that person's dog. It was their son's girlfriend's parents' new dog. And I have had a couple rabbits, hedgehogs, one person had a fox as a pet—and a lot of babies, too."

Seventh location! Those two words instantly elevated Felena's status in my eyes, even though I had never met her or spoken with her. Felena's story, consisting of a single sentence, is very different than Rachel's, yet they have the same effect.*

I love the out-of-office message because it's a low-heat strategy that even the most fearful self-promoters can use. You don't have to look anyone in the eye while you write about your Assertiveness and Warmth, and your self-promotion is hidden in the explicit purpose of the message—letting people know your response may be delayed. Although the above examples are in the context of work for pay, this strategy can just as easily be used with your personal email.

I also love the efficiency of an automated email: Everyone who emails you will see a single message, allowing you to build your reputation with many people while you're off doing other things. To boost the time efficiency even further, consider creating email templates for common out-of-office situations like Rachel does. In addition to the "onstage" template, she has a template for traveling, and another for focused work. When she's in one of these situations, she quickly customizes the template, and the out-of-office message is posted within minutes.

> **THE OUT-OF-OFFICE STRATEGY**
> Promote yourself through email with a two-part automated reply. State the awesome thing you're doing, then add a few details that showcase your likeability, humor, or helpfulness.

---

* If Felena asked me for advice—which she has not—I would suggest she add one more sentence to her reply message to highlight her Warmth. Something like "This expansion of our business will enable us to serve and support even more women entrepreneurs in their journeys." If you're a fan of short and sweet, two sentences is generally all it takes to build your reputation, as we saw with Stacey Abrams—one to showcase your Assertiveness, and another to showcase your Warmth.

Praise

One of my favorite storytelling strategies also relies on email, although you could easily adapt this to in-person conversations. When appropriate, I send messages to high-power, high-status people making them aware of my work, while also offering genuine appreciation for the great work of others. In other words, I look for opportunities to promote myself and promote others at the same time. I'm not alone. Meghana, for example, employed the same strategy through her "shout out" emails.

Although I've been doing this for years, recent research supports my logic—combining self-promotion with other-promotion is an effective strategy to convey both Assertiveness and Warmth and helps to create a more favorable impression than self-promotion alone. I also like it because it gives me an authentic opportunity to elevate the talents of others, which is central to my identity as a sponsor and advocate. You might find this strategy to be slightly higher heat than setting your out-of-office message, but only by a few degrees.

Here's an example of a recent message I sent. I organized and moderated a virtual panel discussion for prospective applicants to my university, and recruited three stellar alumni to take part, all now distinguished professionals in their respective careers. This was a non-promotable task for all of us, but I agreed because it was an easy lift, and it was important to the school. The panel was a huge success, but I knew that my colleagues would have no idea it happened if I didn't tell them. I also felt that the three alums deserved more recognition than a thank-you from me. To address both of these concerns, I sent the following message to my dean—a powerful and busy man:

> Hi [Dean],
>   Yesterday . . . I moderated a LinkedIn Live webinar on Negotiation and Advocacy for Women with three star alums: J, C, and S. All three were incredibly generous with their time and advice and helped us show the very best side of what we offer. The session was very well attended and well received, all thanks to them.

I thought you would appreciate knowing what great ambassadors they are for women's advancement, DEI more broadly, and our program.

Best,
Alison

He didn't respond to this message, but knowing him I assume he read it, and then immediately went on to the next email in his inbox or meeting on his calendar—which is exactly what I intended. I wanted him to pay just enough attention that my underlying message—Alison and the three alums are all likeable badasses—would set up camp in his nonconscious brain.

> **THE BRAG AND THANK STRATEGY**
> When you have an accomplishment that may go unnoticed, make people aware by offering sincere praise for those who contributed to your success.

Outsource

"I really loved writing my résumé," said no one ever. Telling your story on a résumé feels hard, no matter how old or experienced you are. *If I don't toot my own horn enough, I won't impress my audience,* you fret. *But if I toot my horn too much, people will think I'm exaggerating or see me as a braggart.* It often feels like an impossible tightrope to navigate. This goes for more than résumés; we struggle to find the perfect balance of horn tooting for bios, social media pages, school application essays, and many other types of documents meant for self-promotion.

Robynn Storey, founder of Storeyline Resumes, an executive résumé-writing service, has seen this dynamic play out a million times, particularly among women:

"When you read someone's résumé, 99.999% of the time they are describing their job and not their accomplishments. Everyone struggles with this, but women have a particular habit of underselling who they are in this process. They don't want to brag—but a résumé is the place to brag! They don't know how to describe the value of what they do. Men are much better at being master of the universe, espousing their successes."

Rather than face this struggle alone, enlist a partner. Give a list of your accomplishments and accolades to someone else and ask them to write the document for you. This is the value of a high-quality résumé-writing service like Robynn's: they craft your story for you. The incredible demand for these services is evidence of how helpful a trusted partner can be. For example, in 2022, Storeyline Resumes alone grossed $10 million in revenue and employed sixty-five people.

Although paying for the expertise of a professional storytelling firm may be well worth it in certain situations, you don't necessarily need to spend money to employ this strategy. Give your résumé, bio, or social media profile to a friend and ask them to write it for you. Yes, you're asking for a favor, but if they already think you're a likeable badass, they'll be happy to do it. Not only do they want you to be successful, but it's also a simple request for a friend to fulfill. Bragging about someone else is way easier, and more fun, than bragging about yourself, so a bio that would take you a week to write might take your friend an hour.

When they have a draft, you can edit it—as long as you don't cut out all of the nice things they said about you. If you want to go one step further, offer to return the favor and write their document, making the exchange mutually beneficial.

To get the most from this process, consider following the steps that Robynn uses with her clients:

- Send your current documents (résumé, bio, social media profiles) to your partner. Don't edit them, don't judge them, just send them as they are.

- Set aside an hour for your partner to interview you (over coffee, wine, or a walk—whatever makes it feel fun). Have them ask questions to pull your story out of you, such as:
  - Walk me through your life from your first job until now.
  - What were the challenges you faced in each job, or at each stage of your life?
  - Tell me a story about something that happened in your life that was a mess, and how you dealt with it.
  - When you look back over that time in your life, what would you consider your legacy to be?
  - What outcomes have you achieved, and how are those outcomes measured? As Robynn says, "Everyone has outcomes they can measure. If you're a janitor and you negotiated with your company's mop head supplier to reduce costs and save $800, that belongs in your story."
- Find two quotes about yourself from other people, such as comments from your boss in your last performance review, or a compliment you received about a social media post.
- Your partner will review all this information and draft your story.
- You review what your partner has written, and you collaborate on edits. It's common for new accolades to be added at this point. "It's hard to get people to open up about their accomplishments at first," Robynn observes, "but once they start thinking about it, they realize they have more!"

Enlisting a partner in this process can be transformational. Looking at your story through another person's eyes, you may not even recognize yourself. That's exactly what happened to one of Robynn's clients, a chief technology officer for a medical company. Initially, her résumé stated, *"I manage a small team of IT professionals, including our help desk."* Through the interview process, however, Robynn's team uncovered the full story. The CTO knew her firm was struggling to compete because they lacked adequate technology to manage orders and shipments. Sales were tracked manually on spreadsheets, and mistakes were frequent. The CTO secured a $2 million investment to craft a company-wide technology and process overhaul. However, this accomplishment was nowhere to be found in the story she was telling on her résumé and may never have emerged if she hadn't enlisted the help of a third party. Working with Robynn, her story was transformed: *"I spearheaded an entire enterprise-wide digital transformation initiative that eliminated antiquated systems and empowered the organization with the proper technology tools to increase revenue by $4 million annually."** Compare that statement to the one she started with and it's hard to believe they describe the same person. In the likeable badass version, words like "spearheaded," "enterprise-wide," and "empowered" all showcase Assertiveness. Highlighting that she solved a costly problem for her organization conveys that she uses her talents for the benefit of others, which signals Warmth.

THE GHOSTWRITER STRATEGY
Enlist a partner to write your brag documents—
résumé, bio, social media profile, etc.

Practice

When Erin Moriarty asked Stacey Abrams if she aspired to the presidency, Abrams's well-crafted response appeared unscripted, off the cuff. However, as a media pro and experienced political debater, Abrams surely knew this question was coming (as it likely had many times before). Her response seemed spontaneous and effortless precisely because it wasn't. It was her behind-the-scenes preparation that enabled Abrams to deliver responses that were both natural and effective.

Telling a strong story isn't about being quick on your feet. It's about thoughtful preparation and practice. Just like Abrams, each of us is

---

* Details of this story have been modified to conceal the identity of the client.

interviewed multiple times a day. Don't believe me? How often are you asked the following:

How are you?
How's work?
What have you been up to?

Just because these questions aren't asked on national television doesn't mean that no one's watching. Each of these questions is an opportunity to tell your story, so don't let them slip away. For example, how many times have you responded to *"How are you?"* by saying *"Fine"* or *"Busy!"* These are terrible answers.* They convey no useful information, and any inferences the listener would make from these responses would not make them think you were particularly likeable or badass.

Like Abrams, you know these questions are coming, so prepare for them! This is how you come up with answers that are honest, feel natural, and build your status. The options here are endless, but to get you thinking, here are a few ideas for responding to *"How are you?"*:

- Say something positive that inspires follow-up questions: "I had a great win at work today."
- Say something that conveys Warmth: "Wonderful, now that I'm talking to you!"
- Say something that conveys Assertiveness: "Great. Heading to California tomorrow to present to our board of directors."

You don't need or want a thirty-minute response. With only a few more words than "Fine" or "Busy" you can answer the question in a socially appropriate way, and still offer a small piece of your story. These types of responses are more likely to spark conversation, which then gives you the chance to elaborate on the longer version of your

---

* "Busy" is particularly awful. It suggests your life is out of control, as if you're on a treadmill moving too fast. Not the answer of a likeable badass. Not. One. Bit.

likeable badass story. This same approach can be used with any question, like when you're asked in a job interview to describe a challenge you overcame, or when your boss asks you for a status update on a project.

Do you need to do this *every* time you respond to a question? No, of course not. But whatever your response, it should be a conscious choice, not simply a habit. And you shouldn't opt out due to fear. I saved this one for last because it's a higher-heat strategy. If you want to start slowly, try this in low-risk situations, like talking with your friends and family or strangers you'll never see again. Telling your story to those next to you in line at the airport is a much more productive way to pass the time than doom-scrolling your phone!

Also, you don't necessarily need to say you're doing great when you're not. Every day for two years someone asked me, "How's the book coming?" Some days my honest feeling was *"Spectacular."* Other days it was *"Ugh, slowly."* Before responding, though, I would ask myself whether I wanted that person's support in that moment. If the answer was yes, then I was forthcoming about my current state. Often, though, I would live by famed football coach Lou Holtz's philosophy: *"Don't tell your problems to people. Eighty percent don't care and the other twenty percent are glad you have them."* In those cases, I would say something honest, but still status-building, like "I just interviewed two amazing CEOs who had great likeable badass tips." Remember, you can be both authentic *and* strategic.

THE THROWAWAY QUESTION STRATEGY
Prepare answers to two questions you commonly receive. Each answer should highlight your Assertiveness, Warmth, or both.

The goal with these types of strategies is to be like M—without being like M. As I promised you, none of these strategies require you to add additional tasks to your to-do list or behave in fundamentally different ways. Rather, telling a strong story is mainly about tweaking things you're already doing, like sending emails and answering questions, to help people realize what a likeable badass you are.

I also suspect that reading these suggestions has surfaced other storytelling strategies for you, perhaps ones that are already in your toolkit. Use them. There's no formula you need to use, or any limit on the creative ways to tell your story. Any idea that helps you talk about yourself in ways that convey Assertiveness and Warmth is a great one.

PLAYS TO PRACTICE

🔥 If storytelling is hard for you and you need inspiration, go to a coffee shop (or other public place) and eavesdrop on strangers' conversations. Rate how much you perceive them as a likeable badass based on how they show up. What did they do well (be specific)? What could they have done differently to improve your impression of them?

🔥🔥 Identify your biggest win of the week and tell two people about it. Any small win (e.g., exercising three times) counts, and telling strangers is permitted.

🔥🔥🔥 Expand your storytelling to social media. Commit to posting at least one success per week for a month on your most active social media channel. While you're there, leave a positive comment for someone else who posted about their own success—they were probably as nervous as you were to post and will appreciate your kind words.

CHAPTER 5

Recruit an Army of Other-Promoters

Picture this:[*] You're attending a dinner party among friends, acquaintances, and strangers. As the wine flows, so does the conversation, moving back and forth across topics, from politics to sports to blockbuster movies. At some point, the person next to you announces, "I'm having lunch with Stacie Mitchell[†] next week." How does the group respond? Generally, initial responses to this type of statement fall in one of four categories:

Response 1: "Who's Stacie Mitchell?" (unknown response)
Response 2: "Oh, nice," then immediately changes subject
   (neutral response)
Response 3: "*Really?* What do you think of her?"
   (negative response)
Response 4: "OMG, LOVE Stacie. She's a rockstar."
   (positive response)

---

[*] This is an homage to *The Golden Girls*. I consider myself a superfan.
[†] Random name I made up. Any similarity to real-life Stacie Mitchells is pure coincidence. And if your name is Stacie Mitchell, hurray! You're in a book!

Now, imagine that *you* are Stacie Mitchell, and your name has come up at a dinner party you're not attending. Which response do you want others to have?

Imagine a future in which your name is guaranteed to come up at every dinner party worldwide, and the mention of your name always generates a version of "OMG, LOVE Stacie." Every time you walked into a room you would feel confident that everyone in it would see you as the likeable badass you are. Imagine the opportunities this would create for you. This is what we're going for—to become a "household name" in the best way possible. Is this a Big Hairy Audacious Goal? Yes, of course. But we've established that ambitious goals drive better performance. Aim high.

You are the origin of your story. But many others then have a chance to retell and shape that story, at dinner parties, in conference rooms, via emails, hallway gossip, and more. A compelling story without an audience is simply a tree falling in the woods without a sound. Your story is only as valuable as the number of people who hear it, believe it . . . and repeat it. These people are your "other-promoters"—those who describe you as a likeable badass to others, building your status when you're not around. In this chapter we focus on other-promoters and answer two questions: Why are other-promoters so valuable? And how do we get more of them?

THE VALUE OF OTHER-PROMOTERS

Anyone who describes themselves as "self-made" is lying to you (and themselves). No one succeeds alone, and that's particularly true when it comes to building status. Other people will always tell your story more *effectively* and *efficiently*.

Other-Promoters Are More Effective

As we've established, self-promotion is necessary, it's not as risky as we think, and there are ways to do it artfully. Done well, self-promotion can feel comfortable (or at least tolerable) and can generate great status benefits. But, even under the best of circumstances, self-promotion is never more effective than having someone else sing your praises. Why? Other-promoters are generally seen as very credible. A person may exaggerate their own accomplishments, but there's not as much motive for someone else to say nice things about you unless they're true. This is one reason Robynn Storey asks her résumé clients to find quotes about themselves from their past performance reviews. As she's realized, "What someone else says about you is more impactful than what you say about yourself." Other-promoters are also effective because they eliminate any possible Warmth penalty that could arise from self-promotion. Imagine learning that Amy won a prestigious award. Would you see this as boastful, and perhaps like Amy less, if this news came from Amy herself? Hopefully not, but maybe. But what if you learned about Amy's award from Steve? Would Amy seem boastful then? Of course not. When another person promotes you, the risk to your perceived Warmth is essentially zero.

Adam Grant and I demonstrated this in our research on self-promotion. Recall that the more distracted the audience, the less likely they are to remember the source of the message, and the more effective self-promotion is for gaining status. However, in this work, we also compared self-promotion to other-promotion. Specifically, we varied whether the promoting information came from the job applicant themself (their "cover letter") or the applicant's former manager (a recommendation letter). Even under the most favorable conditions for self-promotion, we found across multiple studies that the applicant always gained as much or more status when someone else promoted them. The job applicant was seen as equally Assertive regardless of the source of information, but Warmer when promoted by others. The moral of the story: Self-promotion is good, and other-promotion is even better.

I know what you're thinking: If other-promotion is better than self-promotion, I can just avoid all of that uncomfortable self-promotion and let other people do it for me. Nice try, but no. Knowing how effective other-promotion is doesn't absolve you of the need to tell your story, it just shows you that a strong story alone isn't enough. You're the author of the story, and your other-promoters are your microphone.

Other-Promoters Are More Efficient

Basic math: There's only one you, but billions of others—over eight billion others, in fact. If you wanted to build your reputation directly with everyone in the world, you would need to have eight billion points of contact—that's obviously not happening. But what if you could build your reputation with two thousand people, who each promoted you to two thousand people, and each of those people in turn promoted you to another two thousand people? Voilà, eight billion people now think you're a likeable badass. That may still feel out of reach, but you get the idea—it's certainly more doable than the first option. The more people who build our status for us, the less effort we have to expend. Similar to how a diversified investment portfolio is a strategy to build financial wealth, a large, diverse set of other-promoters who sing your praises is the most efficient way to increase your status while you sleep.

CULTIVATING OTHER-PROMOTERS

However many other-promoters you currently have, you would benefit from having more of them—lots more of them. The bigger your army of other-promoters, the more value you will derive from it.

For a person to become an other-promoter for you, three things need to happen:

1. They need to know who you are.
2. They need to see you as a likeable badass.
3. They need to be motivated to share this news with others.

For each step, I'll walk you through how to build your army effectively and efficiently (along with, of course, the psychology of why you should do it).

STEP 1: DRAW A BIG CIRCLE

The first rule of other-promotion is this: People can't sing your praises if they've never heard of you. The people who say "Who's that?" when your name comes up at the dinner party aren't yet able to be your other-promoters. To visualize your possible set of other-promoters, think about it like this:

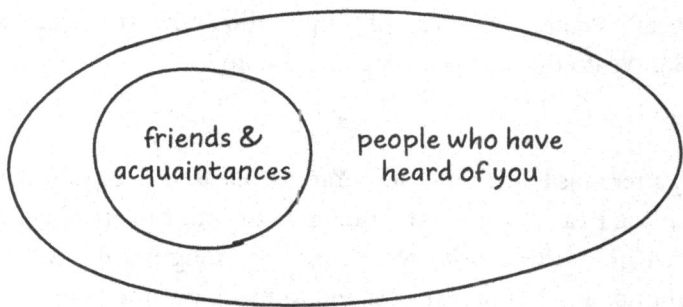

Your maximum possible set of other-promoters is all the people in the world who have heard of you. Within that group, there's a smaller set of people you actually know on some level, your friends and acquaintances. Your friends and acquaintances are a great source of other-promotion, but this set can only get so big. In the early 1990s, British anthropologist Robin Dunbar found a correlation between the size of primates' brains and their average social group size. Extrapolating this correlation to humans, Dunbar predicted that the average person could maintain about 150 social relationships, commonly referred to as "Dunbar's number." Dunbar described this set of people as "the number of people you would not feel embarrassed about joining uninvited for a drink if you happened to bump into them in a bar." Dunbar's number was always conjecture, and a more recent study challenged the idea that we can meaningfully measure a cognitive limit for human group size. However, a 2,000-person study for Evite conducted by OnePoll found that, in practice, many people do have friendship circles that are close in size to Dunbar's estimate. The 2019 survey revealed that the average American had 157 "friends," distributed as follows: Three best friends, five good friends, eight people they like but don't spend one-on-one time with, fifty acquaintances, and ninety-one social media friends.

Other-promoters don't necessarily have to be friends and acquaintances, but they do need to be in the set of people who have heard about you. I consider myself a great promoter for Oprah Winfrey, even though I'm not (yet) in her circle of friends and acquaintances. So the first step in cultivating a large number of other-promoters is acting strategically to make the circle of people who know we exist as large as possible. We do this by becoming "Despacito."

★

Shortly after Luis Fonsi and Daddy Yankee released "Despacito" in 2017, I was sitting in a Chicago restaurant talking with a dear college friend, Misong Kim, visiting from New York. The song played in the noisy background, and it was hard for me to make out the words. Misong was excitedly singing along, so I asked her what it was. When she told me, I shrugged and said, "Never heard of it," convinced this was a song she knew because she spoke Spanish. However, after that night I heard the song everywhere I went—on the radio, from my kids at the dinner table, in every bar, and on every party playlist. In a matter of weeks, I went from "What song is this?" to "Turn it up, I love this song!" And I know I'm not alone. Within six months of its release, "Despacito" and its remix captured the then-record for the most-streamed song of all time, with over 4.6 billion streams.

Whether or not you do, or ever did, love "Despacito," you surely have your set of "Turn it up, I love this song!" favorites. Whatever those songs are, I guarantee you like them more now than the first time you heard them, thanks to the well-documented psychological phenomenon of *mere exposure:* The more we're exposed to something, the more we like it. Although "absence makes the heart grow fonder" is a romantic notion, "out of sight, out of mind" is much more accurate. Fondness follows not from absence, but from frequency and familiarity. The word *mere* is used because it generally takes only a few minimal exposures for liking to increase.

Anything can benefit from mere exposure—a song on the radio, a word, an idea, or an object. The Eiffel Tower, now considered one of the world's most iconic and beloved structures, didn't enjoy this reputation from the outset. Not long after construction began in 1887, approximately forty influential French artists penned a front-page article in *Le Temps*, a prestigious daily newspaper. Titled "Protests by artists against the tower of Mr. Eiffel," the article delivered a scathing attack against the "useless and monstrous" structure that "even the commercial Americans didn't want" and would "without a doubt dishonor Paris." Similar protests and at least one lawsuit followed. With strong support of the government, construction continued despite the protests—which eventually subsided. Thankfully, for all who have traveled the world just to lay eyes on it, mere exposure has been credited with changing public perception of the Eiffel Tower over time. Its physical size makes it hard to avoid or ignore, so eventually, as it became a familiar part of the Paris skyline, it became more widely accepted.

Most important for our purposes, mere exposure can also benefit people. One of the first studies to demonstrate this was conducted with women in the 1960s who taste-tested different beverages. Half of the women were given varieties of Kool-Aid, while the other half tasted unpleasant drinks, like quinine and vinegar. The women moved between cubicles for each round of tasting such that, by the conclusion of the study, each woman had been seated with every other woman 0, 1, 2, 5, or 10 times. They then rated each other on "likeability." The more often two women were seated together, the more they liked each other, even among the women who met each other under the unpleasant circumstance of drinking nasty liquids.

I didn't have to get very far in my graduate training at Stanford to learn about mere exposure, but I don't think I would have understood its power for managing status if it wasn't for my academic "big sister," Katherine (Kathy) Phillips.* In one of our early conversations, Kathy

---

* This is one of many idiosyncrasies of academia: Unrelated people refer to each other as relatives. Your advisor is your academic "parent," your advisor's advisor is your academic "grandparent," and your advisor's other students are your "big" or "little" siblings, depending on whether they graduated before you or after you. Strange, I know.

stressed the importance of "staying in front of the faculty." Doctoral work was very independent and solitary, she cautioned, and many students made the mistake of sequestering in their cubicle for months, thinking big thoughts, all the while being completely out of faculty sight and mind. Knowing this risk, Kathy took strategic action and passed her tactic on to me: "Walk the hallway once a day." She would strike up a short conversation with every person she passed, whether she already knew them or not—ask a question, offer some assistance, or simply say hello and ask about their day. She employed the same strategy at national conferences, walking up to faculty in hotel lobbies or ballrooms to introduce herself and say hello. After five years of executing this strategy consistently, Kathy had become a household name—the Despacito of our program. I still vividly remember walking alongside her on the streets of Chicago in 1999 when Kathy was serving as my tour guide at our field's premier academic conference. I had been in graduate school all of two weeks. Kathy had just graduated from our program and accepted a prestigious faculty appointment at the Kellogg School of Management at Northwestern University. Shadowing Kathy was fun, but slow—we couldn't take more than two steps before she was recognized by yet another conference attendee who would exclaim "Kathy!" and stop to talk with her. It appeared she had achieved "OMG, LOVE Stacie" status with all of Chicago.

Kathy was a brilliant academic, of course. Before her untimely death at forty-seven, she became the first Black woman to receive tenure at Kellogg, and then again at Columbia University Business School, where she ultimately attained the prestigious rank of chaired professor. But there are lots of brilliant academics. One of the things that set Kathy apart was her ability to think strategically about building her status from a young age, and at the beginning of her career. She had always been a likeable badass, but she helped others recognize that by staying top of mind for them—just by chatting people up for a few minutes every day.

Once you understand the power of mere exposure like Kathy did, acting strategically to maximize it is straightforward.

Get your name and face out there. You may have been taught it's not polite to "name-drop," but when it comes to your own name you should make an exception. You benefit from mere exposure when others hear your name or see it in print.* You can also benefit from others seeing your face. Multiple studies have examined mere exposure using photographs and found that the more a person's photo was shown, the more others liked them.†

In person, the most straightforward way to benefit from both name and face recognition is by introducing yourself with your first and last name. I'll admit, "Hi, I'm Alison" feels like a more natural introduction for me, and it took me some practice to consistently add "Fragale." If your first name is memorable, like Oprah, Cher, or Beyoncé, you might be able to get away with this more casual intro. But if you have a more common first name, like me, then using your full name is probably better.‡

Done properly, introducing yourself is an act of Assertive Warmth—sustained eye contact, a confident tone of voice, and a smile. Get in the habit of doing it everywhere you go—at the grocery store, the playground, on the bus or airplane, since you never know where your next other-promoter will come from.

Beyond the artful introduction, you can also get mere exposure through your written name. Consider:

- If you use email, create an email signature, and always include it. If it's appropriate, include your photo in your signature as well. Even if the person you're writing to already knows you well, making mere exposure less valuable, they may forward your message to someone who doesn't.

---

* A 1969 study asked participants to rate more than 200 Americans who had appeared on the cover of *Time* or *Newsweek* magazines between the 1940s and the 1960s. The more familiar the person was, the more they were liked by participants.
† In one study, participants were shown photos of men's graduation portraits 0, 1, 2, 5, 10, or 25 times. Those who saw a given graduation portrait more often rated the person more favorably. A later experiment found that these effects held across gender and race.
‡ So strong is my belief in the value of mere exposure that it played a role in my decision to keep my maiden name when I got married. Fragale is an uncommon last name, so people usually remember it (even though they mispronounce it). In explaining my decision to my husband, I told him that I couldn't "waste thirty good years of mere exposure on a name change." He didn't seem to care, nor did he have any idea what I was talking about.

- Carbon copy (cc) email recipients liberally, as appropriate, to put your name in as many inboxes as possible.
- When you create online documents, include your name in the file name, especially if there's a chance others will eventually see these documents.
- If you ever make presentations, put your name in the footer of every slide.
- At an event where name tags are provided, wear yours.[*]
- Dust off your business cards and start distributing them. Will they get thrown away? Maybe. But the person is likely to glance at the card before tossing it. Mere exposure achieved!
- Get some letterhead and stationery with your name on it. In the age of digital communication, a written note stands out.
- Social media, used with intention, is an unparalleled mere-exposure machine. Rather than mindlessly scrolling, use your time on social media to increase your followers or connections. The more connections you have, the more people are reminded of you every time you post or comment.

Be uniquely you. When Robin Arzón approached the starting line for her first ultramarathon, she felt exposed. It was before dawn and most runners looked as you might expect, as if they had rolled out of bed for an early-morning workout. Robin looked different. She sported gold jewelry, black winged eyeliner, red lipstick, and a fanny pack to hold her Nikon camera (this was pre-smartphone). When she stopped during the race to take photos or reapply her lipstick, other runners looked on, confused. Not in a judgmental way—Robin always found the running community "incredibly welcoming"—but out of sheer curiosity. They had never seen a competitor who looked and behaved quite like Robin. At the time, she was not the internationally known Peloton head instructor, executive, and global wellness icon she is today. She was a former attorney who wanted to make a career pivot

---

[*] Just remember to take it off before you leave the event and head out in public. Yes, you can get mere exposure wearing a name tag on the sidewalk, but it may not be worth the embarrassment.

into wellness and liked to run. And, although running a fifty-mile race at any speed sounds damn impressive to most of us, Robin wasn't an elite runner in that crowd. She worried: "I'm not a five-minute miler, I'm not competing in the Olympics. If I show up with a red lip, people will think I'm a joke." But she did it scared, because it represented her authentic self, and she never regretted it. This is one of the moments that Robin remembers when she thinks about one of her signature pieces of advice: "Leverage your differences. Stay weird. No one remembers normal."

You don't have to be a celebrity or media personality to embrace your uniqueness. Recall Rachel Sheerin, master of the out-of-office email. The only reason I even know Rachel is because she "stayed weird." We met when we serendipitously sat next to each other at an airport bar. I was quietly sipping my drink when I overheard Rachel tell the bartender that she was a keynote speaker. I, too, was returning from a speaking event and this shared similarity prompted me to strike up a conversation with her. As I stood to leave, she handed me her business card. I looked down to see a glossy teal and pink three-by-five-inch postcard with a flamingo on it—the wackiest, most "unbusinesslike" business card I had ever received. I couldn't reciprocate (my business cards were 1,500 miles away, in my bedroom closet), but I tucked this work of art in my bag and promised to contact her. My promise was sincere at the time, but by the time I got back to my previously organized home that had been turned to chaos by three kids in my absence, Rachel was far from my mind. It wasn't until days later, when I was finally unpacking my suitcase, that I came across the flamingo. I put the card on my desk—it was just so darn cute—and a few days after that I emailed Rachel to reconnect. That was the beginning of a friendship and professional relationship that is still going strong to this day. Rachel has been one of my most effective other-promoters—making introductions for me, recommending me to clients, singing my praises on social media—and I like to think that I've been equally promoting of her. And none of it would have happened if I hadn't introduced myself to a random stranger in a bar, and she hadn't handed me a paper flamingo.

Although any form of mere exposure is valuable, the more unique you are the easier it will be for people to remember you (which is why I recommend introducing yourself with your last name). Don't pretend to be something you're not (that's a smuggler's move). But don't be afraid to let your true self shine through, as Robin and Rachel did. What makes you different makes you memorable.

Volunteer strategically. Often, we make choices about how to spend our free time, both at work and at home. Should I volunteer for this nonprofit? Should I join the parent association? Should I raise my hand for the conference planning committee at the office? Like many women do, I used to have a "first come, first served" approach to handling these requests. I would feel a generalized obligation to always say "yes," so I would . . . again, and again, and again . . . until I was so overwhelmed and overworked that I would eventually have to say "no." Unfortunately, I often found that the request I had to say no to was way more interesting than the ten requests I had accepted, and I then regretted my prior choices. So, I changed my approach. Now, when considering a discretionary activity, I ask myself three questions:

First: *Am I uniquely qualified to contribute?* If I feel that I have unique expertise, I know it will be fairly easy for me to show up as a likeable badass. Remember, offering up our skills and knowledge for the benefit of others is a surefire way to convey Assertive Warmth. However, if I think many other people can do what's being asked of me as well or better, I often pass on the request. Showing up Assertively and Warmly is much harder if I feel that the task at hand is either over my head or a poor use of my scarce free time.

Second: *Will this bring joy to my life?* If I don't think it will be fun, or that I'll learn anything new, this is another good reason to pass. Again, it's hard to show up as your likeable badass self if you're bored, annoyed, or resentful.

And third: *Who will I meet?* This is the most relevant question for building your other-promoter army. One of the perks of these service opportunities is that they provide an easy chance to bring new people into your network. Simply showing up (in person or virtually) gives you repeated mere exposure to people who wouldn't otherwise know you.

Kate, the likeable badass you met in chapter 2, achieved great results using this rule. For example, she volunteered to be on the planning committee for the Texas event where we met. She realized that this all-firm event was a great way to quickly get to know lots of influential people "across offices and functions, all working toward the same goal," as she put it. And, the chief of staff position she was ultimately offered had its origins in the mere exposure she got from volunteering as a diversity and inclusion liaison at her firm. Through that role, she became connected to one of the firm's external advisors, who became one of her mentors. When she mentioned applying for chief of staff, he thought she would be great in the role and took it upon himself to be her other-promoter—singing her praises to the CEO and COO, whom he knew well.

You don't need to volunteer for everything, or anything for that matter. Like walking the hallway once a day, volunteering for low-effort assignments is just one means to achieve the desired end—to get your name and face in front of as many people as possible, as often as possible. Increasing the set of people who have heard of you is the first critical step in cultivating other-promoters.

GETTING STARTED

- Looking at your schedule for today and tomorrow, where are there opportunities to introduce yourself to new people?
- What is one new practice you can adopt that increases mere exposure to your name or face (e.g., at every work conference introduce yourself to at least 20 people)?
- What can you do to get your name in front of 100 new people this week? 1,000 people? 10,000 people?

STEP 2: MASTER THE ART OF THE SMALL DEPOSIT

"Despacito" undoubtedly benefited from mere exposure. But it also helps that it's a very catchy song. Playing a recording of my nine-year-old's drum practice wouldn't generate such widespread acclaim no matter how much you heard it, trust me. Mere exposure helps grow the circle of people who have heard of you, but they need to think of you as the catchy tune they can't get out of their head before they'll become valuable other-promoters. This doesn't mean they need to know you very well, but they do need to see you as likeable enough and badass enough to want to sing your praises. Once you've introduced yourself to someone, you can use the conversation that follows to tell your story. Beyond your words, you also build status through actions. Kate initially built status through her "make other people's lives easier" strategy. It was effective, but it was also the product of significant work on her part. When we're trying to cast a wide net around potential other-promoters, though, we need to find actions that don't take a lot of time or energy. I call these low-effort actions "small deposits," and the likeable badass is a master of them.

To understand what a small deposit is and how it works, consider the following experiment. A trade association mailed a paper survey to its members—a boring, detailed, and time-consuming questionnaire concerning the respondents' health insurance. One group of members simply received the survey, with no financial incentive. A second group received the survey with a promise of a notable payment: Return the survey, the cover letter said, and the association would send the respondent a check for $50. A third group received the survey with $1 attached. The $1 was theirs to keep, regardless of whether they returned the survey. As you can see from the response rates below, the promise of the $50 payment produced only a modest increase in responsiveness compared to no incentive at all, but offering a paltry $1 doubled the response rate from baseline!

Condition 1: Survey with no financial incentive, 20.7%
Condition 2: Survey with $50 payment if returned, 23.3%
Condition 3: Survey with $1 enclosed, 40.7%

Notice that Conditions 2 and 3 both rely on the norm of reciprocity—you do something good for me, and I'll do something good for you. However, the reciprocity invoked in Condition 3 is both significantly cheaper and more effective—more surveys are returned at a much lower cost. The problem with Condition 2 is that it asks the other person to invest in you first, based on the promise that you will return the favor. Condition 3, in contrast, is an example of a "small deposit": offering a token of goodwill, like a dollar, that the recipient can't easily reject or return.

Receiving anything, even a small thing that you didn't want or ask for, pulls you to reciprocate. Just ask Phillip Kunz. As part of an experiment, Kunz, then a sociologist at Brigham Young University, and his colleague sent hundreds of Christmas cards to strangers in and around Chicago, Illinois, in 1974. Kunz was surprised to receive hundreds of replies—not just cards, but photos of families he never knew, along with many handwritten letters that were multiple pages long. The reciprocity extended beyond a single holiday season, with some families including Kunz on their mailing list for about fifteen years!

Other-promoters will be more willing to promote you if they feel that they owe you, and that sense of obligation comes from the value you have already delivered to them. Because a small deposit is something easy to give, you won't be annoyed or burdened if you don't get anything back. We all understand the value of investing in relationships, but too often we make large investments in a select few, and then end up disappointed and disadvantaged if those investments don't pay off. The search for a sponsor at work is a good example. To advance, you set your sights on a person in your organization who could be your advocate. You put all your metaphorical eggs in this basket by doing everything you can to help them and impress them—but at the expense of investing in other relationships. If the strategy pays off and this person becomes a strong other-promoter for you, like Kate's colleagues did for her, great! But if they don't, you're left broke and betrayed, with nowhere else to turn.

We don't need to abandon these larger investments, but we do need to make more Condition 3 investments—small deposits in the accounts of many. This is how we cultivate a large army of other-promoters. Visualize walking down the street handing a dollar to everyone who passes you. As we see in the questionnaire study, not every investment will pay off—60 percent of the participants took the dollar and didn't return the survey—but that's OK! We have plenty of dollars to spend, and we know that enough of them will land in the hands of our future other-promoters to yield a significant return.

Any small deposit can be valuable for cultivating other-promoters. As women, however, we need to choose them carefully. There are relational benefits of being a "giver," but there is a fine line between making strategic small deposits and being saddled with nonpromotable work. The trick is to switch from simply giving *more* to giving *more Assertively*. That is, we need to give selectively in ways that boost perceptions of not only our Warmth, but also our Assertiveness. The likeable badass looks for easy ways to add value to others while also showcasing her confidence, competence, and contributions.

Meghana Dhar, who learned to tell a strong story after watching her colleague Walt, also learned to improve her small deposits. Early in her career, she loved raising her hand for volunteer opportunities at work, but over time she realized that many of the things she had signed up for were classic examples of nonpromotable work. "The guys were working, and I was party planning," she recalled. She didn't stop giving, but she started giving more strategically. When COVID-19 forced everyone to retreat to their homes, Meghana, in California, worried about staying visible to her colleagues and bosses who were in New York. And, as a self-described "in-person person," she worried that her Warmth and Assertiveness would be muted behind the screen. She pitched an idea to her new boss—during the next virtual monthly meeting, which would be attended by lots of people across the organization, Meghana would interview him as a way of introducing him to the company, showcasing his expertise and leadership style. He was excited about the idea and agreed. Meghana got to shine doing what she loved, and her boss was so pleased with how it went that he recommended she do the same thing with the new senior vice president, global head of sales, a woman in one of the most powerful positions in the company. Meghana's interview with the SVP was livestreamed across the entire organization. From those two events, Meghana garnered extensive mere exposure, as well as recognition from her boss and her boss's boss—these were mentioned specifically in her next performance review—all with a lot less effort than it took to plan the company holiday party.

Meeting countless likeable badasses over the years, I've found they all have their unique ways to give Assertively. Take Clare Hart. The story of how I met Clare is a textbook example of how small deposits build other-promoters. I was introduced to Clare through a mutual friend, Eden Abrahams, who insisted that I needed to know Clare. "You'll love her," Eden vowed. Her brief other-promotion of Clare included only two details: Clare was CEO at Williams Lea, and she had compiled a list of "twenty ways to say no" that she shared with women in her network. This latter point intrigued me because it sounded like a great example of a small deposit. I found it noteworthy that of all Clare's impressive professional accomplishments, including being CEO at four different organizations in her more than thirty-year career, this list was what came to Eden's mind when singing her praises.

Talking with Clare, I was struck by three principles that enabled her to add maximum value to others with minimum effort.

If you found it helpful, share it, because others will, too: Turns out Clare didn't create the original list of nos. She came across the list years ago and found it valuable, so she started sharing it with others. Over time, she added her own ideas to the list. The authorship of the original list wasn't what people cared about—all they remembered was that it was valuable information that came from Clare.

Put your advice on paper: Clare is a master of writing out her advice—lists of nos, book recommendations, tips from a panel she moderated, and so on. Once you write it down, you can share it with others in seconds through email or text.

Use texts to stay connected and top of mind: Whether it's a restaurant meal or piece of museum art, any time Clare enjoys something enough to take a picture of it, she asks herself, "Who else would appreciate this?" and will text them the photo with a brief "thought you would enjoy this" message.

Although Clare's small deposits differ from Meghana's, the overarching philosophy is the same: Find low-effort ways to achieve mere exposure while adding value to others. "You don't need to meet someone for coffee to stay connected," Clare advises. "There's nothing wrong with that, but you can't stay in touch with enough people that way."

Giving advice, assuming the advice is welcome, is a small deposit that conveys both Warmth and Assertiveness, and is one of the best tools in the likeable badass toolkit. The beauty of giving advice is that everyone can do it well—we're all experts in something. Figure out what you're naturally good at, develop a few key pieces of advice, write them down, and look for opportunities to share what you've learned. Like Clare, I have found success with this strategy using my professional skills, but I've found equal success using expertise from my personal life. For example, I'm exceptionally good at hiring childcare providers—everything from finding qualified candidates to setting up workplace expectations—and I'm aware that this is an area where many parents, especially mothers, struggle. I don't walk around shouting my opinions from rooftops, but I do listen carefully to the conversations around me. Whenever I hear of someone who's grappling with childcare decisions, I'm not shy about offering suggestions. As an example, a professional acquaintance posted the following to a WhatsApp group: *"Does anyone have a good contact who can share ideas on babysitting options as a single parent? My friend is General Counsel for a public company and needs to find options for overnight care when she travels for work."* Although not a single parent, I knew that I could help, so I immediately responded, *"I consider myself an unofficial expert on this!!! Share my number with her if helpful!"* A few days later, I was on the phone with the mom and gave her some of my key tips (e.g., where to find the best candidates, how to conduct a professional background check) and followed up via email, per her request, by sharing some hiring documents I had created (employment contract, job description). She was incredibly grateful and, as reciprocity predicts, offered to repay the favor in any way she could. I received a similar message of thanks from the woman who introduced us—after all, I made her look like a hero because she was able to solve her friend's problem. In about twenty minutes, I was able to turn both a stranger and an acquaintance into potential other-promoters, just by capitalizing on an opportunity to talk about an area that I know well and enjoy discussing. However, reflecting afterward, I saw an opportunity to improve my advice-giving efficiency by writing it down. When I first talked to my new mom connection, my advice was mainly in my head, which forced me to deliver it in a live conversation. After talking with Clare, I realized that writing my ideas down would let me help more people in less time.

To develop your own small-deposit rules, start by thinking of the things you enjoy doing for others. Then, consider two tweaks. First, are there ways to make your contributions more time efficient? I use (otherwise unproductive) airport time to comment on others' social media posts; Clare makes lists. Both serve the same purpose of enabling us to add value to more people without taking time away from other things. Second, could you modify your contributions to make them more Assertive? As a relative newcomer to social media, I quickly realized that a thumbs-up or a heart is one of the easiest small deposits. It takes only one finger and a fraction of a second, but it can be highly valued by the person who receives it—a person who may be feeling vulnerable after they hit "post," wondering how others will react to what they shared. However, I also realized that a simple modification—adding a comment with a link to a reference or an insight—was an easy way for me to show up more Assertively. I've also tweaked my time in the kitchen for the same purpose. I love to cook for others, but I'm far from a professional chef. I've discovered, though, there are two things I do better than any amateur I know: I make killer homemade baked beans, and I'm a master of the Instagram-worthy cheese board.* So, I made an adjustment: Every time I'm asked or volunteer to contribute

---

* The secret is no empty space. It doesn't matter what you put on your cheese board, or in what position, as long as you cover every millimeter of the board. I got this advice years ago from the owner of a cheese shop and it has never failed me. Try it. When you look like a hero at your next party, send me a bottle of wine to say thanks.

food to a gathering, I only bring one of these two things. Having a signature contribution allows me to give by doing something I enjoy and distinguishes me as talented and unique. I can tell that it's working because most dinner party invitations now start with some version of the following message: "Alison, you're invited, but only because we want you to bring the cheese board."

> **GETTING STARTED**
>
> - What are your favorite small deposits to make? (Examples: writing thank-you notes, commenting on social media posts, sharing book recommendations.) Rate each on a 1 (low) to 5 (high) scale of Assertiveness.
>
> - How can you make these small deposits more efficient? (Examples: write the advice down, create templates for thank-you notes, use commuting time.)
>
> - How could you make these small deposits more Assertive by showcasing your competence, skills, and achievements? (Examples: start a book club at work, when you have a success to share write a thank-you note to anyone who contributed to it.)
>
> - How can you increase the number of small deposits you make today, by either contributing in new ways or to new people?

STEP 3: GIVE YOUR OTHER-PROMOTERS A REASON TO PICK UP THE MICROPHONE

Once people know who you are and see you as a likeable badass, the third step in cultivating other-promoters is motivating them to sing your praises far and wide. Often, simply making small deposits is enough to cultivate other-promoters, as we saw with Eden's promotion of Clare. As a coach to senior executives, Eden knows, and could introduce me to, dozens of CEOs. Yet, the person she chose to recommend to me was Clare—a woman who had set herself apart in Eden's mind not because of her title, but because of her list of nos.

There are two other straightforward actions we can take to increase the chances that others will promote us. One is simply to promote them first. That is, one of the best ways to cultivate other-promoters is to become one yourself. When you spot a likeable badass—especially women, people of color, and members of other systemically excluded groups—spread the word: send a group email complimenting their great work, give them a public "thank you" at a gathering, or send a social media shout out. Promoting others is a very specific form of small deposit. Although not every behavior is reciprocated with the identical kindness, many are—as Phillip Kunz experienced, one holiday card begets another. So, if you pay for lunch this time, I'm more likely to pay for lunch next time. And, if you sing my praises today, and you do so publicly, so that I know about it, I'm more likely to sing your praises tomorrow. Too often, though, we let these easy opportunities for other-promotion slip away. As American author William Arthur Ward reportedly cautioned, "Feeling gratitude and not expressing it is like wrapping a present and not giving it." So every time that voice in your head says, "That person is amazing," don't let the moment pass you by. Commit to promoting them to at least one other person—and many more if you can! Not only is it the right thing to do, but you'll probably gain an other-promoter in return.

The second simple step we can take to get others to promote us is—wait for it—to ask them! Every time I get in front of an audience to talk about negotiation skills, the most important message I always convey is that negotiation is not limited to discussions that involve money. Have you ever heard the advice that you should negotiate your salary? I bet my unnecessarily large collection of overpriced handbags that you have. Have you ever heard that you should negotiate how your fan club talks about you? I'll wager my (equally indulgent) shoe collection that you haven't. Negotiation is simply a tool we use to get other people to do what we want them to do. You can negotiate anything—children's bedtimes, authorship order, meeting time, red or white wine, and so on. But because much of the well-publicized negotiation advice, especially for women, focuses on strategies to negotiate for more power, like salaries and promotion, we often forget about the millions of other "asks" from which we can benefit.

To illustrate how you can negotiate for other-promotion, below is an excerpt from a text string I sent to a male colleague before a meeting we were both going to attend. He and I were both deans of academic programs and worked closely together. However, these administrative responsibilities often caused me to miss other meetings in the school where my presence was expected. I didn't want my absences to damage my reputation with my other colleagues, especially when these absences were a direct result of my service to the school. I knew my fellow dean saw me as a likeable badass—I had made many small, and some large, deposits into that account over the years—and I knew he had high status in the eyes of the other meeting attendees. So, I texted him:

> ME: You need to make sure to mention how awesome I am so that other people in the meeting hear that message.
> HIM: Subtle. True point.
> ME: Don't ask, don't get.
> HIM: You should teach this stuff, you might be good at it.

And guess what? He took ten seconds in the meeting to comment on my great work! I texted him again afterward to thank him and he responded that he was happy to help, which I'm sure he was. This was a small deposit for him that had a lot of value to me and he, like all of us, wants a large return on his relationship investments. What I'm sure of, though, is that he wouldn't have thought to speak about my contributions in that meeting had I not asked him. The reality is that no one cares about your life as much as you do—not even your mom. Your other-promoters are willing to promote you, but they don't walk around all day thinking about how they can help you. They're too busy thinking about how they can help themselves. But if they already see you as a likeable badass, they're happy to share that fact with others. All they need is a little nudge from you to make it happen.

I recognize that asking people to promote you might feel just as scary as asking for a raise. But remember, you're only asking this of people who already think highly of you. Imagine if the situation were reversed—a person who has repeatedly added value to you, and whom you hold in the highest regard, has asked you to share these feelings with other people. Would you feel burdened or annoyed? No, just the opposite. You want to be helpful to them, so you would be grateful that they gave you specific guidance about what they needed. And what they asked for is both easy and enjoyable for you. Your other-promoters are just like you, and that's exactly how they'll feel when you make the ask.

> **GETTING STARTED**
>
> - Think of all the likeable badasses in your world. Who can you promote this week, and to whom?
> - Identify up to three people you would like to be other-promoters for you. How and when can you ask them to promote you?

STOP BUYING COFFEE, START MAKING INTRODUCTIONS

Thus far, we've discussed the three steps required to build an army of other-promoters:

1. Get as many people as possible to know who you are (mere exposure)
2. Get them to see you as a likeable badass (small deposits)
3. Get them to sing your praises to others (by promoting them, and asking them to promote you)

In my own life, I've found that one simple behavior, executed consistently, has generated more other-promotion for me than all my other efforts combined. I consider *the email introduction* to be my secret weapon, and I'm sharing it with you in the hope that it brings you similar benefit. Here's what I do: Every time I have a conversation with a new person, I end our time together by offering to introduce them to two people in my network. When they accept (which they always do), I make these introductions by email within twenty-four hours of our meeting. I adhere to two guidelines when making these connections: I need to believe that each introduction will be beneficial to both parties; and I am effusively (and genuinely) complimentary to both parties when introducing them.

This isn't something I've always done. I often meet new connections for coffee or lunch, and, as many people do in that situation, I always offer to pick up the check. Beyond basic rules of etiquette, buying someone's coffee or lunch seemed like an easy small deposit to make. The problem, I realized, is that buying someone's coffee is a kindness that anyone else could give just as easily, which makes it totally forgettable. In other words, my small deposit was high on likeable, but low on badass. Once I recognized this, I realized I needed a better strategy. I experimented with the email introduction as my alternative and found such success with it that I ultimately established it as my signature small deposit.[*]

The story of how I met and came to know Eden Abrahams, the woman who introduced me to Clare Hart, illustrates both what I do and the tremendous benefit these introductions provide. Although this story is one of my favorites, it's not an outlier. I have been able to add value to dozens (maybe hundreds) of people, generating years of goodwill and reciprocity in return, just by looking for opportunities to bring great people in my network together.

2019

In complete small-world fashion, this story begins with Kate, who reached out (along with her colleague) to ask if I offered executive leadership coaching. I don't do that type of work, but—taking a page

---

[*] Yes, I do still offer to pay for coffee or lunch in these situations, but only because my Italian grandmother would expect nothing less. I no longer do it with the expectation of building status.

from Kate's playbook—I didn't want to simply say, "Sorry, I can't help you." Instead, I saw it as a great opportunity to build my status with Kate and her colleague by making an introduction. The only problem was that I didn't know any executive coaches in New York, where they wanted the coaching to take place. So I emailed a close friend with strong New York connections, and she connected me to Eden. Eden and I had a brief introductory phone conversation, I sensed immediately that she was a likeable badass, I introduced her to Kate, and she got the job. I looked like a hero to Kate, and even more so to Eden—in the span of two weeks I went from a total stranger to a person who got her a lucrative assignment.

My time spent in 2019: One hour

2020

As reciprocity predicts, Eden then became a great other-promoter for me. She introduced me to several people who could be potential clients. Then, when Eden became a partner in a consulting firm, she called to ask if I had any interest in a job there. I wasn't in the market for a new career, but I was flattered. And I saw it as great evidence for the value of my strategy—after making one introduction for her the prior year, Eden valued me enough to consider hiring me. I also asked Eden to be an other-promoter for me by recommending me to join Chief, an organization built to elevate senior women in their careers. She agreed, and I was ultimately invited to join.[*]

My time spent in 2020: 30–45 minutes

2021

Sheldon Bernard, an MBA student I had taught over a decade prior, reached out asking for advice about starting his own behavioral science consulting firm. As I listened to his story, I did what I now always do—mentally scanned my list of contacts to identify potential intro-

---

[*] Thanks also to likeable badass extraordinaire Michelle Pecak, a dear friend and fellow Chief who also nominated me and introduced me to the Chicago Chief community.

ductions for him. I ended our thirty-minute conversation offering to put him in touch with two people, one of whom was Eden. I wasn't sure if Eden would see this introduction as mutually beneficial—one of my criteria—so I emailed her first asking permission to make the introduction, and she welcomed it. I then connected them via this email:

> Sheldon—I sent Eden your LinkedIn page and told her briefly about your expertise in decision science and desire to do more of this work. Eden is a partner at . . . an advisory firm that specializes in senior leadership development services.
>
> Eden—I met Sheldon a decade ago when he was a standout MBA student in my leadership class. Clearly, I made a very favorable impression on him, as he has now become a de facto organizational psychologist in his free time!
>
> You are both crazy smart, gregarious people with interesting life stories, so I know you will enjoy talking with each other. I'll get out of the way and let you take it from here!

A month later, I made another, unrelated introduction for Eden. As part of that email exchange, she wrote:

> I don't know if Sheldon told you,* but after he and I met I was speaking to my good friend who runs strategy at a company, and something she said made me realize that he could be a potentially helpful resource to her, so I introduced them, and it sounds like they're going to continue the conversation.

A few months after that, I received an update from Sheldon:

> Hi Alison,
> Just wanted to tell you that, thanks to Eden, I've landed a corporate client. There was no chance I'd have this opportunity

---

* He hadn't.

had you not made the introduction (and had Eden not opened up her Rolodex . . . does anyone even have a Rolodex anymore??).* I'm in full swing this week working with them to get an executive committee workshop ready . . . but wanted to pause and just say thank you.

My time spent in 2021: 45 minutes

2022

Sheldon sent me another update. His side hustle had now become his full-time job:

Thanks again for all your support last year, it was tremendously helpful. This year I'll be nearly full time with my start-up and I don't know if we would have gotten started without your counsel and support.

Note that my "counsel and support" to Sheldon was nothing more than a short meeting and an email to Eden. But from that small deposit he gained tremendous benefit—his first paying corporate client, which was the springboard for him achieving his professional dream of starting his own company. Sheldon credits that to the introduction that I made for him. If my name came up tomorrow at a dinner party that Sheldon was attending, how do you think he would respond? And if I asked him to be an other-promoter for me in a specific way, do you think he would agree? In comparison, reread these two questions again, but assume that, instead of introducing him to Eden, I simply bought Sheldon's coffee when we met in 2021. See what I mean? A simple tweak in my giving—from a behavior that was just likeable to a behavior that was both likeable and badass—earned me an other-promoter for life.

Around this time, I finally met Eden in person. Let that sink in for a minute. My entire relationship with Eden had been built through

---

* See what I mean? I'm not the only one who still uses this reference.

emails and video chats. We would only connect a few times per year, but by making small deposits I was able to deepen the relationship. When Eden finally traveled to my hometown for work, she invited me to lunch. At that lunch, she thanked me for introducing her to Sheldon, and told me that she continued to find more opportunities for him. It was at this point that she offered to introduce me to Clare Hart.

Then, in late 2022, Dawn Morrow entered the mix. As with Sheldon, I knew Dawn from her days as an MBA student. Like Sheldon, she had entrepreneurial aspirations and didn't know where to begin, so she reached out to talk with me. And guess what I did at the end of that conversation? I introduced her to Eden and Sheldon! By this point I knew that Eden and Sheldon would do what they could to help Dawn, simply because I was the one who asked. Of course, I was right. Soon after, I received an email from Dawn with the subject line: *GOLD!* and the following message:

> Alison—
> Your recommendations were gold. I talked to Sheldon already. He connected me with a friend of his who is a partner at a firm that does leadership development and culture work and I'm talking with him tomorrow.
> And I'm going to chat with Eden early in the new year.
> Amazing. Thank you so much.
> Dawn

Although I haven't yet tested it, I feel confident from this message that Dawn has now joined my set of other-promoters.

My time spent in 2022: 90 minutes (including lunch)

By my count, a few mutually beneficial introductions earned me one new friend (Eden), a potential job offer, multiple speaking engagement referrals, an invitation to join a women's leadership group (Chief), a book interview (Clare), and four other-promoters (Kate, Eden, Sheldon, and Dawn). Not a bad return on a few minutes of my time a month. And I could go on for days with similar examples from my other relationships.

I could also give you just as many examples when my introduction fizzled. For instance, following my rule, I also introduced Sheldon to a second person at the same time as Eden. To my knowledge, nothing came from that connection. Not every small deposit yields returns, but again, that's OK. Because the effort required is low, I can make a lot of introductions.

The reason I think the email introduction is the single best strategy we can employ to build our army of other-promoters is because it hits all of the steps I've outlined in this chapter, each in a few minutes or less:

- An introduction gives you a great reason to contact someone you might not have otherwise connected with today, thereby staying top of mind for them. Mere exposure achieved.
- Because the introduction is mutually beneficial, this small deposit is both Assertive and Warm. You're connecting each person to someone who might benefit them, while also showing your value—you're a person who knows people.
- An introduction is a natural opportunity for other-promotion. When you sing each person's praises as you describe them, you increase the likelihood they will reciprocate by promoting you in the future.
- It's highly efficient: All the above benefits are doubled, because one email is sent to two people.

★

When we build an army of other-promoters, we no longer live in fear of others "talking behind our backs." Quite the opposite, we're happy to have our names come up at dinner parties across the world, knowing that others will be talking about what likeable badasses we are.

PLAYS TO PRACTICE

🔥 Cultivate a daily connection habit. Find a convenient time to reach out to one person each day, either a new person or someone you already know. I have two daily practices: I send one LinkedIn direct message to someone I'd like to connect with while I drink my early-morning coffee, and I send one text to someone I already know while I'm waiting to pick up my kids after their evening activities. Whenever I think, "Oh, I should reach out to so-and-so," I add their name to a list I keep on my phone, and I refer back to the list at these two points in the day.

🔥🔥 Identify an area where people seek you out for advice (e.g., public speaking), and write down your top tips. Post these on social media.

🔥🔥🔥 The next time you're tempted to volunteer for a discretionary activity (e.g., committee at work, nonprofit in your community) ask yourself "Who will I meet?" and use the answer to guide your decision. Be willing to say "no" if needed, so you can save your "yes" for a better mere exposure opportunity.

CHAPTER 6

Get What You Want (and Make Them Love You for It)

"I ruined my career in less time than it takes to order a latte." That's how Kathryn Valentine describes "the incident" now.

At the time of the incident, Kathryn was completing her MBA. After college, she spent two years as a consultant for McKinsey, a year working for Teach for America, and then she helped develop the growth strategy that rocketed Lilly Pulitzer's revenues from $100 million to $300 million in a few short years. After all of that, still just twenty-seven years old, she was now at a top-ranked business school with her pick of summer internships. She chose to work at a Fortune 50 company in the southeastern United States for one reason—so she and her husband could live in the same city upon her graduation. Kathryn knew these internships were essentially "three-month job interviews," so she was determined to bring her A-game and secure a full-time offer by the end of the summer.

The problem was, Kathryn found her boss insufferable and quickly realized that he didn't have the respect of his peers. Because he was insecure about his low status, she feared he might not be a great other-promoter for her. So Kathryn decided that she needed a new boss, one who could be a better advocate for her in the end-of-summer job offer discussions. She knew she couldn't just complain her way onto a new team, she needed to earn a new spot. She came up with what she thought was a brilliant plan: Finish her assigned project quickly, so she could ask the intern coordinator to assign her to a second project on someone else's team. Kathryn put her head down and finished the project that was supposed to take her ten weeks in under a month. She did it fast, and she did it well. No one could dispute that.

Kathryn requested a meeting with the intern coordinator, which was scheduled for 10 a.m. on Monday. All weekend, she rehearsed what she was going to say and made her mother practice the script with her for hours—"That's just love," Kathryn, now a mom herself, recalls fondly.

When Monday morning arrived, Kathryn walked into the meeting, recited the script, and ended with her grand finale: the request to be moved to another team. She waited for the praise, hoping for something like "Oh, Kathryn, how wonderful. No other intern has ever done such great work so quickly. We would love to use your superior skills on a second project." It never came. Instead, the coordinator's eyes narrowed and a rush of criticism spewed forth, including a phrase that still rings in Kathryn's ears over a decade later—she wasn't a "culture fit." Kathryn knew instantly there was no way to recover. She would not be getting a full-time job offer. And if she wasn't going to get the job, there was no point in staying one minute longer. She needed to use the rest of the summer to find a different job in that city. She managed to choke back shock and tears to mutter two words: "I agree." Recognizing the mutual decision to part ways, the intern coordinator picked up the phone and called security; per company policy, anyone who quit or was fired was escorted out immediately. "A security guard walked me to my desk, stood there while I packed up, and showed me out of the building. I never even got a chance to say goodbye to the other interns." She sat in her car in the office parking lot, wondering what the hell had just happened, and looked at her watch. It was not yet 10:30 a.m.

★

If a group of women were sitting around a campfire, the scary stories they'd tell wouldn't be of ghosts or axe-wielding serial killers. Instead, they would tell stories like Kathryn's, where a high-performing woman's attempt to advocate for herself resulted in backlash—criticism, insults, damaged relationships, and more.

Showing up as a likeable badass seems feasible when you're thinking about telling your story or making small deposits. But it may sound more challenging when you think about advocating for yourself. As women, we live with the pervasive worry that we won't get what we want, even if we push for it, and we'll be liked less—even despised— just for asking. Every story we hear like Kathryn's only serves to justify our fears. Even if security has never escorted you out of a building, you've probably found yourself concerned about other negative outcomes on many occasions. For example:

> If I ask for the raise, will my boss think I'm greedy or unappreciative?
> If I refuse to play games in the pool with my kids, will they think I'm boring or selfish?
> If I cancel dinner with my girlfriends, will they be mad at me?

These decisions all involve an assumed tradeoff between Assertiveness and Warmth, and often provoke anxiety. If you advocate for your own interests, maybe the other person will like you less and you'll spend some of the Warmth you worked so hard to build. You can probably maintain your Warmth by doing what you think will make the other person happy, but then you don't get what you want.

Fortunately, it's very possible to ask for what you want in a way that builds your status, rather than destroys it. Remember, no one cares about your life more than you do, so getting what you want requires advocating for yourself. If that notion scares the hell out of you, here's my pep talk: For every story I've heard like Kathryn's over the past twenty years, I've heard fifty success stories. This week alone I received a message from a former student who successfully advocated for a better employment agreement and a friend who was able to extend her maternity leave by two months. Even Kathryn's story ends better than you'd think.

All we need is a little bit of sleuthing. You don't get out of bed looking for reasons to say no to other people. Neither does anyone else. People *want* to say yes, and they *will* if you create the right conditions. This means using your Assertiveness to get what you want, while showcasing your Warmth. That's the likeable badass way.

THERE IS ALWAYS AN ALPHA DOG

Hopefully by now I've convinced you that you should always look for ways to lean into your Assertiveness, not suppress it. The more Assertive you are, the more status you gain. There is, however, yet another benefit of Assertiveness: it changes how others behave in your presence, to your advantage.

After M, the second-most-memorable person from my consulting days was my worst client. He was nearing the end of his career and made it clear that he wanted to do as little work as possible while maintaining his reputation in the eyes of his supervisors. Each week, I put together a presentation for the supervisors, full of charts, graphs, and analyses summarizing my team's progress. My client's contributions consisted of occasionally looking over my shoulder and hiding from me when I came to his office to ask questions. But during the meetings, he would repeatedly interrupt me to take credit for my work. When I complained about this to one of my older, wiser teammates, he simply replied, "Stand up." I cocked my head like a confused dog, so he elaborated: "Next time, as soon as that guy takes over the conversation, get out of your chair and stand up. Then, start talking again and see what happens." So I did. And it was magic. In the next meeting, I started my update as usual, and my client interrupted me as usual. I immediately stood up and walked to the front of the room, as if I urgently needed to point out something on the projection screen. As I did, I continued my update, talking over my client for the first few beats. Quickly, he stopped speaking and stared at me, looking stunned. After a few more moments he leaned back in his chair and looked downward, as if he had completely disengaged from the conversation. He didn't speak again for the rest of the meeting.

At the time, I didn't understand why getting out of my seat altered my client's behavior so dramatically, nor did I have any ambition to become a psychologist. However, a few years later, one of my first research projects uncovered the science behind this exchange. Ahead of our time, my dear colleague and likeable badass mentor, Larissa (Lara) Tiedens, and I studied "manspreading." We brought people into our lab to work on a task (describing abstract paintings) with a same-gender partner they didn't know. In actuality, the partner was a trained actor, who was instructed to convey either Assertiveness or Submissiveness through their nonverbal behaviors. In the Assertive condition, imagine the worst airplane seatmate you've ever had: The actor draped their arm over the back of an adjacent chair, while putting their right ankle on their left thigh, allowing their leg to protrude out beyond their seat. In the Submissive condition, the actor folded in on themselves, legs together, hands in their lap, shoulders slouched.

We measured how the participants behaved in response. We found that in every interaction there was one—and only one—alpha dog. That is, when the actor conveyed Submissiveness, the participant got more Assertive and expanded their body over the course of the interaction. However, when facing a "manspreading" partner, participants constricted their own bodies over time, taking up less physical space as a sign of Submission. This is why standing up in that meeting many years ago stopped my client in his tracks—as soon as I asserted myself as the top dog, he instinctively submitted and became a member of the beta pack. Subsequent research has demonstrated that this finding isn't limited to nonverbal behaviors and applies to both work relationships, where people are completing shared tasks, and social relationships. Regardless of how it's conveyed and to whom, Assertiveness from one person tends to be complemented with Submissive responses from others, and vice versa.

Importantly, we also found that people *enjoyed* these complementary relationships more than they enjoyed relationships characterized by mutual Assertiveness or Submission. In a second study, we posed both the actor and the participant to create three types of interactions: (1) mutual Assertiveness, with both parties taking up a lot of physical space; (2) mutual Submission, where both parties were physically constricted; and (3) complementarity. After about thirty minutes of working together, we measured how much the participants *liked* their partner and how *comfortable* they found the interaction. Those in Condition 3—where one party was Assertive and the other Submissive—reported the most liking and comfort, regardless of which position they were in.

Two takeaways from this research are relevant to our discussion of self-advocacy. First, every relationship has an alpha dog, so if it's not you, it's them. Advocating for yourself is often scary, but the alternative is more frightening. If you always stay quiet and do whatever you think will make other people happy, they'll (justifiably) start to see you as more Submissive. Over time, they'll ask you to do more and offer you less. Your Submissiveness emboldens their Assertiveness. This is one reason women are disproportionately saddled with "office housework"—we can always sniff out the person most likely to say yes. Failing to be an Assertive advocate for yourself sets you up for a lifetime of fending off rabid alpha dogs.

The second takeaway from our research is that when you make a habit of showing up as Assertive, self-advocacy will start to take less effort. Over time, people will alter their behavior to be more Submissive in your presence, which means you no longer need to push as hard to get what you want. In some cases, people may even go so far as to anticipate what you want and give it to you without asking. For example, most of us have been witness to the maddening double standard of a woman having to negotiate tirelessly to get a benefit, such as a raise, that's given to a man outright. One explanation for this difference is the perceived Assertiveness of the beneficiary. If people think your male colleague will always make the ask, they'll spare themselves the time and start fulfilling his unstated requests proactively.

Fortunately, women can benefit from this reputation as much as men. In my case, I vividly remember an administrator of an executive leadership program asking me if I could shift the date of my workshop for the third time. However, when she asked, she also offered me a surprising concession: She had arranged for my favorite breakfast to be served on the day I would be teaching. The facility where I taught served set meal options on a ten-day rotation. Before asking me to move my date, she had called the catering team, found out when the breakfast pizza (a comforting, caloric concoction of dough, cheese, and egg) was being served, and negotiated with them to change the weekly menu—across the entire facility—just to make me happy. I was thankful, and a bit uncomfortable. I would have said yes to the date change anyway, and I was embarrassed that an entire kitchen staff and hundreds of program attendees would be disrupted for a benefit I didn't request. At the same time, the likeable badass in me felt satisfied because this unrequested perk signaled that I had sufficiently developed a reputation for being Assertive.*

DIALING UP THE WARMTH

Being Assertive isn't without risk, however, which is why advocating for ourselves often provokes anxiety. In Kathryn's case, she had been very Assertive in her conversation with the intern coordinator: She took control of the discussion from the first moment, listed all her credentials and accomplishments, and made the case that she had earned the right to a second assignment. Because her conversation had gone sideways, it's natural to wonder if she should have been more Submissive. Imagine, though, that she entered the conversation *timid, meek, self-doubting, and weak*, hallmark characteristics of Submissiveness. Would she have achieved a better outcome? Probably not. She might not have been escorted out of the building at that moment, but she wouldn't have conveyed the impression that she was worthy of a full-time role, which was her ultimate objective. As women, we often seek refuge in Submissive behaviors because we operate under a common misconception—we face backlash when we are Assertive. That's not true. Women are not penalized for the *presence* of Assertiveness,

---

* Of course, I was equally satisfied to show up that day and eat my fill of breakfast pizza.

they're penalized for the *absence* of Warmth. Although that truth is infuriating, it's also helpful because it informs a path forward. Advocating for ourselves is an Assertive act, and Assertiveness serves us well. We shouldn't shy away from it. Instead, we need to follow the advice that my grandmother (and yours, too, probably) always offered: "You catch more flies with honey than with vinegar." As a child, I thought it was just something old ladies said to remind you to be nice to your siblings, but I now see the adage differently. Catching a fly is an Assertive act—one that doesn't end well for the fly. The advice to use honey was really Grandma's way of instructing me how a likeable badass gets what she wants—not by toning down the Assertive, but by dialing up the Warmth.

Here's why. Unlike Assertiveness, which is countered, Warmth is mimicked. If someone smiles at us, we smile back. If someone is rude, we're more likely to be unkind in turn. Whereas Assertiveness begets Submissiveness, Warmth begets Warmth. Thus, showing up as a likeable badass, combining Assertiveness with Warmth, creates the best possible conditions for self-advocacy. Those around you will probably alter their behavior to be Submissive (in response to your Assertiveness) and Warm (in response to your Warmth), which means you will face an audience of friendly, agreeable people who want to make you happy. This doesn't mean you'll always get everything you want, but you'll have created the most favorable environment for a "yes" to emerge.

There are many ways we can do this. Below, I provide several evidence-based examples. As always, you don't need to do everything on this list every time. You just need to do something. And, if your favorite way of advocating Warmly isn't mentioned here, keep doing what works for you.

Importantly, each of these strategies has been proven effective in situations where the interacting parties are strangers, meaning you can use them even with someone you're meeting for the first time. That said, you'll always get results as good or better if your audience already sees you as a likeable badass, rather than having to build that reputation during the conversation. So, whenever possible, I implore you to build your status using the strategies in chapters 4 and 5 first, before starting to advocate.

> **STOP.**
> **DO NOT PASS GO. DO NOT COLLECT $200.**
>
> Before you read further, pause to answer this question:
>
> *What is one thing I want at this moment that another person could give me?*
>
> Kathryn wanted to work on a second project and secure a full-time job offer. I want my contractor to finish the renovation on my house by the end of summer. Yesterday, I spoke with a colleague who wants to attract more paid coaching clients, and today my daughter wants me to take her to the aquarium.
>
> Whatever you want most at this moment, big or small, identify it now and keep it front of mind as you review these strategies. Think about which ones could work best in your situation, and how you could implement them.

Start Early

It's tempting to put off asking for what we want. We worry about the reputational consequences of asking, and we don't want to be told no. Like any form of procrastination, this is generally a bad idea. Unless you can state a very specific reason that delaying a conversation improves your chances of getting a good outcome, the best time to make the ask is the moment you think of it. Ninety-nine percent of the time, I've found, delaying a conversation only creates problems.

This was true for Kathryn. Two weeks into her internship, and only two weeks before the ill-fated conversation, she had lunch with the intern coordinator. "We enjoyed each other," she remembers, "but I totally missed the opportunity to make her an ally." Kathryn had already formulated her plan to ask for a second assignment, but she didn't let on, thinking it would be better to finish the assignment first. "Had I brought it up at lunch, I'm sure she would have solved this problem with me. She would have told me exactly what I needed to do if I wanted to work on a second team, like getting my boss on board, and I would have done it."

There are real emergencies, and there are emergencies of our own making. Don't create an emergency by waiting until the last minute to ask for what you want. It forces the other person to answer instantly, which doesn't work in your favor. Remember the concept of mere exposure? Expecting someone to love your idea the first time you mention it is like asking them to love a song they've only heard once—possible but challenging. A better approach is to float an idea early, before you need an answer. Their first reaction may be a "no," but with repeated exposure they may warm to it by the time you need them to say yes.

Meet Face-to-Face

If you have a choice, advocate in person or on a video call, rather than by email.* It's easier to signal Warmth live (rather than asynchronously), and with visible nonverbal and paraverbal signals (gestures, facial expressions, emphasis, tone of voice).

Unfortunately, we're not as good as we think at conveying Warmth (or any other intent) over email. In one study, email senders thought recipients would be able to accurately identify their intent (e.g., sarcastic, serious) 80 percent of the time, but in actuality the recipients were only correct about half of the time—no better than flipping a coin. And rereading our messages before we send them generally doesn't help because we read them with a tone that the reader obviously can't hear. Advocating via email risks the possibility that you could come across as more aggressive or argumentative than you intend. So, if you can choose your medium, opt for one where the other person can see your friendly face, or at least hear your voice.†

---

* The only exception to this advice is situations where the parties are very hostile toward each other (e.g., contentious divorce). In those cases, email can be better than face-to-face. But that's a rare situation; in general, face-to-face is better than email.
† If you do need to use email to self-advocate, the best strategy is to ask another person to read the message and identify which emotions you're trying to convey before you send it. If they guess wrong, your recipient may, too.

Chit-Chat Warmly

Many task-related conversations start with some exchange of pleasantries before discussing the business at hand. Used purposefully, this small talk is an opportunity to show or remind your audience of your Warmth, so it's top of (nonconscious) mind for them as you advocate. Because you have only a few minutes, you need to rely on Warmth cues that can be conveyed quickly, such as humor, gratitude, compliments, or smiles.

In addition to these tools, another fast way to showcase Warmth—and one of my favorites—is to highlight a similarity between you and your audience. In short, similarity is one of the greatest bases of liking and attraction that psychology has ever documented. Put simply, we like people who are like us, and the similarity doesn't need to be substantive or relevant to the conversation to boost attraction. Studies have shown that strangers like each other more once they know they share trivial similarities, such as the same fingerprint type or first initial. If you've ever crossed paths with someone wearing a hat or shirt with your favorite sports team or alma mater and felt compelled to strike up a conversation, or at least wave hello, you can thank the similarity-attraction effect.

My all-time favorite story of the power of similarity comes from a dear friend and co-author, Greg Northcraft, who credited his longevity and success in senior leadership roles to his ability to build personal connections through common interests. An avid golfer, the first thing Greg would do whenever he met a new person was figure out if that person liked golf. As he explained, "If I can meet a fellow golfer, I can make a friend. And if I can make a friend, I know I will have a much easier time getting what I need. People often share with friends what they won't share with strangers."

Sometimes, the people he met weren't golfers, so he would need to move to other points of similarity (like dogs). However, the "talk about golf" strategy paid off more than once, including in his most memorable success. He was arranging a meeting with a fellow administrator he'd never met (let's call him Bill) to advocate for the favorable division of money (always a scarce resource) between their two groups. Greg deliberately offered to meet in Bill's office solely to scan Bill's physical space and identify points of connection. As he shook Bill's hand, he glanced over Bill's shoulder looking for clues. He couldn't believe his luck. Behind Bill's desk was a hole-in-one trophy. As Greg recounted, "If you're a golfer and you ever see a hole-in-one trophy, you know two things are true. There is a heck of a story behind the trophy, and the person behind the desk is *dying* to tell you what it is." So, he asked, with genuine interest, about Bill's hole-in-one, and shared the story of his own. I'm sure you can figure out by now how this movie ended. Of the sixty minutes scheduled for this discussion, they spent the first fifty-five minutes discussing golf. By that point, they were friends. Greg was able to successfully advocate for his ideal split of the money, while still leaving Bill's office more liked than when he had walked in.

No doubt, Greg got lucky that day. But the part that isn't luck—the part each of us can and should replicate—is Greg's long-term commitment, day in and day out, to finding a genuine point of connection with each person he meets. The key word, of course, is "genuine." I don't talk golf because I don't like golf. Doing so would come off as flat or phony. But I guarantee that Bill and I would have some true point of similarity we could discuss—if I made the deliberate effort to find it.

Highlighting similarities may feel more challenging when you look different than those around you. However, not only is it possible in these situations, it's even more important.

Remember Felecia Carty, the woman who applied to 104 customer success jobs in technology firms? She noticed that for the three companies where she advanced to the final interview round, she was referred by a current employee, and all those referrals came from fellow Black women. The similarities of race and gender may have helped Felecia get her foot in the door at those companies, but she couldn't rely on those commonalities in her interviews, which were with different people. For the job she ultimately accepted, her final interview was with four different people, three women and one man, all of whom were white. But that didn't mean that she didn't have something in common with each of them. The season was changing, and they all bonded over "soup, weather, and sweaters." None of these things was relevant to the job at hand, but they helped her come across as "someone people could see themselves working with." She also took care to speak the language of the tech industry, rather than retail—instead of "merchandise," she said "product"; instead of "store," she said "location" or "facility." Using their terms was another way she signaled that they were birds of a feather. And it worked. Felecia messaged her internal contact right after the interview, only to learn that her contact had already been messaged by the interview team—"Felecia was great!"

Similarly, a military officer in one of my training programs described the challenges of building relationships while deployed overseas. He would interact with country leaders of different races and ethnicities, who spoke different languages and often weren't very pleased to have the United States military in their country at all. Yet, even in the face of multiple glaring differences, he still found a way to highlight similarity—through his children. "No matter where you go in the world," he said, "you know that all parents adore their kids and would love nothing more than to tell you about them." He had found great success building relationships by talking about his children and asking foreign leaders about theirs. No matter how different they may appear at first glance, between any two people there exist multiple points of true similarity. Discover them, bring them into the conversation, and you will build Warmth.

This is another strategy Kathryn realized she should have used. When they had lunch, Kathryn learned the intern coordinator had only been at the company a few months and they bonded over "finding their way." When Kathryn finally sat down to ask for a new role, she could have found a way to bring that similarity back into the conversation to set a Warm tone, perhaps by asking the intern coordinator for some advice about how to handle a situation as a newcomer, or telling a funny story about a novice mishap, like getting lost on the way to the bathroom.

Move First

In a negotiation, should you make the first offer, or sit back and hear what the other person has to say first? When I ask this question in my negotiation programs, most people think the second mover has the upper hand. They've been conditioned to believe that "she who talks first, loses." However, the science shows the opposite is true: The person who makes the first offer in a negotiation ends up with a better deal than the person who makes the second offer.

Being a first-mover makes it easier to get what you want without sacrificing Warmth, because it shapes the other party's definition of a "good deal." In many cases, people—even those with expertise—don't know how to evaluate the worth of what's being discussed. In situations where the receiving party isn't 100 percent sure what a "fair" or "good" outcome would be, they're highly susceptible to using the first offer to determine what's reasonable and assume that the person making it has a valid justification for asking for what they want. To use a common example, job candidates often lament that they don't know how much a given role will typically pay. Similarly, job recruiters may be working within a specified pay range, but don't always know how to evaluate the potential skills of a given candidate to determine whether they should be at the bottom or top of that range.

If the recruiter moves first and offers a $50,000 salary, several thoughts are likely to run through the candidate's mind:

> This must be the going rate for this type of job. If I can get them to increase the starting offer by 10 percent, that will be a victory.
> There are a lot of layoffs in the market right now, so companies don't need to pay as much for talent.
> I was hoping for a $100,000 salary, but I can't ask for that now. I'll seem crazy. Maybe I'll ask for $75,000 instead.

The recruiter's offer shapes how the candidate defines a "good deal." As a result, research shows that the candidate will lower their expectations, make a counteroffer (the second offer) that's lower than what they would have asked for if they had moved first, and the outcome will be closer to the recruiter's ideal of $50,000 than the candidate's ideal of $100,000. The same thoughts and behaviors would be equally likely to happen with the recruiter, just in reverse, if the candidate made the first offer.

One of my favorite examples of the first-mover tactic came from Annie Duke, the professional poker player turned educator who always shares great wisdom in my book authors' group. Of all her stellar suggestions, I found this one to be most life-changing: Whenever you get a request to speak at an event, offer to do a conversation-style interview (often called a fireside chat) instead of a traditional presentation.

Mic dropped. Mind blown.

I instantly recognized the potential of this advice to reduce my workload and stress. Successful speakers make their job look very easy, like they just rolled out of bed telling stories and cracking jokes. However, there's a ton of exhausting work behind the scenes (at least for me). I'll spare you the details, but the important thing is that with a conversation between the speaker and a moderator most of my stresses would disappear. Preparation is minimal—there are no slides to make, and as an expert in your topic, you're able to answer the moderator's questions spontaneously. If the event runs long or short, you just answer fewer or more questions, no need to rework your entire presentation on the fly. What's more, fireside chats are usually done seated, so you can wear great shoes without torturing your feet.

Annie developed this idea for a slightly different reason—her dislike of virtual presentations, which became commonplace during the COVID-19 pandemic. She found staring into a webcam while clicking through slides was terribly boring for both her and the audience. Switching to a conversation eliminated one of her most despised tasks—making slides—and enabled her to reclaim the human engagement that energized her when speaking onstage.

Whenever Annie received a speaking inquiry, she would immediately suggest her preferred format. By moving first, she was able to shape her clients' perception of a good deal. Clients usually didn't know, or have a strong opinion, about what form Annie's appearance would take, and they didn't have any idea of how easy or difficult various formats were for her, or what rates she would charge. They simply knew they wanted her at their event, and they wanted the event to be a hit. As a result, they were very likely to accept and be happy with whatever she suggested. When promoting the 2022 release of her book *Quit: The Power of Knowing When to Walk Away,* Annie offered only fireside chats and not a single client refused. Within a year, she had done more than a hundred of them. They were so well received that fireside chats are now her standard speaking offering, not just for virtual events but in-person ones, too. Given her success with this format, I'd bet money that none of these clients saw her as less Warm. Quite the opposite, they were pleased with the events and grateful to have her speak.

Further, by offering the fireside chat at the outset of the negotiation, Annie wouldn't have to be the first to say "no." If she had waited for her clients to request a standard speaker-with-slides presentation, and then counteroffered with a different format, she would essentially be saying no to their ask. Saying no always risks putting a little ding in your perceived Warmth. The risk may not be that big, and there are some situations where that risk is worth it, but it's still there. Conversely, by moving first one of two things will happen: You'll get a yes, like Annie did, or the other party will have to be the first one to say "no" (perhaps implicitly by making a counterproposal). Either option threatens your Warmth less than being the first to disagree.

Present Three Solutions

Despite strong evidence supporting the first-mover advantage, the notion still scares people. *If my first proposal is too extreme, couldn't that backfire and damage my reputation?* This fear is frequent in salary negotiations, for example, which are a common topic among those who seek me out for advice.

Technically, this risk is real. If you're looking for someone to mow your lawn and you ask them to do it at 3 a.m. for $5, you probably won't make a friend (and you'll certainly be mowing your own lawn). This is why people often feel more comfortable moving second: If you hear what the other person has to say, you can avoid the risk of asking for too much (or offering too little) by counteroffering not far from their initial proposal. This may preserve your Warmth, but at the expense of Asserting your interests. Rather than moving second, a better way to manage the fear of a "too extreme" first offer is to use the "multiple equivalent offers" strategy. You still make the first move, but with *three* offers at the same time, instead of one.

My first memory of seeing this strategy in action was watching Adam Grant manage his calendar. Even though we were office neighbors at the time, we would often email each other from adjacent rooms. Every time we needed to meet, Adam would send an email with three available times on his calendar. Sometimes, his availability was comically limited—6 a.m. or 8 p.m. options six weeks out. But at least one of the options usually worked for me and I would pick the best one from the set. I eventually realized he was doing this to group like activities together—putting all of his meetings on one day a week, for example, to leave the other days free for thinking and writing.

The contrast between our approaches was stark. At the time, I was a "second-mover" with my calendar. I would receive a meeting request via email and, in a desire to clear my inbox as fast as possible, I would fire back a *"Sure, let me know what works for you"* reply. As I deleted the message, I would feel victorious . . . for a hot second. Moments later I would receive the response: *"How about 7 a.m. on Wednesday?"* Ugh. Seven a.m. was far from ideal for me. I'd have to give up my morning workout and my kids' school drop-off. Yet I hesitated to say no, worrying I would take a hit to my Warmth or my Assertiveness by implicitly admitting I wasn't willing to work 24-7. I felt I had no good option but to agree with a *"Sounds great, talk then!"* (which really meant, *"OMG my life is so out of control, how many more years until I retire?"*). Not surprisingly, years of this behavior resulted in early-morning and late-night meetings, and an overwhelming feeling of burnout. Notably, though, I held no ill will toward the people consuming my off-hours. I simply reasoned that they were offering me the next opening in their busy schedules. I could have easily capitalized on the power of a first offer by responding to meeting requests with my ideal time, yet I repeatedly gave this advantage away.

I don't think we ever spoke of it, but watching Adam manage his calendar finally convinced me to become a first-mover with my own schedule, using the multiple options approach. I'm now a master of efficiency who turns otherwise dead spots in my calendar into productive time, like scheduling phone calls during taxi rides to and from airports.

The advantage of providing multiple options is that you maintain the first-mover advantage by anchoring the conversation around options that are equally good for you, while also successfully preserving your Warmth. Letting the other person choose makes it more likely to end up with an outcome they like, and they'll feel positively about you as a result. Further, people like choice, and they like people who give them choices. When you present multiple choices, research shows that you're perceived as more trustworthy, flexible, cooperative, and sincere (all signals of Warmth), in comparison to making a single offer.

Notably, three is not an arbitrary number. Paradoxically, although people love choice, too much choice can be overwhelming. Three offers has been shown to be sufficient to generate the reputational benefits detailed above, so no need to go beyond that and risk confusing people.

Once you start looking for them, you'll find nearly limitless opportunities to use the three-offer strategy. If you wanted to ask your boss for a raise, for example, you could identify three different opportunities to volunteer for discretionary activities at work, such as taking on a leadership role in your organization's women's group, completing a high-visibility research project for the company, or mentoring a new member of your team. You wouldn't want these ideas to be nonpromotable work, but instead activities that interested you and would build your status in the organization. When you asked for the raise, you could also ask your boss which of the three possible contributions had the most value to the organization and would put her in the strongest position to justify your well-deserved raise to her superiors. This subtle shift allows you to appear more "collaborative" and less "demanding" without reducing your ask.

In a very different context, this same approach has become integral to my parenting. I'm pretty sure all moms can be divided into two categories: those who like swimming with their kids and those who don't. I'm squarely on team "reading in the lounge chair." As I've explained to my kids, the only reason I had three of them was so they could entertain each other in the pool. Until I became a first-mover in these discussions, my summers were always filled with broken promises (I'll get in the pool in five minutes), endless nagging (C'mon, water tag is really fun, Mom), and lots of parental guilt. Now, I use the three-offer approach to make everyone happy. Knowing that we'll be spending the day near water, I identify three pool games that don't involve me getting wet (e.g., I will judge the "best cannonball contest"). Before we even get out of the car, I move first by saying, "I'll give you three choices," and putting my options to a vote. Occasionally I need to bring in a fourth choice to break a stalemate, but I'm almost always successful at getting them to agree on one of the selections. I then sit back smugly as "fun mom," while I stay warm and dry in the sun, exactly as I wanted.

Always Answer "What's in It for Me?"

The easiest way to get someone to love you is to figure out what they want and give it to them. If I want my child to be quiet while I take a call, I can make both of us happy by giving her an iPad. My contractor may joyfully work at a quicker pace if I offer him a financial bonus for finishing the project by a given date. If you have resources that the other person will value, offering them is a surefire way to get what you want while maintaining your Warmth. Before you make an ask, pause for a moment and put yourself in the head of the other person. What do they want out of your exchange? Then think creatively about anything you could provide that would address their wants. If the iPad is out of battery life, I could offer a lollipop. Instead of money, I could promise my contractor a second project once the first is complete. The benefit you offer doesn't need to be a tangible item. Even without a budget or candy, you can still add value by using your time and effort to solve the other person's problem.

Of all the things Kathryn could have done differently, this is the one we both agreed would have been most impactful. Kathryn spent a ton of time preparing for the conversation, but she didn't spend any time thinking about the one question that mattered most: how the intern coordinator would benefit from Kathryn's request. "I was so focused on proving I had earned what I was asking for, I missed that it wasn't about that," she now sees in hindsight. "It was about her liking me and me helping her look good. I could have tried to help her shine. I could have said, 'This internship program is so great, and I'd love to help you show the rest of the company how innovative this program is. If each intern works on two teams, you'll get more feedback on each intern's performance and you'll have better information for hiring decisions. I've finished my project, and I'd love to be your test case.' If I had only said that, I might still be working there now."

Just like in Kathryn's case, the thing you want may also be beneficial to the other person, but they're unlikely to see the value unless you point it out. The other person hasn't been thinking about this idea as long as you have, and they have other things on their mind (like all the things they want from other people), so you need to make it easy for them to see how they benefit. What's more, highlighting the benefits to the other person signals that you care about their well-being, too, which subtly conveys your Warmth.

Helping others find value in your ask is one of the superpowers of a likeable badass. Sheryl Sandberg used this approach to negotiate her compensation at Facebook. She told Mark Zuckerberg: *"Of course you realize that you're hiring me to run your deal team, so you want me to be a good negotiator. This is the only time you and I will ever be on opposite sides of the table."* I LOVE this response. One of the reasons salary negotiations give people so much anxiety is the worry that the ask will come across as self-interested. It may be hard to imagine how paying you more could benefit the other person. However, by highlighting her unique contributions to the company and Zuckerberg, Sheryl was able to convey that Facebook was getting a *bargain*, no matter the cost. And, like Stacey Abrams's interview response, she needed only two sentences to do it. Her first sentence highlighted her negotiation skills and her second sentence conveyed her fierce loyalty—both valued assets that signal concern for others. Showcasing them in her ask was a masterful way for Sheryl to be an Assertive advocate for her interests while conveying Warmth.

Similarly, selling fireside chats was good for Annie Duke. She made no secret of this when speaking to clients. She was clear that she wouldn't be the best version of herself if she had to stare into a camera and click through a slide deck. "People assume that if you say, 'this is better for me,' people will be turned off, but that's not true," she advised. Her clients wanted the experience to be great for everyone, including her. But Annie also fiercely believed that a more enjoyable talk for her would also be better for her clients—and she let this be known as well. She explained how a fireside chat would be more *engaging* for the audience and would give the client more *control* over the event. After a prep meeting to learn about the client and their goals, she gave them full freedom to develop the question list. This enabled the client to focus the conversation on topics that were most relevant for the attendees. By pointing out these benefits, Annie got exactly what she wanted while also answering "What's in it for me?" for her clients.

Even canceling dinner with friends can be reframed as an act of generosity. For example, assuming it's true, you could tell them how important it is for you to be present and positive when you're together, and you're too tired, mentally and physically, to bring that energy to dinner this time. You could go one step further and offer to take responsibility for scheduling the next dinner (and maybe even buy the first round of drinks). In this way, canceling is an act of love, not selfishness. In sum, drawing attention to the benefit to others is how a likeable badass can be both strategic *and* authentic while advocating for herself.

Get an Agent

Not every request that benefits you needs to be made by you. Sometimes, you may not be the best messenger. Maybe your audience doesn't know you, or worse, doesn't like or respect you. In these cases, a better strategy is to ask someone else to be your agent—advocating to person A that they should advocate to person B on your behalf.

Every time I want something from another person, the first question I ask myself is *"Who is most likely to get this person to do what I want them to do?"* If I know someone who may be more likely to get a yes than me, I'll ask that person to be my agent. My message to the agent always follows a simple formula: "I want X from Person Y. Person Y thinks highly of you. Would you be willing to ask them on my behalf? If it helps you, I'll draft the email request and you can edit it." No one has ever said no. I've used this approach to negotiate my teaching schedule, book speaking engagements, secure media appearances, hire vendors, and even book reservations at "sold out" restaurants.

I've also found this question transformational for my parenting. Alas, I've realized that literally anyone—from the mail carrier to the person sitting next to me on the train—is more likely to get a "yes" out of my children than I am. Despite being a professional educator, I have outsourced almost every aspect of my kids' learning and development. After a summer of fighting my oldest son to put his head in the water when he swam, I hired a high schooler from the swim team to assist. Less than an hour later, he was swimming with his head underwater. I did the same thing when it was time for my youngest to learn to ride a bike. I've outsourced everything from math tutoring to driving lessons to etiquette classes. I don't do this because I lack the necessary knowledge—I was a math major in college, and I can swim, bike, drive a car, and put my napkin in my lap. I outsource because I realize that I'm not the best person to advocate for what I want in these situations. I'm more likely to get my children to comply if I use an agent, so I do.

COLLECTING NOS

Many of the things we want in life require the cooperation of other people. When we shy away from these asks out of fear of being seen as greedy, selfish, "too much," or anything else, we squander the potential to live our most successful and satisfying lives. If you advocated for yourself just once a day, and only half of those attempts resulted in a "yes," that would add up to thousands of happier days over your lifetime.

The strategies above can help you get to "yes" without bankrupting your Warmth. But, sometimes, despite your best likeable badassery, the answer will be "no." Another common reason that people, especially women, fail to advocate for themselves is because they assume the other person will never agree. The anticipation of the "no" keeps us from asking in the first place.

But where is the boundary between a "yes" and a "no"? How much could you ask for before others will deny your requests? Are you asking for enough, or is there more room to advocate for yourself? Are your assumptions about what people will agree to correct?

To answer these questions, I encourage you to complete the Collecting Nos exercise. Instead of trying to get people to say "yes," the goal of this exercise is to get people to say "no" to you. That is, you want to push the limits of your requests until you go too far, asking people for things they won't give. Although it may sound scary at first, my experience doing this with thousands of people is that it's great fun once you get into it (we likeable badasses love a challenge).

This is one of my favorite ways to practice advocating for yourself. For one, it can be easily modified to turn the heat up or down. Also, almost everyone finds getting ten "nos" more difficult than they anticipate—because they get several unexpected "yes"es! Studies show that we're more reluctant to ask for help than we should be; we overestimate how much our asks will inconvenience others and underestimate how willing they are to help and how positively they feel when they do. For most people, the boundary between a "yes" and a "no" is further out than they assumed. Not only are you likely to get more than you expect through this exercise, but you will also realize that a "no" is nowhere near as bad as you imagined and may even be a good thing. In the sage words of Jada Pinkett Smith:

> "Have the courage to say what you need in the moment. Most people aren't mind readers. Two things will happen: You'll either get

what you need or realize that the source you are asking doesn't have the capacity to deliver. Both are gifts."

There are many different variants of the Collecting Nos exercise available online. Here are the rules I use.

What to Do

Make asks of other people until *ten* different people tell you "no" in response to *ten* different requests. Ask for anything that has value to you, no matter how big or small. This way, you can't lose. If the person says "yes," you get something you wanted! If they say "no," you've completed one request for this challenge.

If you want to make it very low risk, you can make requests of strangers you'll never see again (e.g., asking a salesperson for a discount). For a more intense experience, you could make all your requests at work, with peers, superiors, and customers.

Keep track of each request and what the other person said when they responded. This will be helpful for reflecting after the experience is complete.

Reflection Questions

Getting the ten "nos" is step one. Step two is reflecting on what you learned from them. These are the questions my students answer when they complete this assignment for a grade. Obviously, I have no reward or punishment to offer you here, but I encourage you to complete them for your own benefit (likeable badass honor)!

1. How many requests did you have to make to get ten "no"s?
2. Looking across your requests, what seemed to make it easier or harder for people to say no?
3. How many of these people saw you as a likeable badass before you made the request? For those who didn't, what could you have done to build this reputation before you made the ask?
4. How many different ways did people say no? How many

actually said the word "no" versus something else that you took to mean "no"? If they didn't say "no" outright, why do you think this was?
5. How did you feel or react when people said "no"? Why did you feel or react this way?
6. What are the most important things you learned about yourself through this exercise?
7. What is one lesson from this experience that you can apply in your future asks? How can you put that lesson into practice this week?

★

You might be wondering what happened to Kathryn. She returned for her final year of business school (without a job offer), still ruminating on the abrupt and confusing end to her internship. She kept asking herself, and others, "What should I have done differently?" One professor pointed her to emerging research on gender and negotiation, so Kathryn took the list of recommendations to the library and started reading. One article led her to another, then another, until Kathryn had an entire binder of research, dog-eared and highlighted. She was able to secure a teaching assistant position for a negotiation course in her program and as part of that effort wrote a "How to Negotiate as a Woman" guide, based on everything she had read and learned. She shared it with twenty friends, who found it so valuable they forwarded it to their friends. Soon, Kathryn started fielding calls from women she had never met who had questions about negotiating their job offers.

This continued for years, after she graduated and returned to McKinsey (in the city where her husband lived), took a job at an apparel company (which she eventually helped sell), and started her own apparel consulting firm. All the while, helping women negotiate was something she did "just for fun." She had great success with it. She helped one friend transition from a middle-management role in one company to a C-level role in another company (with an 84 percent pay increase), and supported several others in their job negotiations with firms like

Peloton and Uber. Then, when the COVID-19 pandemic forced Kathryn to work from home with two small children underfoot, she started writing while they napped to keep herself from "going crazy." She wrote an article titled "Dear Working Women: Before You Go, Negotiate," which offered tips on how working moms, buried under pandemic-related childcare demands, could negotiate more flexible employment terms instead of quitting. A friend of a friend (i.e., Kathryn's agent) got the article placed in *Adweek,* a weekly national marketing and advertising trade publication in the United States. From that article, companies started reaching out to Kathryn with messages of "Yes, we need this type of advice for women!" and her newest company, Worthmore, was born. Today, leveraging research to help women succeed is no longer a hobby, it's her company's central mission. Kathryn is a nationally recognized thought leader on women's advancement, and her insights have been featured in publications like *Harvard Business Review, The Wall Street Journal,* and *Fast Company.* She and her team of facilitators offer a suite of programs aimed at accelerating women's career progress, including developing negotiation skills. Kathryn estimates that in the first three years after founding Worthmore she has shared her trademarked approach to negotiating as a woman with more than thirty thousand people. None of which would have happened if she hadn't "ruined her career in less time than it takes to order a latte."

PLAYS TO PRACTICE

🔥 Strike up conversations with ten strangers with the goal of finding a point of genuine similarity with each person.

🔥🔥 Be an agent for someone else (without them asking). Identify a situation where you're well positioned to help another person get something they want, and make the ask on their behalf. For example, I'm fortunate to have many medical doctors as personal friends. Whenever I hear of someone struggling to get a timely doctor's appointment, I will often jump in as their agent and ask one of my doctor friends to make time for them.

🔥🔥🔥 Make one ask that scares the hell out of you (e.g., inviting a senior colleague to lunch, asking someone to introduce you to a powerful person in your network, asking for a raise or a discount). If you need inspiration, I just advised a woman to email the COO of her company and offer to update him on one of her projects. She was terrified, and assumed he would say no, but she did it. She sent me the update: He scheduled a meeting with her for the following week, and she was very excited.

CHAPTER 7

Start with the End

In my consulting days, accumulating airline miles was considered a perk of the "road warrior" lifestyle. Some took it to extremes: One of my colleagues would check out of his hotel room every morning, only to check back in at night so he could earn the "500 airline miles at check-in" perk every day, instead of once a week. The irony was, we were all working hard to accumulate more miles than we'd ever spend. I would always fantasize about saving up enough miles to book a first-class ticket to Australia, even though I had no plans to go there. Instead, I would pay for tickets to go back and forth to my hometown of Pittsburgh, while I stockpiled enough miles to get me to the sun and back. Now, almost thirty years later, I still feel a twinge of worry every time I use my obscenely large balance of airline miles to book a ticket. I may need those miles tomorrow if someone invites me on the trip of a lifetime—to Australia, no doubt.

So, I chuckled when I read Amy Schulman's analogy comparing this all-too-familiar behavior with a much worse form of hoarding: our tendency to hoard status. Speaking to *The New York Times* during her tenure as general counsel for Pfizer, Schulman observed that women often conserve their status "as if [it] were airline miles. But 'when we really need them' may never come. The trips are not going to happen, and we'll be left with 800,000 . . . miles."

The urge to conserve our status is understandable. We often need to do more than men to earn others' respect, so it's logical that we don't want to lose any. It's also natural to worry that our status is finite, so we need to save it up in case an urgent need arises tomorrow. But if we take this fear to the extreme and never use the status we've earned, we might as well spare ourselves the trouble of earning it at all. Having status that you aren't willing to leverage is no different than banking airline miles you'll never redeem or storing two hundred cans of beans in your basement.

When I think of a woman who was brilliant at using her status, I think of my maternal grandmother, Marge. She wasn't formally educated beyond high school, but she was a master at building relationships. She turned strangers into acquaintances into friends by the hundreds through her favorite small deposits. She would chat with people on the bus or the street. Next thing we knew, she was mixing a cocktail for them at her kitchen counter. An avid gambler, she would invite the neighborhood over for impromptu poker games (teaching me to play while I sat in her lap). She used humor to charm, and I'd like to think I inherited her knack for memorable one-liners. When she worked as a hairstylist, her customers would exclaim, "Make me beautiful, Marge." She'd reply, "I just do hair, I don't fix faces." One by one, she built a legion of fans. If she called someone in the middle of the night to ask a favor, the number of people who would jump out of bed to help, no questions asked, would easily be in the hundreds. And she often picked up the phone. Not necessarily in the middle of the night, but my grandmother wasn't afraid to cash in on the goodwill she had built in her community to help her get things done. She was a highly respected political activist and cared deeply about both local and national politics. When it was election season, everyone knew that it was time to "return the favor" to Marge by volunteering at one of the voting call centers she had organized. As a teenager, when Grandma "volunteered" me to work the phones, too, I was both proud and surprised by how many adults would show up, looking lost, mumbling, "Um, Marge told me to come here today." They weren't sure what they had agreed to, but they wouldn't dare refuse a request from Marge. This cycle repeated her entire life: build status, use status, build status, use status. When she died, the attendance at her funeral convinced me that the number of people who admired her had only increased over her lifetime.

★

Of all the everyday choices we make, some of the most difficult are those that put our status at risk—taking an action that *might* result in someone seeing us as less Assertive or Warm than they do now. I emphasize the word "might" because this danger may not always be as likely as we imagine. Advocating for ourselves often feels uncomfortable because we worry that asking for what we want will kill our Warmth. But as we saw in chapter 6, and in Grandma Marge's story, it's very possible to get what you want without burning status. Also, thanks to confirmation bias, once others see you as a likeable badass, they're likely to continue seeing you that way, even when you occasionally behave to the contrary. We shouldn't assume that every time we ask, disagree, say no, or speak up that we will necessarily lose status. But any time you make a decision that impacts other people there's always a chance (even a small one) you could lose some respect in their eyes.

Consider the unfortunate dilemma of Samantha, my former colleague turned friend and travel partner.* In her early fifties, Samantha worked as a senior leader in a global technology firm. Typically confident and decisive, she was unusually uncertain the day we met for lunch, as she recounted an incident that happened during a recent business trip. She had traveled across the country with her female colleague and male boss, let's call them Kim and Matt, to meet with a potential client. As they checked into their hotel on a Tuesday evening, they discussed plans for the next morning. When Samantha suggested they meet for breakfast at 8:30 a.m., before the midday client meeting, Matt quipped, "8:30! Aren't you going to do any work in the morning?" Having worked with Matt for years, Samantha found

---

* Not her real name—Samantha is the name her father allegedly wanted her to have.

his response annoyingly predictable. A proud workaholic (driven by his disorganization, rather than his work ethic), Matt was known for dropping snide comments about everyone else's relative "slacking." Samantha and Kim brushed it off and went to bed. Wednesday morning, after Matt bowed out of breakfast, the two women chose to catch up on business over a walk instead. As they were leaving the hotel, they ran into Matt. After a short conversation, Samantha and Kim excused themselves for their "walking meeting." They meandered their new surroundings for an hour, enjoying the fresh air, exercise, and productive work discussion. That evening, Samantha, Kim, and Matt reconvened with the clients over dinner. The conversation turned to the beautiful southern weather and one of the clients asked if their midwestern guests had been able to get outside and enjoy it. Matt jumped in: "I'm the only one who did any work this morning. These two [gesturing to Samantha and Kim] just played outside."

Samantha was pissed. Matt was trying to build his own status with the client by destroying hers—and with a lie, to boot. She glanced around the table to see discomfort on her clients' faces, and embarrassment on Kim's. She didn't know how to respond. If she stayed silent, she risked her status with her clients, who might see her as less dedicated and driven thanks to Matt's false allegation. But if she spoke up, she would be publicly disagreeing with her boss, and would surely lose status with him. No matter which choice she made, she felt she would take a reputational hit. Ultimately, she stayed silent (and seething) at dinner, but doubt about her choice lingered. Weeks later, when she finally told me the story, it was still haunting her. She felt angry that she hadn't put Matt in his place. She felt guilty that she hadn't defended Kim. "Did I do the right thing?" she asked, more to herself than to me.

I felt for Samantha. There was very little she could do to prevent this situation from happening. Since she was meeting with clients, I would have advised her to use the conversation to build her status, as appropriate. She should have been telling a strong story about herself by highlighting her accomplishments, building rapport through similarity, and finding easy ways to add value to these new relationships. But she couldn't know that the subject of the weather would lead Matt to disparage her, and any status-building tactics she had employed to that point might not have been sufficient to guarantee that Matt's insult wouldn't sway the clients. She also didn't have a perfectly "safe" choice—staying silent and speaking up both risked her status in different ways. And she had only a split second to decide how to respond. All around, it was a perfect storm.

Hopefully you'll never be in Samantha's exact situation, but you've undoubtedly faced a choice that could endanger your hard-earned Assertiveness or Warmth. For example:

- Should I turn down the work trip, or the relocation, due to family obligations, if it risks my co-workers, family, or friends seeing me as less "ambitious"?
- Should I speak up in the meeting with an alternative to my colleague's proposal, if it risks her seeing me as less of a "team player"?
- Should I accept the stretch assignment knowing I'll have a steep learning curve, if it risks my new boss seeing me as "inept"?
- Should I act counter to my superior's advice at the risk of being labeled "insubordinate," "incompetent," or both?
- Should I stand up for someone I think is being undervalued, if it risks my being seen as "difficult"?

When faced with these types of hard decisions, there are two instinctive responses, both of which are problematic. One instinct is to choose what feels *safest*, which is often *inaction*—staying silent, preserving the status quo, or going along with the crowd. The problem with always picking the safe choice, as Amy Schulman points out, is that it leads to status hoarding: If you wait "for the perfect moment to spend that [political] capital, you're going to be sidelined your whole career waiting to ... enter the ring."

The other instinct is to choose *reaction*, which often feels most *satisfying*, at least in the moment. The challenge is that this response often leads to buyer's remorse—burning status on impulse in the moment and waking up tomorrow regretting it. When your cousin starts spouting his political views at the dinner table, you may feel compelled to refute him. But after the argument gets heated, other relatives leave the table and hide in another room, and your cousin gives you a frosty greeting at breakfast the next morning, you may quickly lose the satisfaction you felt the night before. Disagreeing simply because you think the other person is incorrect is a common form of reaction that often leads to unnecessary status losses.

LET YOUR FUTURE SELF DECIDE

Both inaction and reaction are knee-jerk responses that don't necessarily pay off in the long run. A better alternative—the one the likeable badass uses—is to use your long-term priorities to guide today's decisions. A wealth of psychological evidence suggests that people aren't always skilled at accounting for the future when making choices today. Another glass of wine tonight seems like a great idea, but less so when the alarm goes off early tomorrow morning. Procrastinating on your work this week is regretted when you have to pull an all-nighter next week. As psychologist Hal Hershfield, author of *Your Future Self: How to Make Tomorrow Better Today*, points out, we "think of our future selves as if they're other people."

Hershfield stresses the importance of getting to know your future self so that you can account for their preferences in the decisions you make today. This is particularly true when it comes to decisions that involve status. Whether or not it's worth using your status today depends, in part, on what you want from tomorrow (and all the days that follow). Rather than choose impulsively in the moment and cross your fingers that you'll still think you made the right choice down the road, you can work in reverse. When you "start with the end," you identify a milestone in the future, specify what you want it to look like, and use progress toward that milestone to guide today's choices.

This will prove harder than it sounds at first, but it's well worth it. Knowing what really matters to you eliminates status hoarding, buyer's remorse, and all the associated "should I or shouldn't I" anxieties we often experience in the face of tough choices. Just like your finances, decisions about how to use your status are highly personal. Only you can decide what's best for you, and it's perfectly valid if your choice differs from your neighbor's. When Samantha wondered if she "did the right thing," I couldn't answer that question for her. But I told her what I'll tell you: The right thing isn't defined by *what* decision you made, but *why* you made it. If Samantha chose inaction to play it safe, refraining from speaking up against Matt because she was fearful of taking any hit to her status, I would question the choice. But if she stayed silent because she felt that preserving her Warmth with Matt was important to accomplishing her long-term goals, then it was the right call for her. Similarly, I would advise her against speaking up to Matt simply because he made her mad. But, if she addressed Matt's insult because she believed that defending Kim and managing her status with her clients would best serve her in the long term, then this would have been the right choice. Once you've identified your long-term priorities, the "right thing" becomes easier to define and measure against—it's the decision that provides a possible future benefit that's greater than any short-term hit to your status today.

You'll know your long-term priorities are clear when you can answer this question without hesitation: *"How likely is it that risking some of my likeable badass reputation today will advance one or more of my long-term goals?"* It's hard to know for sure that anything we do today is guaranteed to benefit us tomorrow, which is why I phrase this question in terms of likelihood. If you think there's a "good chance" that risking a little Warmth or Assertiveness now may benefit you in the future, then it's probably worth it. If you think chances are "slim," then you may want to save your status for another day.

There are two different exercises I recommend trying to help you clarify your long-term priorities. I think they're useful in different ways, so I advise you to do both. But if one resonates much more than the other, it won't hurt my feelings if you pick your favorite. I also encourage you to complete these exercises now. Waiting until a critical spending decision is urgent is a mistake. Unfortunately, at that point, your mind will be too clouded to develop meaningful priorities. Like Samantha experienced, you may have mere seconds to decide, without the luxury of time to contemplate your future.

EXERCISE 1: YOUR RETIREMENT PARTY SPEECHES

Imagine your retirement party. It will be a splendid affair in a glamorous location, filled with friends, family, and colleagues. You will, as always, look fabulous and be having a great hair day. There will be speeches and toasts, of course. Many people will line up to say wonderful things about you. *What do you want them to say?* Think about those speeches and identify:

1. The *top three contributions* you most want people to mention. A contribution is a mark you want to make on the world—anything that adds value to other people (customers, employees, family, strangers). You'll likely derive personal benefit or a sense of accomplishment from these contributions, too. As a rule of thumb, a contribution is something that might be listed on a résumé or bio (even in the fun facts section), such as:

   - After more than twenty years as a successful attorney, she founded her first company—a bakery—in her fifties.
   - She takes pride in her perfect attendance record at her three kids' games, recitals, and plays, never missing a single event in more than twenty-six years.
   - She was the CEO of Amazon.
   - She ran a yearly marathon for fifteen years to raise funds for the children's cancer hospital in her community.

2. The *top three characteristics* you most want people to use to describe you (other than likeable badass—that's a given). A characteristic is an adjective that describes you or a quality you embody, such as:

   - Fun-loving
   - Forgiving
   - Open-minded
   - Decisive

I've been using this exercise with students and leaders for close to a decade, since I saw an interview with Dutch-born pharmaceutical executive Marijn Dekkers describing the value he got from a similar experience. Dekkers quickly advanced through the ranks of General Electric and Allied Signal, before being promoted to his first CEO role, at Thermo Electron, in his early forties. Michael Porter, a renowned Harvard Business School professor, sat on the company's board and invited Dekkers to attend a Harvard leadership course designed for new CEOs. The first assignment of the program was for each CEO to give their "going-away speech"—the public address they would want to make years in the future at the company party held to celebrate the end of their successful tenure. Reflecting over fifteen years later, after he had left Thermo Fisher Scientific (as it had been renamed) to become CEO of Bayer AG, one of the world's largest pharmaceutical companies, the speech Dekkers wrote at Harvard still stood out as "the best lesson" he ever learned. Preparing his parting words at the "*beginning* of his tenure, rather than the end," he realized, gave him "clarity," and served as a "tremendous guide for the ten years [he] was there."

The retirement party exercise is inspired by Dekkers's story. I use a retirement party rather than a going-away speech to broaden your aspirations beyond a single organization or experience. And I've changed the perspective from what you want to be able to say about yourself to what other people will say about you. Dekkers was using the speech to identify how he wanted to shape the organization—what *he* wanted to be able to say about *his own* contributions at the end. We're focused on status, which is what *other* people think and say about us—not just what we *did*, but also who we *are*.[*]

To start the exercise, I recommend identifying as many contributions and characteristics as you can think of. After all, people will certainly say more than three good things about you in each category, so it's valuable to think about the full list. Then, once you have several ideas listed, narrow them down to your top three in each category. I

---

[*] You could accomplish a similar objective using the more common "write your own obituary" assignment. I prefer the retirement party because thinking about a party in my honor is less depressing than thinking about my own death.

force you to prioritize because tradeoffs in life are inevitable. You can't be everything to everyone at all times, so you need to decide what you most want to be. A 100-item list of priorities is the same as no priorities at all.

I also think that surveying your friends and colleagues is a great way to get ideas about who you are and what contributions and characteristics you might want to put on the list. This is what happened to me—albeit unintentionally. Long before I was using this exercise, I faced the difficult decision of whether I should testify in a legal proceeding. Refusing to testify felt safer—if I stayed silent, I wouldn't make any enemies. But if I didn't speak up, someone I thought could be a threat to others—particularly women—might avoid punishment and even be rewarded.

This decision caused me a lot of angst. For a long time I was able to kick it to the back of my mind, but as the deadline approached, I stopped sleeping well, my hair was falling out, and I was staring at my computer screen for days pretending to work—still no closer to a decision. Out of time and options, I called a dear friend for advice.[*] Her response remains one of the most influential things anyone has ever said to me. After reassuring me that there was no right or wrong decision, she said, "But, Alison, I've always thought of you as a very principled person, and I think it's one of your best qualities." As soon as her words hit the air, I knew I would testify.

Those words forever changed how I saw myself and have influenced numerous decisions since.

Principled.

It fit me. It was my word.

If I had to lose Warmth with some people for others to see me as "principled" (including myself), that was a trade worth making. Understanding that "principled" was part of my end story gave me the same clarity that Marijn Dekkers experienced from his going-away speech. It also gave me a rule for choosing between difficult options—when in doubt, choose the more principled route. And I never would

---

[*] Given the story, I won't name her, but she's one of the most likeable badasses I know.

have found my word, at least at that point in time, if I hadn't heard my friend describe me that way.

Since that day, I've completed the retirement party exercise, and have identified my top three contributions and characteristics. If you're curious, they are (in no particular order):

Contributions
- Wrote a book (check!)
- Was a fierce women's advocate, giving women the science and confidence to kick ass in a biased world (in process)
- Although unable to do a cartwheel, she was a lifelong, relentless cheerleader for her students—always willing to meet with them and support their careers, even decades after they graduated (ongoing)

Characteristics
- Principled
- Entertaining
- Generous

Not every likeable badass I've met has done my version of this exercise, but I find that most successful women are very confident and decisive about how they use their status because they have figured out, one way or another, what they value. For example, Victoria Pelletier, the woman who earned a reputation as the Iron Maiden early in her career, realized she would need to be very "intentional and consistent" if she was going to break free from this image and rebrand herself as a likeable badass. She started to think about her legacy and realized, "If I had a tombstone, it's not going to talk about the sales, revenue, and profit I delivered for the companies I work for, it would talk about what I stood for in the communities I served." That realization led her to choose the key pillars of her personal brand, which helped her not only build her status, but decide how to use it. One of Victoria's chosen characteristics is to be an "advocate," especially for diversity, inclusion, and equal rights. Once she identified this, it became easier for her to speak up against injustice toward members of systemically marginalized groups, even if it risked her status. In fact, Victoria's outspoken advocacy is what led me to meet her. A woman I know, Mary,[*] sent me a message that Victoria was a likeable badass and I should interview her. Although they had never met in person, Victoria's allyship earned Mary's respect. When Accenture, where both Mary and Victoria worked, announced layoffs at the executive level, many social media posts emerged, including from current and former employees, about how white men were being disproportionately impacted. Mary, a Black female managing director who was laid off, found these posts "psychologically harmful," but didn't want to speak up and "be attacked for noting the privilege of white males." However, Victoria, who has a large following on LinkedIn, immediately posted her disagreement, citing her power and privilege as a white woman to call out the explicit and implicit racial bias in her colleagues' posts. Mary appreciated Victoria's advocacy, which inspired her to recommend Victoria to me. But Victoria's posts probably weren't appreciated by everyone, especially the colleagues she was contradicting. Victoria knew her views would cost her status with some people, but that didn't give her a moment of hesitation. Because she knew being an advocate for equality was one of her defining characteristics, the choice to speak up in that moment was obvious—just as choosing "principled" as one of my values made testifying an easy choice for me. In fact, Victoria's clarity on her personal brand, combined with her value of advocacy, inspired her to write a book to help others do the same, *Influence Unleashed: Forging a Lasting Legacy Through Personal Branding*.

Clarifying your contributions and characteristics also helps you decide when *not* to speak up. One of the biggest forms of discipline I've learned through this exercise is the value of *disagreeing with purpose*. I really like to be right. I mean REALLY like it.[†] In my less experienced days, the joy of "winning" an argument—any argument—was intoxicating. But it was also killing my Warmth without any real upside. Now, before I disagree with someone, I pause for a moment to ponder

---

[*] Name changed.
[†] People who know me are falling off their chairs laughing at how true this is.

what benefit or contribution could result from my counterpoint. If, like Victoria, I can state how the disagreement moves me a step closer to one or more of my retirement party goals, I do it. If not, I keep my mouth shut and save my status for another day.*

> ### EXERCISE 2: THE VIEW FROM THE ROCKING CHAIR
>
> After your retirement party (which was amazing, by the way), you begin to enjoy a new stage of life. You start and end each day sitting in the rocking chair on your front porch. Look around you. *What do you see?* In your mind, draw a detailed picture of your life at this moment. For example:
>
> - Who, if anyone, is rocking next to you? Who comes to visit?
> - Where is the rocking chair? Is it in a different location than where you live now? Is it on a farm, a beach, a yacht?
> - What are you doing in the chair? Knitting, day-trading, meditating? What are you thinking about, and not thinking about?
> - When you get up from the rocking chair, how will you spend your day? What hobbies and interests do you pursue?

The origin of this exercise is a conversation I had when I was in my early thirties with my dear friend and colleague, Mabel Miguel. I was newly married, and confided in Mabel that I was uncertain about

---

* I find this particularly useful on social media—aka the land of inflammatory comments and pointless arguments. Every day I see people engaged in comment wars with total strangers. I always marvel, "What are they possibly hoping to achieve in that debate?" Though I never get to ask, I'm sure the answer is that they have absolutely no idea. They're potentially burning through reputation in front of a worldwide audience with no stated purpose in mind. Instead, I scroll past most things I don't agree with and try to use social media to be "entertaining" and "generous" with a larger audience—making people laugh, making them feel seen and valued. But I'm only able to show up that way with intention because I took the time to complete the retirement party exercise and I keep it front of mind.

whether I wanted children. Mabel, by this point a mother of two grown kids, confessed to being similarly ambivalent about motherhood at my age. When I asked her how she eventually decided she wanted children, she explained a version of this exercise to me. Mabel had expressed her uncertainty to a friend, who told Mabel to close her eyes and imagine herself in her rocking chair. "Look around," the friend said. "Who do you see?" As Mabel scanned her mind's eye, she realized that there were lots of people around her. "As much as I love my husband," Mabel realized, "we weren't the only two in that picture." After hearing her story, I pictured my own rocking chair and found that I, too, was surrounded by family. Fast-forward fifteen years, and I'm now the proud mother of three awesome likeable badasses in training. I can't say that I would never have had kids if not for that conversation, but it certainly gave me needed clarity.

I realized that this same exercise could be broadened to make decisions about status. Looking at the full picture of your life—where are you, who's with you, what are you doing—helps you make decisions today toward that future vision. Although I don't draw a strict work/life delineation between the two exercises, my experience is that the retirement party exercise is very helpful for thinking about professional aspirations and the rocking chair exercise is useful for thinking about personal ones.

In Samantha's case, the rocking chair exercise was particularly helpful as we analyzed, postmortem, whether she had "done the right thing" by letting Matt's insult slide. When I asked her what was important to her, she replied, "Making as much money as I can at this point in life." As I dug deeper, I could see her view from the porch. In her future, she wanted to be financially secure enough that she could take care of herself and her aging parents as a single woman. She wanted to be able to leave her industry and pursue a career in hospitality technology before retirement. She wanted to travel and eat all the best food all over the world. But to afford this vision, she felt strongly that she needed to maximize her income over the next five to ten years. Once we established these aims, I asked her which choice—preserving her Warmth with Matt by staying silent or preserving her and Kim's Assertiveness with the clients—best helped her achieve this goal. Put in this context, she was able to answer quickly: Preserving her relationship with Matt was more important. She liked her current job, and thought she was well compensated. If she eventually switched jobs in her industry, she would benefit from Matt's support. And she certainly didn't want to risk Matt becoming an other-*demoter* for her, badmouthing her behind her back because he was mad. "That settles it," I reassured her. "You did the right thing." Given two bad choices, Samantha chose the one that best supported her view from the rocking chair.

If you had been in Samantha's situation, you may have responded differently. Again, the choice of how to use your status is up to you, and you alone. You deserve to have the future *you* want. It doesn't matter if your future looks different than someone else's, but it does matter that you recognize what you're working toward. The clearer you are on where you're going, the better you can use your status to help you get there.

For me, the rocking chair exercise has been helpful in making career decisions that impact my family. From my porch, one of my clearest visions is having strong relationships with my three children when they're adults. I want them to like me, not just love me. I want them to enjoy spending time with me, not just do it once a year out of obligation. I want them to seek me out for advice because they value my opinion, even when they no longer need it. I want to travel with them, shop with them, drink wine with them, and play poker with them. I want their spouses to like me as much as they like their own mothers. This clarity has proven immensely valuable in deciding when to prioritize my job over my family, and when to do the opposite.

These types of choices—job vs. family—are particularly fraught for women because we have to navigate the "motherhood penalty"—the tendency for people to judge mothers as less Assertive than nonmothers.[*] Aware of the motherhood penalty, I know that every time I make

---

[*] In one experimental study, participants compared résumés of two same-gender (male or female), same race (white or Black) job applicants who differed only in parental status (parent or nonparent). Both Black and white mothers were judged less competent and committed than equally qualified nonmothers of the same race, but fathers were not penalized over nonfathers. In a subsequent field study, the same researchers found that nonmothers were twice as likely to land a job interview than mothers, though there was no difference between nonfathers and fathers.

a decision that highlights my mom status and prioritizes family over work, I risk further eroding my Assertiveness. In these moments, I return to my view from the rocking chair. I'll ask myself whether the decision I face is likely to impact how my grown children feel about me and I base my choice on that answer. For example, I'm pretty sure I missed all my kids' "firsts"—first laughs, first words, first steps. Many mothers prioritize being there for those moments or feel guilty if they miss them. I didn't even try to stick around, and it didn't bother me one bit. I knew they wouldn't remember those things, and therefore my presence or absence in those moments was irrelevant to how they'll feel about our relationship as adults. I also felt sure that the first time I saw them walk, talk, or laugh would be amazing, whether or not they'd done it before. So I went to work and learned about most of my kids' development from birth to age three from their wonderful daycare teachers. For me, it wasn't worth risking any Assertiveness with my colleagues and clients to be there in those moments. I was (and am) perfectly content with being average (or below average) on any aspect of parenthood that I don't think will matter twenty years from now.

However, when my husband and I considered a move to Chicago for his job, envisioning this same future helped me make the choice to pick family over career. I didn't want to leave my faculty position at the University of North Carolina and I knew most people in my field would see working remotely as an unorthodox decision. I felt confident that being less present in the hallways because I had—gasp!—"followed my husband" would be a career-limiting move. As much as I loved—and still love—my work, though, the move was an easy decision for me. I knew that my rocking chair wouldn't be in North Carolina—it would be in Chicago. And, it being one of the largest cities in the United States, I knew that the chances of living near my grown children were greater if they were raised in Chicago. I didn't care if I had to spend every ounce of status I had built with my colleagues if it meant even a slightly better chance that my adult children would visit me more often.

Although I never got to ask my Grandma Marge about the view from her rocking chair, I observed her long enough to have a sense of what she valued. As much as I know she loved us, I feel confident that none of us were in the picture. Instead, I see her reading the newspaper—the political election results specifically—hoping to learn that her preferred party won in a landslide. This is why she didn't hesitate to get into arguments with friends and family members on the opposite political side, or to nag and badger her friends to make phone calls, carry signs, and wear buttons come election season. To her, the best use of the status she built was to convince as many people as she could to vote for "the good people." I don't share Grandma's political activism, so I would never use my status the exact ways she did. But I do share her commitment to using her status to create the life and the world that she wanted.

★

Use your status (and your airline miles) for your own long-term benefit, and for the benefit of others. As Amy Schulman points out, women underestimate "the role that we can play in the success of other people." She advises us to "be unafraid to introduce people, compliment somebody when it's deserved and stand up for something you really believe in . . . being a fighter for the people on your team when appropriate, and . . . arguing for principles that matter." I couldn't agree more.

Don't sell yourself short. When you've earned respect and admiration, you're in a privileged position to do a lot of good, both for yourself and for others. You built your status to use it, so use it well. Your future self will thank you.

PLAYS TO PRACTICE

🔥 Once you've completed the retirement party exercise, keep your contributions and characteristics top of mind by posting them somewhere you will see them every day. For example, make your three characteristics part of your internet passwords so you think of them every time you type them. Or list your contributions as your screensaver so you see them every time you sit down at your computer.

🔥🔥 Pick one of your desired contributions. List three people who could help move you one step closer to achieving that goal. Make a plan to build your status with each of these people over the next six months. What could you do to show up as Assertive and Warm?

🔥🔥🔥 Follow Amy Schulman's advice. This week, use your status to speak up or stand up for someone or something you believe in.

Part III

Coach Others

CHAPTER 8

Teach and Learn

I arrived at Stanford in July 1999, three months ahead of my soon-to-be classmates. I did this because my new advisor, Maggie Neale, told me to—there was a lot for me to learn and no time to waste. I quit my job, packed my things, and moved across the country. My furniture was delayed in transit, so I spent the first nights in my new apartment sleeping on the floor. But when I showed up in Maggie's office—jet-lagged and stiff, but ready to work—she told me that she didn't have time for me. More accurately, she told me that she wouldn't be able to start a project with me until the end of the summer, when she would finish her time-consuming service as an associate dean. Until then, she gave me a status-building assignment to complete (although she didn't describe it as such). I was to walk the hallways and knock on every professor's door, offering help on their research projects. I was to work for anyone who accepted my assistance, regardless of how menial the tasks, and I should ask for nothing in return. I was to do this, and do it well, until Maggie was ready to work with me. I felt confused and rejected that I had changed my summer plans to *not* work with Maggie. And I wasn't excited about the assignment. But, at over six feet tall with a world-renowned reputation as a negotiation scholar, Maggie is literally and figuratively a giant in the field of organizational psychology. I was not going to tell her no. So, I did as she said.

The doors of the faculty offices were comically massive—dark, thick wood with no windows, as if to communicate "the person inside is thinking big thoughts, please don't bother them." I felt like a door-to-door salesperson, rehearsing my pitch in my head while I knocked, secretly hoping no one would answer.

But people did answer.

They gave me work.

And it changed my life.

My hallway pacing not only led to fruitful research collaborations, but also gave me mere exposure to many faculty who ultimately became, and remain to this day, my other-promoters. For example, I met Larissa Tiedens, who was a new professor in the department and studied status. I had come to graduate school to research negotiation, so I didn't know much about status research at that time or have any inspiration to study it. However, per my instructions, I agreed to help Lara on a new project—the manspreading study I discussed in chapter 6—and it altered the course of my career. I fell in love with studying status, and Lara became an influential mentor and advocate in my life. She served on my dissertation committee, she wrote job recommendations for me, and she sang my praises to influential people in her own network (which was different than Maggie's). None of that would've happened if Maggie hadn't told me to knock on her door. Whereas other advisors might have suggested that I bide my time with solo activities, such as "immersing myself in the literature" or "brainstorming a list of research ideas," Maggie prioritized doing something arguably more valuable, gaining firsthand research experience, that also had the secondary benefit of building my status with powerful people from the outset.

Maggie's assignment was my first experience deliberately investing in my likeable badass reputation. She offered me this type of guidance almost daily. For example, I developed my three criteria for choosing discretionary activities (what will I contribute, will it bring me joy, and who will I meet) based on advice from Maggie. Almost every professor offers the same advice to young faculty and graduate students: "Say no to everything other than research." The intent of this advice is sound—research is important and you need to preserve time for it. However, Maggie realized that this advice, taken literally, which it usually is, kept people from saying yes to activities that could build their status without much cost. Instead of "protect your time," Maggie's standard refrain was "the world runs on reciprocity." When faced with a request for my time, Maggie wouldn't reflexively tell me to avoid it. Instead, she would analyze it. How difficult was the request? Who was the person making it? How likely was that person to be an other-promoter for me at some point, and who was in their network? If I said yes (or no), how would I show up as Assertive and Warm? Over time, Maggie's voice became the one in my head every time I faced a decision about building or leveraging my status, and I became better at anticipating her advice and acting accordingly.

At the time, I falsely assumed that every student benefited from similar wisdom. It wasn't until I became a professor that I saw my colleagues and students squander countless opportunities to build their status. Silently and out loud, I asked, "Didn't anyone ever teach you this stuff?" I found it impossible to stay silent when I saw someone on the verge of making a status faux-pas, so I started offering unsolicited advice. Eventually, younger faculty and students began coming to me with their status challenges. I would ask myself, "What would Maggie do?" Unintentionally, I started mentoring others to show up as likeable badasses simply by regurgitating the lessons I learned from Maggie.

★

Today my mentoring—and this book—are based on science and stories gleaned from my career as a professor and speaker. However, I *never* would have found this path without Maggie's guidance. My grandmother showed me what a likeable badass could do, but Maggie was the first person in my life who articulated *why* being a likeable badass was important. To grow as a likeable badass yourself, you *need* a Maggie (actually, multiple Maggies) in your life. One of the most effective ways to manage your status is to model yourself after the likeable badasses you admire. Watching them, you learn their strategies, and can adopt the ones that work for you. Equally important, I want to convince you that you need to *be* a Maggie for one or more people. Mentoring others is a likeable badass act that builds your status and confidence and creates a better path for the women who come after you.

I've devoted an entire chapter to mentoring for three reasons. In a nutshell, we all need mentoring, women don't get enough of it, and likeable badass mentoring is particularly necessary.

Everyone needs mentoring, always. If I told you about an athlete who had eight coaches (a strength coach, a nutritionist, a psychologist, a yoga teacher, and so on), you would probably infer that they're an elite performer. In sports, we think of coaching as a lifelong necessity, and something we invest more in, not less, as we advance. However, outside of athletics, we often adopt the opposite view—mentorship is for the young and inexperienced, something you should grow out of if you're successful enough. I don't agree with this mindset. Neither does Dr. Atul Gawande. In his popular 2017 TED Talk (viewed close to four million times), Dr. Gawande, a surgeon and bestselling writer, challenges the widely held view that "expertise means not needing to be coached." Like many of us, Dr. Gawande was socialized to believe that the definition of a *professional* is "someone who is capable of managing their own improvement." The problem with this view, he realized, is that "somewhere along the way you stop improving." Dr. Gawande was concerned this was happening to him; after several years of seeing his surgical complication rates drop, he hit a plateau. He decided to experiment with coaching and invited one of his former professors into his operating room. He thought the first case that day was perfectly executed—until his mentor handed over a full page of notes at the end. Until that point, he had started to feel that he was as good a surgeon as he was ever going to be. However, after two months of coaching he found himself improving again, and after a year he saw his complication rates drop further.

We never outgrow mentoring because it provides an outside perspective, which is always valuable. When I give advice, I'm often praised for being so "wise." I'll accept the gratitude for my time, but

I'll also retort with one of my favorite adages, adapted from the HBO drama *In Treatment:* "You can't look at yourself through your own binoculars." I'm wise in these conversations for only one reason: It's not my life. It's easy to hear another person's story and instantly see how they could improve, but nearly impossible to do this for yourself. Great coaches, Dr. Gawande realized, "are your external eyes and ears, providing a more accurate picture of your reality . . . they're breaking your actions down and then helping you build them back up again." This is true whether you're trying to be a better ice skater, a better surgeon, or a better likeable badass.

Women get less mentoring. Even in academia, a profession built on the relationship between student and advisor, I saw that good mentorship like Maggie's was rare. Across industries, quality mentorship is even more elusive for women and people of color, and this is yet another obstacle in their quest for equitable power, status, and advancement. For example, formal mentoring programs in organizations have been shown to boost the managerial representation of systemically excluded groups by 9 to 24 percent. However, the majority of women—63 percent, according to one widely cited study—report that they have never had a formal mentor. Further, women report that they're 24 percent less likely than men to get advice from senior leaders, and 62 percent of women of color in law firms say that the lack of an influential mentor holds them back. Women would benefit from a mentor like Maggie, but many don't have one.

We crave likeable badass mentorship. In 2022, Menttium, an industry leader in professional mentoring experiences, surveyed 270 of their mentees to identify their three key development needs—areas where they most wanted mentoring.

I'd be lying if I said this list didn't make me happy. Although they didn't use my term, these people clearly wanted guidance on how to show up as a likeable badass. "Career planning" is about the quest for power, status, achievement, and fulfillment, which are all fundamental human needs. And "authentic self-promotion" is a key tool for building status. It's exactly what we're talking about here—how to be authentically strategic (or strategically authentic) in shaping how oth-

TOP THREE MOST REQUESTED DEVELOPMENT GOALS IN 2022

Career Planning

- Constructing a career plan/pathway; deciding on career next steps; being proactive; taking control of career
- Promotion advice; positioning for next role
- Identify blindspots in their own development

Executive Presence

- How to influence executives (up and across)
- Executive-level presentations; strategy, content and delivery
- Concise and clear communication; verbal and written

Authentic Self-Promotion

- Self-confidence; asking for wants and needs; less self-doubt; awareness of how to manage imposter syndrome
- Being visible to the broader organization
- Demonstrating professional strengths to executives

ers see you. Looking at these results, I see that my instincts are right—everyone wants a Maggie in their life.

Many people fortunate enough to have a mentor focus on the first category—career planning. As Missy Chicre, CEO of Menttium, has observed, "When people think about mentoring, their first inclination is to find somebody just like them who followed a very similar career path and is a little further along. There's value in that, but it's not all you need."

The most valuable mentorship I got from Maggie was not her career advice (although that was also very good). It was her encouragement and guidance about how to succeed as a professional woman, how to build name recognition for myself in the field, how to get people to advocate for me, how to effectively advocate for myself, how to avoid burning a bridge, and how to decide when it was time to burn the whole damn city down. While many professors gave great research and teaching advice, Maggie was teaching a master class on how to be a likeable badass. We see from the Menttium survey that people want this advice just as much as career planning, but not as many people are giving or getting it.

Likeable badass mentorship can be your competitive advantage. Talking to hundreds of women in my work, I've noticed a clear pattern—the ones who give off strong likeable badass vibes always have mentors who have taught them to think about status. For example, when Felecia Carty wanted to transition from retail to customer success in technology, she sought out formal mentorship through a competitive program. Her assigned mentor was in the industry, but it was his guidance on telling her story and showcasing her Warmth that made the biggest difference for her. When he observed Felecia in mock interviews, he noticed a shift—she got "robotic and serious," and her smile disappeared. In short, he observed that Felecia was engaging in compensatory impression management—when she wanted to show up as Assertive, she did it by downplaying her Warmth. Her mentor coached Felecia on presence ("people need to like you and want to work with you") and fostering similarity ("you can chat about personal things"). This advice went against everything Felecia had been taught in retail, where she was conditioned to be uber-professional and "buttoned-up." But she trusted her mentor and was willing to give it a try. Notably, her best effort led to her best outcome. She showed up to the final-round interview for the job she ultimately received determined to showcase her authentic Warmth. She could feel how much more friendly and personable her interviewers were in response (remember, Warmth begets Warmth). At long last, her 104-application job search had come to a happy conclusion, thanks to her mentor's likeable badass guidance.

Kathryn Valentine, whose abrupt internship end led her to found a highly successful training and development company for women leaders, also learned her likeable badass moves from her mentor. Her boss at Lilly Pulitzer was the first woman Kathryn ever saw lead with "warmth and credibility," and Kathryn wanted to be just like her. When I asked Kathryn to describe how her boss earned this likeable badass reputation, she immediately repeated her boss's three small-deposit rules:

One, always hold the door open for other people. Two, if you're having a difficult conversation, you go to them (like the time her boss flew to Chicago to have a hard conversation with one of their vendors). And three, determine who in your network you interact with frequently and figure out how to help them at least twice a year. Kathryn started living by these rules herself, and they helped her build her large army of other-promoters. For example, working in analytics at Lilly Pulitzer, Kathryn had access to lots of data. Twice a year, she would give her colleague statistics to put in her performance review and show the impact of her work. "My friend couldn't quantify the impact of her great work, but I had the data and could help her." However, Kathryn might not have thought to do that without the likeable badass mentorship she received from her former boss.

HOW TO FIND YOUR LIKEABLE BADASS MENTORS

A LinkedIn survey of nearly 1,000 professional women found that about 20 percent never had a mentor, and over half of the mentor-less women (52 percent) reported it was because they "never encountered someone appropriate." Read that again to let the absurdity sink in. The notion that a person has *never* crossed paths with someone who could coach, advise, or teach them anything is preposterous. I find that people say this because they have an unrealistic mental model of what mentorship is supposed to be. They've been falsely socialized to believe they're searching for a unicorn—a single person who can teach them everything they need to know *and* will make a lifelong commitment to them. If that's the standard, then I agree—mentorship will be *very* hard for most people to find, and we'll be setting ourselves up for failure and disappointment.

Rather than search the kingdom for one person who fits the glass slipper, I advocate for a different model, which I call *fractional mentorship*. With fractional mentorship, we seek out multiple "imperfect" mentors who each embody some, but not all, of the characteristics we want to emulate. Only a fraction of our total mentorship comes from any one person, but across the full set of mentors we get 100 percent of the guidance we need. I think of it like a vacation time-share, but for life advice. You don't need to spend the rest of your life vacationing in only one place; you can spend a little time each year in your favorite place and still have vacation days left over to explore new destinations.

This model has two noteworthy advantages over the traditional one-mentor model. First, it lowers the stakes on both sides of the relationship. If you only get to pick one person, then you feel pressure to pick perfectly. And if a mentor believes they'll have only one mentee, they'll feel a similar pressure to choose well. You might relish that kind of stress in your life, but I don't. When you pursue fractional mentorship, finding what you need becomes much easier. You don't need to find a person who can teach you *everything*, you just need to find a person who can teach you *something*. Then, you can find other mentors to fill in the gaps.

This was one of Felecia's biggest realizations going through her job search—"Anyone who knows more than you is a mentor. Your kid can be your mentor." She had traditionally thought that mentorship was something you got from one person, but as she learned from each person she met in her job search she realized there were mentors all around her—people she met on social media, presenters in her certification programs, and everyone she invited for a coffee chat. When I asked her how many people mentored her in her career switch, she said, "Upwards of forty. I've had over forty coffee chats and there is something I took from each conversation."

The second advantage of the fractional mentorship model is that you'll get better, more holistic guidance because you can select people for specific skills, such as executive presence or authentic self-promotion. Maybe your career mentor would give good advice in these domains, too, but just as likely they wouldn't. If you open yourself up to multiple mentors, you can choose a wide variety of people who collectively broaden your perspective. For example, *The No Club: Putting a Stop to Women's Dead-End Work* originated from a peer mentoring group—five female colleagues who got together to advise each other how to muster Assertive Warmth when saying no. Although peers may lack the experience of those more senior, their experiences are current, and they don't preface every piece of advice with "back in my day." If you have only one mentor, you probably wouldn't choose a peer or choose someone solely because they're skilled at saying "no," but then you would miss out on this type of guidance.

In my case, sometimes I really need a likeable badass cheerleader—someone to silence any limiting mindsets that are getting louder and reset my outlook. For that, I'll hop on my Peloton bike for a ride led by Robin Arzón, the queen of imposter-crushing mantras, like "You can turn up the volume on your inner critic or turn up the volume on your inner bad bitch. I choose the bad bitch." Having both Maggie and Robin in my life, in very different ways, meets more of my development needs than either would be able to do alone.

You don't need to be formulaic about how many or what type of fractional mentors you choose. As a starting point, consider the eight types of mentors leadership coach and speaker Lisa Barrington suggests in her guidance on building a personal board of directors:*

1. Someone in your field (your profession or industry)
2. Someone who has been in your circumstance (e.g., a single parent, someone transitioning careers later in life)
3. Someone who is one of your greatest cheerleaders
4. Someone who will critique you
5. Someone who is a leader in the area in which you aspire to grow or succeed (e.g., professional, spiritual, personal)
6. Someone from a generation older
7. Someone from a generation younger
8. Someone who can introduce you to others (e.g., in your profession or community)

To assemble your fractional mentorship team, do the following:

Take stock of your mentors. List all the people you rely on for advice, and what type of mentorship they're best at offering (e.g.,

---

* If you're wondering how a personal board of directors differs from fractional mentorship, the main difference in my mind is the degree of formality. With a personal board of directors, you often formally ask someone to participate. With fractional mentorship, the person doesn't even need to know you consider them a mentor. To them, you're just a likeable badass who calls them for advice occasionally.

career advice, self-promotion, networking, self-advocacy, stress management, parenting). If you're fortunate enough to be related to people who give good advice, include family members on the list. Consider people you know and talk to, and also those you don't. For example, I count Robin's Peloton rides as mentorship, even though we're not interacting. Funny enough, she and I see eye to eye on this. Speaking of her own mentorship in a 2020 interview, Robin revealed:

> "One of my biggest mentors is someone I haven't even met—Michelle Obama. It's not because I know her personally—I wish—but [because] she demonstrates and lives her life by the principles I aspire to have and the grace I try to have with myself, and with the responsibility of creating a legacy that matters. I think mentors [inspire] us to action, and she is one of mine."

Anyone you model yourself after is a mentor, regardless of your relationship. If you follow thought leaders on social media or read particular authors, add them to your list.

Also, look at the balance between internal mentors, who are in the same organization as you, and external mentors, who sit outside your groups. Missy Chicre of Menttium notes the unique value of external mentors in particular, observing that they give you "a different lens to look at your role, your organization, and its culture." And, she finds that trust and rapport is often built more quickly with external mentors because you don't necessarily have to worry about censoring yourself in front of someone more senior than you. This level of trust is especially valuable for likeable badass mentorship, so that you can be candid about the status challenges you face and plan to manage them, just as Felecia did with the mentor who helped her prepare for interviews.

Figure out what's missing. Cross-reference this list of mentors with the eight categories above. Are any positions vacant? Do you have enough likeable badasses to model Assertive Warmth for you? Is there something you're struggling with at this moment and could use more guidance on?

Return to the "start with the end" exercises from chapter 7. Look at your list of retirement party accolades and your view from the front porch. Ask yourself two questions:

- *What* advice do you need to get from here to there?
- *Who* can offer that advice?

For example, imagine that "engaged community volunteer" is one of your desired contributions, but you're not currently volunteering. Is it because you don't feel that you have time? If so, perhaps mentorship from someone who can help you prioritize or outsource is most helpful. Or is it because you aspire to be on the board of a particular nonprofit, and you've been hesitant to promote yourself to the board member you met at a few neighborhood events? In this case, you may benefit from some likeable badass mentorship, particularly someone who can help you tell a stronger story.

Fill in the gaps. Now it's time to identify additional mentors who can provide the missing guidance. For every need, list as many people as you can think of who have wisdom to offer. Include people you know personally, and those you don't. Looking across your needs, find mentors who show up on more than one list—these may be particularly useful advisors since they can help you in multiple ways. Also consider that no matter how brilliant a person is, not everyone makes a good mentor *for you*. Try to pick someone different enough to provide a novel perspective, but similar enough that you can see yourself emulating them. I've seen people attempt to implement advice from mentors who are radically different, and it always comes off like they're wearing someone else's clothes.

Because you're not constrained to a given number of mentors, you can also identify mentors who excel in critical niches. In my case, perhaps due to my resting bitch face, I've always struggled to ask difficult questions without coming across as critical or judgmental. From the moment I met her, I saw that my co-author Lara had the uncanny ability to ask the most pointed questions, while still coming across as friendly. I felt that my overall likeable badass style was similar enough to hers that I could model myself after her. First, I simply paid close attention to her in meetings and presentations. I noticed that she often prefaced her most difficult questions with the phrase "It's not clear to me that . . ." I tried that a few times, but it didn't seem to work. I still sounded snarky. I then spoke with Lara, told her I admired her skill in this area and asked for her advice. What I learned is that it wasn't the phrase, but the curiosity behind it that mattered. Lara tended to use that phrase when she was trying to learn, not when she was trying to disagree. Sometimes, what she learned led her to take an opposing view, but that was never her initial intent. I realized that one of the reasons my questions often came across as harsh was that I was asking them too late—once I had already made up my mind about the right answer. By watching and talking to Lara, I learned to ask questions earlier in a discussion, while I still have an open mind, so that I authentically convey curiosity (through voice and nonverbals) rather than judgment.

Learning from Lara was very natural because I already knew her and saw her almost daily. Often, though, growing your bench of mentors requires establishing a relationship with someone new. In that case, you need to reach out to them. However, you don't need to have a "promposal"-like* "Will you be my mentor?" conversation, unless you want to. As *Forbes* reported, very few people—14 percent, according to one survey—start their mentor relationships this way. If you do approach someone new for advice, you need to show up with Assertive Warmth, just as you would in any situation. And you need to convey that you value the person—in other words, you need to honor their status by respecting their time and the relationship.

Robin Arzón sees many people who unintentionally annoy their would-be mentors because they haven't been strategic. "When I was a lawyer trying to enter wellness," she remembers, "I was a sponge. Lots of people were generous with their time and energy, but I was also very thoughtful about my approach." She noted two things she did to

---

* I only recently learned of this term from my friends who have older children in high school. Apparently, the process of asking someone to the prom is no longer traumatic enough. The asker is now expected to create some elaborate craft project or grand gesture (like a flash mob) to accompany the request. Add this to the list of reasons I'm glad I'm no longer in high school.

convey her respect and recommends to anyone seeking mentorship, especially from someone who doesn't know you:

Be specific: "If there's someone whose opinion and time you value, they're probably asked for advice on a weekly basis. 'Can I pick your brain?' is one of the most annoying things a person can say. Do your research, come with smart questions."

Be of service: "I would show up at events early, looking for any way I could to add value. 'Can I walk you to the elevator? Carry your bag? Help you with your microphone?' Of course, I was a lawyer so pro bono legal work was something I was able to offer a lot."

Asking for advice is fundamentally no different than asking for a raise. As Robin astutely points out, the more specific your questions, the easier it is for the person to help you. And answering "What's in it for me?" not only conveys Warmth (you care about their benefit), but also shows your Assertiveness (you have value to add).

If you reach out to someone via email, you can convey the same points in a simple four-point structure (illustrated with a hypothetical example):

1. Why you respect them (honor their status)

Hi Amy,
 I've been thinking about your impressive entrepreneurial journey ever since I heard you on Tori Dunlaps's Financial Feminist podcast in November.

2. What value you have to offer (make a small deposit)

If you haven't already, you might enjoy listening to/reading [insert name of another podcast you enjoyed or article you read].

3. What you would like to learn from them (be specific)

I'm about to quit my job to start my own venture and I remember your advice that "leaving your job is like taking a cake out of the oven—too soon and too late are both bad in different ways."

4. An invitation to connect (give options, make it easy)

> Would you be willing to give me your opinion on my exit timing, either via email or talking live, whichever is easier for you? If it's helpful I can send you a short summary of my situation, along with three questions I'm trying to answer.

I've had great success with this approach. I always follow up with a specific thank-you, not just for their time, but also to let them know how I implemented their advice and the positive impact of that advice. If I enjoyed talking with them and found their advice useful, I'll reach out again. Over time, some of these people have become my longest-standing and most influential mentors, but they all started with a single conversation that didn't include the word "mentorship."

Repeat this process as needed. Over time, as your skills and needs evolve, your mentors should, too. Often, new challenges emerge that require you to add mentors. For example, the return to paid work after the birth or adoption of one's first child creates a variety of new challenges for mothers. In addition to navigating a hit to one's Assertiveness and perceived employability (i.e., the "motherhood penalty"), there are also a host of practical dilemmas for mothers that spill over into reputational challenges. In a day packed full of meetings, when should I pump, and how do I explain my absence to my team without announcing to everyone what I'm doing? How do I manage requests for 5 p.m. meetings when I'm rushing to daycare pickup? How do I negotiate for a flexible work arrangement or part-time work without furthering the bias that I'm not serious about my career? Although a woman may feel that she has a great community of likeable badass mentors, the transition to motherhood creates a different set of questions that may require adding new perspectives.[*]

---

[*] Anyone facing this specific issue should add Lauren Smith Brody to your mentorship team. The former executive editor of *Glamour* magazine, Brody is the author of *The Fifth Trimester: The Working Mom's Guide to Style, Sanity, and Success After Baby* and the founder of an education and advocacy company of the same name. Read the book and check out her website: www.thefifthtrimester.com.

Life events, like the birth of a child, present an obvious opportunity to re-evaluate your mentorship needs. However, your needs will still evolve over time, even absent these major milestones. One of my dearest mentors, Andrew Samwick, an economics professor from my undergraduate days at Dartmouth, told me that he makes all his charitable contributions for the year on his birthday. Not only does he enjoy celebrating through giving, but it's also an easy way for him to remember to donate to his favorite organizations each year. I thought this was a great idea that could be applied to any activity that should be repeated annually, from scheduling a mammogram to taking stock of your mentorship. Your birthday is a natural time to reflect on where you've been and where you're going, and what additional guidance may be needed to get you there.

HOW TO MENTOR OTHERS

Mentoring other people is just as important for building your likeable badass reputation as being mentored. Most importantly, as I've mentioned throughout this book, offering advice—showing up as an expert for the benefit of others—is an act of Assertive Warmth. If you wanted to, you could build your likeable badass reputation through mentoring alone. However, this requires that other people are aware of it. If your mentoring isn't broadly visible, you'll have to bring it into your story. Find a way to let people know that you set aside Friday afternoons as "open-door office hours" for your subordinates, or that you have two mentees in your company's formal mentorship program. This information can be worked into your answers to the mundane questions (e.g., What's new? How's work?), your social media posts, or your résumé or bio as appropriate (a good reason to include a "fun facts about me" section).

Another benefit of mentoring is that it forces you to become self-aware of the ways you show up as a likeable badass. As we develop any skill—whether it's singing, driving a car, or likeable badassery—we progress through levels of proficiency, often referred to as the "stages of competence."

Level 1
UNCONSCIOUS INCOMPETENCE
You suck, but you don't know it. For example, you sing off-key,
but it sounds great to you in the shower.

★

Level 2
CONSCIOUS INCOMPETENCE
You're bad and now you're aware of it.
You may be motivated to improve.

★

Level 3
CONSCIOUS COMPETENCE
If you put all your thought and effort into it, you can perform well—
some of the time. If you lose concentration, you'll make mistakes.

★

Level 4
UNCONSCIOUS COMPETENCE
Your performance is more consistent and requires
little conscious thought.

★

Level 5
CONSCIOUS EXCELLENCE
You can analyze your own performance, explain what you're doing
and why you're doing it to teach it to others. You're no longer
on autopilot, but instead have brought conscious attention
back to your (high-level) performance.

For our purposes, I want to focus on Levels 4 and 5. To the outside observer, both levels look like mastery. However, there's an important difference. Those at Level 4 are great at what they do, but they don't understand *why*. Level 5 performers are just as skilled, but they also have conscious awareness of what causes their performance. As a result, only Level 5 performers can explain what they do in a way that a beginner could understand. Only Level 5 performers can *teach*.

In talking to many women in my work, I have been able to observe the difference between Level 4 and Level 5 likeable badasses. Those at Level 5 can explain how they developed their likeable badass reputation. Rachel Sheerin, for example, articulated how she used her out-of-office email messages to build status. However, more often, I come across wildly successful women who are clearly regarded as likeable badasses but can't offer any specifics on what they did well, even when pressed. Level 4 likeable badasses tend to speak in generalities, like "I just try to be myself" or "If I want something I'll go for it." These women are every bit as Assertive and Warm as the women you've read about in this book, but they don't have any insight into how their own behavior shaped their image. As a result, they can't help anyone else get to their level.

Mentoring others forces you to get to Level 5. To give useful advice you need to articulate what you do and why it works. And the more you give this type of advice, the more time you spend assessing and analyzing the causes of your performance. That introspection makes you a better mentor, but it also improves your own skill development. Through teaching, you learn. In my case, I couldn't initially articulate my policy of making two email introductions at the end of every meeting with a new acquaintance. It was just something I did once . . . then twice . . . then almost every time. But I didn't think much about it. It wasn't until I was advising another woman that I said, "Here's a thing I do that you could try." As soon as I put this tactic into words, I was able to connect the dots between a behavior I was doing and an outcome I was getting. And once I became conscious about doing it, I was able to do it even better. I became even more thoughtful about which introductions I made, and I refined my email introduction template.

In addition to building your skill, research shows that mentoring also builds your confidence. Offering advice, or just a listening ear, makes a positive difference in someone else's life and gives you that "I actually know what I'm talking about!" glow. Again, we don't need to be killing our inner imposter, but mentoring does wonders for keeping her in her place. Mentoring is also downright fun and can be a great source of energy and inspiration for you. This is yet another topic on which Robin Arzón and I agree. As she points out, "When you're actually in giving mode . . . empowering . . . communities and loved ones and folks you believe in, that almost feels better than moments where we're empowering ourselves. And when we see that spark... light up in someone else, we actually are reminded of what's possible in our own lives."

As you go forth and mentor others in the ways of the likeable badass, let me offer you three suggestions that I've found helpful in my own mentoring.

Start Now

Don't let the stages of competence model scare you into believing you don't know enough yet to mentor others. Just as your mentors don't need to know everything, neither do you. I guarantee that you're a Level 5 expert in *something*, no matter your age, background, or experience. What's my evidence? Each member of my tech support team is under sixteen years old—I call them my children. They have mastered smartphones, internet research, social media, and even the thermostat in ways that I never will. These are people who can't cook, can't find their way home from two blocks away, and apparently don't understand the purpose of a laundry hamper. If they can be mentors, you certainly can, too. And, like my kids, you don't need to be *the* expert, you just need to be *an* expert. I'm no Martha Stewart, but my cheese board skills are still better than those of most of my friends, so until they become friends with Martha, I'm an expert in their eyes. Make a list of everything you think you do well, think about both professional and personal skills, and don't be ashamed to be very specific (e.g., you write a killer thank-you note). This list is the start of your offerings as a mentor, and it will only grow over time.

Unless you're in a profession like mine, finding people to mentor also takes a bit of thought and effort—perhaps as much as finding people to mentor you. Over two-thirds of women who have never been a mentor report that it's because no one has ever asked them. But remember, a very small number of people find mentorship this way. I've found the one-conversation-at-a-time process works just as well in this direction. I simply invite people to coffee or lunch, tell them how awesome I think they are, and start asking questions about their life. As they talk, I listen for areas where I may be able to add guidance. I'll casually mention offers of assistance or "something that worked for me in that situation" and see if they respond with interest. If I'm meeting someone for the first time, I'll always end the conversation with my offer for two introductions and a general invitation for them to reach out if I can be helpful in the future. I'll also try to find an opportunity to ask them for advice on something, based on what I've learned about their expertise. Knowing reciprocity rules the world, I find that people are more likely to continue reaching out to me for guidance if they expect that they'll be able to return the favor and advise me, too.

Be Honest About Your Shit

There are times when I feel like Supermom, and others when the mom guilt sits so heavy on my chest I can barely breathe. I desperately want to time-travel to the future to ask my adult children, "Did I do OK? Did I give you a good life? Do you like me?" As a professor, I have moments when I think no one does it better, and moments when I think my PhD should be revoked. It's almost comical how quickly I can oscillate between extreme confidence and paralyzing doubt. Your imposter is your friend, but that doesn't mean you need to flaunt her to the outside world. We know that putting yourself down is a risky strategy—the likelihood that people will believe what you say about yourself is greater than any benefit of humor or humility. But I do think there's a place to air our failures and anxieties. That place is mentoring. You can't be mentored well unless your mentor understands where you want to grow. The more honest you are about your struggles, both real and perceived, the better guidance they can give you to tackle them. And talking about your challenges makes you a better mentor, too. People you don't even know look up to you and think they want to be you when they grow up. When they learn that your life has its ups and downs, it builds their confidence that one day they can be where you are. Whenever you're on the verge of blurting a self-deprecating thought, ask yourself, "Will sharing this help me learn or help me teach?" If the answer is yes, then share away. If the answer is no, then tell your likeable badass story instead.

Choose Broad or Deep

Maggie invested a lot in me, as she did in her other advisees. Kathy Phillips, for example, my academic big sister who taught me to knock on faculty doors, learned that from Maggie. Despite Maggie's extensive scholarly accomplishments, her mentorship truly set her apart. Her entire career, she was a tireless advisor who prioritized working with women, people of color, and especially women of color. As she approached retirement a few years ago, a group of her mentees, me included, nominated her for a prestigious lifelong mentorship award in our field. Generations of scholars from across the world sent in forty years of stories about Maggie's wisdom and guidance in support of her nomination. And yes, she won the award!

When I became a professor, I was convinced that I would mentor PhD students as Maggie had mentored me. That didn't happen. I had to come to terms with the reality that I didn't love being that kind of mentor. I've advised a few doctoral students, and they are dear to me. We're still close, many years after they graduated, and I feel confident that they see me as a mentor, even now. But I was surprised to discover that I love other forms of mentoring more. I love mentoring the MBA students in my classes. I love mentoring professional women. I particularly love being a cheerleader for spectacular women who haven't yet realized what likeable badasses they are. I use my research, and the field of psychology overall, to give people practical solutions to build their status. And I use social media as a medium for mentoring people I don't know and may never meet—especially people who may not ever get to sit in a graduate business course or a leadership development program.

I feel strongly that everyone needs mentors, and that everyone should be a mentor. When it comes to being mentored, I advocate for having multiple imperfect mentors. When it comes to mentoring others, I'm more agnostic on the approach. One option is mentoring *deeply*. You make a large investment in relatively few people and provide guidance across a wide range of topics. This form of mentorship may also include sponsorship, where you use your power to open doors and create opportunities for others.*

Another—equally valid and not mutually exclusive—approach is to mentor *broadly,* which is essentially the fractional mentorship model applied in the other direction. You aren't making a lifetime commitment to any one person or providing a lot of guidance to them. Instead, you're offering a little mentoring to a lot of people. This is the approach that I take. If you choose this approach, the key is to figure out how to reach as many people as possible, so look for strategies to make your mentoring efficient. In particular:

Find your niche. Fractional mentors are specialists. You're not attempting to teach someone everything they need to know. Instead, focus on what you do best and leave the rest to their other mentors. To start, think about the times that people have sought you out for advice in the past. Are there certain topics that come up again and again in these conversations? If so, that's your niche. In my case, I found that most people who wanted to talk with me wanted advice in two areas: (1) Being an Assertive advocate for their own interests, and (2) Balancing career and parenting. The first area is one I could have predicted—I do teach negotiation and advocacy skills for a living. The second one surprised me. I'm not a work-life balance specialist, and by no means do I think I have this parenting thing figured out. Who was I to give anyone advice? But, upon reflection, I understand why women seek me out on this topic—I'm often older than they are, my casual interpersonal style makes them feel safe sharing their struggles with me, and they have very few other women around them to ask. So I've leaned into this role. Again, when it comes to identifying your niche, you don't need to be *the* expert, just *an* expert.

Put your wisdom on paper. The more efficiently you can share your wisdom, the more people you can reach. Writing things down, like Clare Hart (the CEO I met through Eden Abrahams) did with her list of ways to say no, makes it easier for you to mentor broadly. If you find

---

* Although this chapter focuses on mentorship, a full discussion of mentorship versus sponsorship is beyond the scope of this book. Let me just go on record that both are valuable and to the extent you can do either or both, you should.

yourself repeating the same advice more than three times to different people, take the time to write it down. When the fourth person comes to you, start by sharing what you've written and ask them to read it before you talk. This may eliminate the need for any live conversation. At the very least, it will enable you to have a shorter, more productive conversation focused on their remaining questions. And if you ever write an email full of brilliant advice, copy the text of it into a running document (with a likeable badass title like "This Is Why I'm Awesome") so you can easily access it next time someone asks you the same question. I've learned from experience this is much easier than searching years of sent messages while mumbling, "Who did I send that to?"

Use social media. Social media is very useful for mere exposure. It's equally useful as a tool for broad mentoring. Once you find your niche and start writing things down, it's an easy next step to start mentoring through social channels by posting your experiences and advice. There's no more effective way to spread your wisdom around the world. I would offer you advice on how to achieve star influencer status, but it's not part of my mentoring niche, so you're on your own. However, when you do figure this out, please mentor me.

★

Whatever form of mentorship brings you joy, I'm here for it. All that matters is that you do it. Mentorship changes lives, and it's the oral tradition through which we develop the next generation of likeable badasses. When I was a kid, my dad bought me something (I can't remember what), and I told him that when I grew up, I would pay him back. He responded, "You pay me back by taking good care of your own kids." Those words stuck, and have influenced not just my parenting, but my mentoring overall.

I know I won't be able to eliminate all challenges, including gender-based challenges, for my daughter, or her generation. My hope, though, is that at least she'll get to face *new* challenges, rather than tackling the same ones that her mother, grandmother, and great-grandmother faced. This "likeable or competent, but not both" conversation has gone on too long, and we need to move on to other problems. As we give those who come after us more tools and strategies to control their fate in a biased world, we participate in changing the conversation. Every time you give someone a tip for showing up as a likeable badass, you're giving them a tool to take ownership of their status and power. And you're "paying back" everyone who invested in you.

PLAYS TO PRACTICE

🔥 Make a weekly habit to be mentored by someone you consider to be a likeable badass but you do not know. Watch their TED Talk, read an article written by them or quoting them, watch and listen to them in the next company meeting. What did they teach you about how to be a likeable badass yourself? For example, I love watching 1960s episodes of *The French Chef* with Julia Child (ideally in black and white). I haven't cooked a single thing, but I did pick up a mantra that has really helped my bad habit of self-deprecating: *Never apologize for the food you serve. No one knows how it was supposed to turn out but you.*

🔥🔥 Think of someone whose mentorship made a difference to you, but they may not know it. Write them a note to thank them. Remind them of what they said or did, how you used their advice, and how you benefited from it. Bonus points if you write a paper note, and if you write to someone who mentored you more than ten years ago.

🔥🔥🔥 Identify a likeable badass play that comes easy to you (e.g., accepting and giving compliments, using humor) and offer someone advice on how to improve in this area. Bonus points if you advise someone who is older than you or more senior (known as reverse mentoring).

Conclusion

Well, friends, we've come to the end of our playbook. As I said at the outset, although the rules and the outcomes can be unfair sometimes, games can still be fun if approached with the right attitude. As a psychologist, I find getting into the head of my audience fun. In every interaction, I start by trying to understand what's going through the other person's mind, then work backward to figure out how to get the outcome I want.

How can I convince potential clients that I will be a successful speaker?
How can I convince my children to follow my advice?
How can I convince my students to prioritize the work for my class over their other commitments?
How can I convince everyone that I'm a likeable badass?

Regardless of the audience and the specific goal, I find this type of sleuthing enjoyable. I'm always searching my memory bank for a relevant study to inform my strategy, and I love experimenting to see what works. I wrote this book to help you do the same. By putting some science in your memory bank, including some of my favorite studies, I wanted to help you think like a psychologist when it comes to status and power, and hopefully find satisfaction in managing yours.

As I leave you to practice, let me offer three suggestions for maximizing both your effectiveness and your enjoyment.

Embrace the Pain

We know that practice should make us better, but often it makes us feel inept. The more you start to analyze your performance, the more areas for improvement you can find. This can feel overwhelming and disappointing—as if you're now further from, not closer to, the person you want to be.

This is natural. There's a phenomenon in psychology known as the Dunning-Kruger effect, named for the two psychologists who first documented it: Those with low competence tend to overestimate their skill, whereas those with high competence tend to be more accurate, or even underestimate their ability. In other words, the most skilled often feel they have the most to learn. This happens because those who lack competence also lack metacognition—the ability to distinguish good performance from bad. This explains why those terrible reality singing competition performers seem genuinely shocked when they're told they can't sing. On the stages of excellence, they're at Level 1—unconscious incompetence. They can't hear the difference between their singing and that of a diva. In contrast, professional singers, who are at Level 5, are very attuned to the slightest differences in performance and hear mistakes in their own performances that even a dog wouldn't notice. Their meta-competence makes them feel less competent than the rest of the world perceives them to be.

Maybe you've experienced this yourself as you've become more conscious about showing up as Assertive and Warm. *Ooh, I just deflected a compliment. Why didn't I ask that person to promote me? I just disagreed with my colleague in a meeting for no good reason (except I was hangry).* Noticing all the ways you can be even better may make you feel that showing up as a likeable badass is unachievable. I promise you the opposite is true! The more likeable and badass you are, the more you'll start to see small ways that you can be even more next-level. Welcome to the inevitable torture of being elite!

Pick Your Swing Thought

As you identify more areas for improvement, one of the most important decisions you need to make is what *not* to practice. A former student of mine, Tara Flickinger, summarized this notion brilliantly with a profound statement that I've repeated countless times: *Don't have too many swing thoughts.* As a former Division 1 collegiate golfer, Tara quickly learned that you couldn't make ten improvements in your golf swing at the same time. If you tried to swing the club with that many thoughts in your head, the result was guaranteed to be a mess. Instead, she would focus on the one or two critical improvements she wanted to make and *forget the rest*—for the moment. Once she had developed muscle memory for the current changes, she would then move on to the next one or two swing thoughts. Eventually, all ten swing errors would be corrected, just not all at once.

Effective practice comes in stages. To use another analogy, no one needs too many New Year's resolutions. If you wake up on January 1 vowing to make ninety-six lifestyle changes, your resolution will last all of three minutes. We experience more success (and less stress) when we narrow the focus of our practice. Pick one likeable badass move that you want to practice and put everything else aside for now. Once the new behavior has become a habit, you can move on.

Play the Long Game

By design, I've attempted to provide more ideas in this book than any one person could (or would need to) execute. I do this so everyone can find options and inspiration that feel true to who they are. But don't let the long list of strategies overwhelm or distract you. Remember, our goal is simple: Be as Assertive and Warm as possible, as often as possible, to as many people as possible. This is the behavior most within our control that will help us achieve the status and power we deserve. When we do this, we can go to sleep at night knowing we've done everything we can to help our audiences see us in the most favorable light. It won't always be enough, but that's OK. In the long run, if we keep showing up as the likeable badasses we are, we'll win a lot more games than we lose.

So when you feel overwhelmed, overlooked, or undervalued, return to the basics. Take a breath and ask yourself, "What is one thing I can do in this moment to project Assertive Warmth into the world?" Follow that instinct, then rest easy—you just showed up as a likeable badass.

Alison's Book Recommendations

If you're wondering what to read next, here are the books I referenced throughout *Likeable Badass*. All fabulous books written by fabulous people!

Linda Babcock, Brenda Peyser, Lise Vesterlund, and Laurie Weingart, *The No Club: Putting a Stop to Women's Dead-End Work*
Lauren Smith Brody, *The Fifth Trimester: The Working Mom's Guide to Style, Sanity, and Big Success After Baby*
Annie Duke, *Quit: The Power of Knowing When to Walk Away* (also check out *Thinking in Bets* and *How to Decide*)
Adam Grant, *Give and Take* and *Think Again* (also check out *Originals, Hidden Potential,* and *Option B* [with Sheryl Sandberg])
Felena Hanson, *Flight Club—Rebel, Reinvent, and Thrive: How to Launch Your Dream Business*
Hal Hershfield, *Your Future Self: How to Make Tomorrow Better Today*
Katty Kay and Claire Shipman, *The Power Code: More Joy, Less Ego, Maximum Impact for Women (and Everyone)* (also check out *The Confidence Code*)
Victoria Pelletier, *Influence Unleashed: Forging a Lasting Legacy Through Personal Branding*

Acknowledgments

I'm embarrassed to say that until I started writing my own, I never read the acknowledgments section in any book. But now I do. This is where all the likeable badasses in the author's life appear. Here are mine.

In general, these names are in no particular order, except for Margo Beth Fleming, my inimitable agent, without whom this book would never have existed. She deserves to be at the top of the list. I can't think of a better way to convey my appreciation for her friendship and brilliance except to tell you that I once announced to a crowd that I would have a fourth child just to name her Margo. And, as a true testament to how beloved and respected she is, several others in the room also offered to have more children named Margo. I'm relieved she didn't take me up on my offer, but it still stands. Without fail, Margo ends every conversation by asking, "How can I support you?" Like everything else she's said, I've adopted this line as my own, and it has made me a better friend and mentor. I've also fantasized about a world where all women ask each other the same question. I think we're getting there, and I'm excited to see what it looks like when we do.

I was fortunate to have not just one awesome editor, but two: Kris Puopolo and Carolyn Williams of Doubleday, who believed in me and the book from the beginning and were masterful at providing both freedom and guidance at the same time. Kasandra Brabaw and Suzanne L'Amoreaux were indispensable all along the way, reading chapters, line editing, brainstorming ideas, and generally keeping me sane-ish throughout this long process. All four women shaped this book in profound ways, and I'm grateful. Heather Kreidler, fact-checker extraordinaire, took what we had created and made it even better by meticulously examining every assertion, quote, and reference for accuracy. Working with this dream team, I came to truly understand the meaning of the phrase "It takes a village."

I always quip that I have great taste in people and that is certainly true when it comes to my academic research collaborators, including Sal Affinito, Adam Grant, Maggie Neale, Greg Northcraft, Jen Overbeck, Deirdre Snyder, John Sumanth, and Lara Tiedens.

I owe a special debt of gratitude to Adam Grant, who supported this project in so many ways, not only offering brilliant advice, as always, but also introducing me to many likeable badasses in his network. He has been one of my most steadfast other-promoters for close to twenty years, and I would be thrilled if I lived long enough to be able to repay all of the kindness he has already shown me. And writing this book has finally put to rest a decades-long debate between us—whether there should be one space or two after a period at the end of a typed sentence. When Adam and I collaborate, he takes out all the extra spaces between sentences, only to have me put them right back in. Well, Adam, I stand corrected. Every person who touched this book for copyediting removed my extra spaces. I give up. The correct answer is one space. Let this public admission serve as my apology.

For the science featured in this book, I have David Ernsthausen to thank. He tracked down quotes, studies, and articles at record pace and was kind enough to send me some of them twice, after I lost the first copies. As my colleague Jan-Benedict (JB) Steenkamp noted, if David couldn't find a reference, then it didn't exist. Sadly, David passed away in 2024, before this book went to print. I am sad that he won't get to see what he helped me create, but I hope he knew how invaluable he was. I will miss him.

The stories in this book would not have been possible without the many likeable badasses who sat for interviews with me, some of whom had never heard my name until I showed up asking them for a favor. They trusted me to tell their stories, and I hope I have done them justice. I am beyond impressed with their honesty, vulnerability, advice, and most of all their desire to build a better world for all women.

The members of "book club," Team Onagadori, graciously invited me to free ride on their genius. Every month I look forward to our meetings, not just for what you teach me about the art and science of writing and publishing a book (which is a lot), but for commiserating about all the parts of this process that feel much harder than you think they will. I am particularly grateful that book club brought Kelly Leonard, my Chicago neighbor, into my life, who has been a great source of connections, support, friendship, and all-around awesomeness.

This book was fueled by oatmilk lattes. I lost count around 276. Keeping me caffeinated was a close-to-full-time job for several people, especially the amazing servers and baristas at BIÂN and the Chief Clubhouse in Chicago, my two favorite writing spots.

For all the work that went into this book, and all the wonderful people who assisted me in the process, I would have never written it if I hadn't become a professor. And I wouldn't have become a professor if not for three teachers in my life who made me love school so much, I decided to stay forever. Mrs. Yuss, my second-grade teacher at Fairview Elementary, Mr. Felder, my high school math teacher at Shady Side Academy, and Andrew Samwick, my economics professor at Dartmouth, all transformed how I saw myself—as a student, a critical thinker, and a person with ideas worth sharing. I hope you were fortunate enough to have teachers who did the same for you. If so, you should find them and thank them. Take it from a teacher, it will mean the world to them.

Before I even got that far in life, I was privileged to have the support of my parents, who dedicated their lives to educating me, so that I could have opportunities they never had. There's an urban legend in my family that all the Italian men wanted me, the first child and grandchild, to be a boy. My dad disputes it, but regardless of whether it's true, there is no doubt my dad leaned into being the parent of a daughter. He decided I was the most capable amazing person in the world and told everyone—his barber, strangers in airports, anyone who would listen. If you met him, you'd be convinced I have an Academy Award, a Nobel Prize, and an Olympic gold medal (I have none). Not long ago, my dad had surgery. I walked into the recovery room and the nurse said, "You must be Alison. Your dad told me all about you." How the hell was that possible? He was under general anesthesia. But my dad always finds a way. I'm still no less embarrassed than I was at age ten, but I now also see the payoff. Because of his belief in me, I've never walked into a room and felt that I didn't deserve to be there—even rooms full of men (who sometimes said stupid things). This is partly why I became an educator, and why I wrote this book—to cheer women on, to give them the science and the encouragement to know that whatever life they want is possible, to help them see themselves as the likeable badasses I know them to be.

I am fortunate to be part of many circles of amazing women, who are sources of friendship, wisdom, support, and cocktails. Thank you to my Stanford GSB Women's Circle for accepting me even though I'm not a "real" GSBer. Thank you to LBOC (the Likeable Badasses of Carolina)—Mabel, Val, Jennifer—for twenty years of mentorship and camaraderie; the next round is on me. Thank you to OC 2024, the Power Shoppers, and all of my friends from SSA—thirty-plus years of friendship has gone by in an instant, and I can't wait to see what kind of fun we will be having when we're all eighty. Thank you to my dearest girlfriends (in Chicago and beyond)—too many to name, but likeable badasses all around—who gave me grace when I ignored them for months at a time, texted me with notes of support, encouragement, and offers to help, and raised many glasses of champagne with me to celebrate the many milestones of this "baby with a very long gestation" (as Margo says).

More than anything, I am thankful to my family, Team P.A.J.A.M.A., as we are known. Writing this book spilled over into our home in ways I never anticipated, and I couldn't be more grateful for the grace, love, and understanding they offered me.

Jordan, thank you for always asking, "How's the book going, Mom?" in the most hopeful, earnest voice I've ever heard coming out of a teenage boy's mouth.

Payton, thank you for never asking about the book, and instead giving the best fly-by hugs.

Maddie, thank you for being my illustrator, my staycation buddy, and my likeable badass legacy.

Alex, thank you for wanting me to write this book more than I did, and for picking up more than your share in our life to make it happen. Thank you also for the extremely expensive gift you're going to buy me to celebrate the end of this journey. I can't wait to see what it is. Yes, I just did that. You're welcome.

Maddie, age seven

Notes

1. Ladies, We Have a Status Problem

4   Your *power* is your control: Joe C. Magee and Adam D. Galinsky, "Social Hierarchy: The Self-Reinforcing Nature of Power and Status," *Academy of Management Annals* 2, no. 1 (2008): 351–98. http://dx.doi.org/10.1080/19416520802211628.

5   At the current rate of progress: World Economic Forum, "Global Gender Gap Report 2023," World Economic Forum, June. www.weforum.org/publications/global-gender-gap-report-2023.

5   are more educated: National Center for Education Statistics, "Bachelor's, Master's, and Doctor's Degrees Conferred by Postsecondary Institutions, by Sex of Student and Discipline Division: 2017–18," n.d. https://nces.ed.gov/programs/digest/d19/tables/dt19_318.30.asp.

5   consistently rated as equal: Tracy Brower, "New Study on Women in Leadership: Good News, Bad News and the Way Forward," *Forbes*, October 10, 2021. https://tinyurl.com/6whfsudn.

5   In contrast, those who transition: Kristen Schilt and Matthew Wiswall, "Before and After: Gender Transitions, Human Capital, and Workplace Experiences," *B.E. Journal of Economic Analysis & Policy* 8, no. 1 (September 11, 2008). https://doi.org/10.2202/1935-1682.1862.

5   For every 100 men: LeanIn.Org and McKinsey & Company, "Women in the Workplace 2023," n.d. https://womenintheworkplace.com.

5   Your *status*, on the other hand: Alison R. Fragale, Jennifer R. Overbeck, and Margaret A. Neale, "Resources Versus Respect: Social Judgments Based on Targets' Power and Status Positions," *Journal of Experimental Social Psychology* 47, no. 4 (July 1, 2011): 767–75. https://doi.org/10.1016/j.jesp.2011.03.006.

5   When Tonja Jacobi: Tonja Jacobi and Dylan Schweers, "Justice, Interrupted: Gender, Ideology, and Seniority at Supreme Court Oral Arguments," *Virginia Law Review* 103 (2017): 1379–1496.

6   As the brilliant Stanford sociologist: Cecilia L. Ridgeway, "Gender, Status, and

Leadership," *Journal of Social Issues* 57, no. 4 (Winter 2001): 637–55. https://doi.org/10.1111/0022-4537.00233.

6 When we're not fending: Clemence Michallon, "Woman Coins the Term 'Hepeating' for Corporate World," *Daily Mail Online*, September 26, 2017. www.dailymail.co.uk/femail/article-4922340/Woman-coins-term-hepeating-corporate-world.html.

6 Like our needs: Robert H. Frank, "Choosing the Right Pond: Human Behavior and the Quest for Status," *Public Choice* 56, no. 1 (January 1, 1988): 84–88. https://doi.org/10.1007/bf00052075; David C. McClelland, *Power: The Inner Experience* (Irvington Publishers, 1975).

6 When our aspirations: Cameron Anderson, John Angus D. Hildreth, and Laura Howland, "Is the Desire for Status a Fundamental Human Motive? A Review of the Empirical Literature," *Psychological Bulletin* 141, no. 3 (2015): 574–601. https://doi.org/10.1037/a0038781.

6 *"power's underrated cousins"*: Katty Kay and Claire Shipman, *The Power Code: More Joy, Less Ego, Maximum Impact for Women (and Everyone)* (HarperCollins Publishers, 2023).

6 I chuckled: Lauren Howard, "Women Really Only Want Three Things," January 20, 2023, www.linkedin.com/posts/elletwo_elletwo-teamdifficult-womeninbusiness-activity-7022193519943393280-B0Li/?originalSubdomain=rw.

7 In every format: "Women and Power," *Harvard Business Review*, accessed July 10, 2023. https://hbr.org/search?search_type=&term=Women+and+Power&term=; "Gender and Power," *Harvard Business Review*, accessed July 10, 2023. https://hbr.org/search?search_type=search-all&term=Gender+and+Power; "Women and Respect," *Harvard Business Review*, accessed July 10, 2023. https://hbr.org/search?search_type=search-all&term=women+and+respect; "Women and Status," *Harvard Business Review*, accessed July 10, 2023. hbr.org/search?search_type=search-all&term=women+and+status; "Women and Power," TED, accessed July 10, 2023. www.ted.com/search?q=women%20and%20power; "Gender and Power," TED, accessed July 10, 2023. www.ted.com/search?q=gender+and+power; "Women and Respect," TED, accessed July 10, 2023. www.ted.com/search?q=women+and+respect; "Women and Status," TED, accessed July 10, 2023. www.ted.com/search?q=women+and+status.

8 We keep the focus on power: American Association of University Women, "Equal Payday Calendar," accessed April 6, 2024. https://aauw.org/resources/article/equal-pay-day-calendar.

8 When we look at the research: Elizabeth J. McClean, Sean R. Martin, Kyle J. Emich, and Col. Todd Woodruff, "The Social Consequences of Voice: An Examination of Voice Type and Gender on Status and Subsequent Leader Emergence," *Academy of Management Journal* 61, no. 5 (October 24, 2018): 1869–91. https://doi.org/10.5465/amj.2016.0148.

9 A 2018 study of 4,600 employees: Benjamin Artz, Amanda H. Goodall, and Andrew J. Oswald, "Do Women Ask?," *Industrial Relations* 57, no. 4 (May 9, 2018): 611–36. https://doi.org/10.1111/irel.12214.

9 a survey of students from a top: Laura J. Kray, Jessica A. Kennedy, and Margaret Lee, "Now, Women Do Ask: A Call to Update Beliefs About the Gender Pay Gap," *Academy of Management Discoveries* 10, no. 1 (March 1, 2024). https://doi.org/10.5465/amd.2022.0021.

10 As Mark Twain allegedly quipped: Quoteresearch, "Eat a Live Frog Every Morning, and Nothing Worse Will Happen to You the Rest of the Day," Quote Investigator, April 3, 2013. https://quoteinvestigator.com/2013/04/03/eat-frog.

11 In a clever series: Nicholas A. Hays, "Fear and Loving in Social Hierarchy: Sex Differences in Preferences for Power Versus Status," *Journal of Experimental Social Psychology* 49, no. 6 (2013): 1130–6.
12 After graduating from both: Stacy Brown-Philpot in conversation with the author, November 27, 2023.
13 In 2015 she ranked on *Fortune*'s: "Stacy Brown-Philpot," *Fortune*, July 3, 2019. https://fortune.com/ranking/40-under-40/2015/stacy-brown-philpot.
13 in 2016 the *Financial Times*: Farva Kaukab, "Profile: Stacy Brown-Philpot, TaskRabbit," *Financial Times*, May 26, 2016. www.ft.com/content/282a3896-1e6a-11e6 -a7bc-ee846770ec15#axzz4AYUsz0cU.
13 As more people used the term: Stacy Brown-Philpot in conversation with the author, November 27, 2023.
13 When I pushed Stacy: Stacy Brown-Philpot in conversation with the author, November 27, 2023.
14 In the words: Robin Arzón, 20 Minute Tabata Ride [Peloton class], June 3, 2022. www.onepeloton.com.
15 A game is simply: Jesse Schell, *The Art of Game Design* (CRC Press eBooks, 2008). https://doi.org/10.1201/9780080919171.
16 Some status characteristics: Ralph Linton, *The Study of Man: An Introduction* (D. Appleton-Century, 1936).

2. The Likeable Badass Solution

20 Or, as Kate puts it: Kate in conversation with the author, April 28, 2023.
22 There are a lot of different ways: Jerry S. Wiggins, "A Psychological Taxonomy of Trait-Descriptive Terms: The Interpersonal Domain," *Journal of Personality and Social Psychology* 37, no. 3 (March 1, 1979): 395–412. https://doi.org/10.1037/0022 -3514.37.3.395.
22 We would describe this person: Andrea E. Abele, Amy J. C. Cuddy, Charles M. Judd, and Vincent Y. Yzerbyt, "Fundamental Dimensions of Social Judgment," *European Journal of Social Psychology* 38, no. 7 (November 11, 2008): 1063–65. https://doi.org/10.1002/ejsp.574.
24 When you put the two dimensions: Jerry S. Wiggins, "An Informal History of the Interpersonal Circumplex Tradition," *Journal of Personality Assessment* 66, no. 2 (1996): 217–33. https://doi.org/10.1207/s15327752jpa6602_2; Wikipedia, "Interpersonal Circumplex," June 1, 2023. https://en.wikipedia.org/wiki/Interpersonal _circumplex.
25 If you chose Friendly Strength: Alison R. Fragale, Jennifer R. Overbeck, and Margaret A. Neale, "Resources Versus Respect: Social Judgments Based on Targets' Power and Status Positions," *Journal of Experimental Social Psychology* 47, no. 4 (July 1, 2011): 767–75. https://doi.org/10.1016/j.jesp.2011.03.006.
26 And fortunately for our purposes: Margaret T. Lee and Richard Ofshe, "The Impact of Behavioral Style and Status Characteristics on Social Influence: A Test of Two Competing Theories," *Social Psychology Quarterly* 44, no. 2 (June 1, 1981): 73–82. https://doi.org/10.2307/3033703; Cecilia L. Ridgeway, "Nonverbal Behavior, Dominance, and the Basis of Status in Task Groups," *American Sociological Review* 52, no. 5 (October 1, 1987): 683–94. https://doi.org/10.2307/2095603; James E. Driskell, Beckett Olmstead, and Eduardo Salas, "Task Cues, Dominance Cues, and Influence in Task Groups," *Journal of Applied Psychology* 78, no. 1 (February 1, 1993): 51–60. https://doi.org/10.1037/0021-9010.78.1.51.

26 Evidence for this comes: James E. Driskell, Beckett Olmstead, and Eduardo Salas, "Task Cues, Dominance Cues, and Influence in Task Groups," *Journal of Applied Psychology* 78, no. 1 (February 1, 1993): 51–60. https://doi.org/10.1037/0021-9010.78.1.51.

26 Task cues indicate: Cecilia L. Ridgeway, "Gender, Status, and Leadership," *Journal of Social Issues* 57, no. 4 (January 1, 2001): 637–55. https://doi.org/10.1111/0022-4537.00233; Andrew S. Imada and Milton D. Hakel, "Influence of Nonverbal Communication and Rater Proximity on Impressions and Decisions in Simulated Employment Interviews," *Journal of Applied Psychology* 62, no. 3 (June 1, 1977): 295–300. https://doi.org/10.1037/0021-9010.62.3.295.

26 A faster speech rate: Don Willard and Fred L. Strodtbeck, "Latency of Verbal Response and Participation in Small Groups," *Sociometry* 35, no. 1 (March 1, 1972): 161–75. https://doi.org/10.2307/2786556; Richard L. Street Jr. and Robert M. Brady, "Speech Rate Acceptance Ranges as a Function of Evaluative Domain, Listener Speech Rate, and Communication Context," *Communication Monographs* 49, no. 4 (December 1, 1982): 290–308. https://doi.org/10.1080/03637758209376091.

27 The more you talk: Don Willard and Fred L. Strodtbeck, "Latency of Verbal Response and Participation in Small Groups," *Sociometry* 35, no. 1 (1972): 161–75. https://doi.org/10.2307/2786556.

27 Traditionally, people: Alison R. Fragale, "The Power of Powerless Speech: The Effects of Speech Style and Task Interdependence on Status Conferral," *Organizational Behavior and Human Decision Processes* 101, no. 2 (November 1, 2006): 243–61. https://doi.org/10.1016/j.obhdp.2006.01.004.

27 Instead, we have been advised: Lois P. Frankel, *Nice Girls Don't Get the Corner Office: Unconscious Mistakes Women Make That Sabotage Their Careers* (UK: Hachette, 2014).

27 In reality, some of my: Alison R. Fragale, "The Power of Powerless Speech: The Effects of Speech Style and Task Interdependence on Status Conferral," *Organizational Behavior and Human Decision Processes* 101, no. 2 (November 1, 2006): 243–61. https://doi.org/10.1016/j.obhdp.2006.01.004.

28 Eye contact also boosts: Andrew S. Imada and Milton D. Hakel, "Influence of Nonverbal Communication and Rater Proximity on Impressions and Decisions in Simulated Employment Interviews," *Journal of Applied Psychology* 62, no. 3 (June 1, 1977): 295–300. https://doi.org/10.1037/0021-9010.62.3.295.

28 That one minute: Eugene A. Rosa and Allan Mazur, "Incipient Status in Small Groups," *Social Forces* 58, no. 1 (September 1, 1979): 18–37. https://doi.org/10.1093/sf/58.1.18.

28 In one study, researchers explored: Charlan Nemeth and Joel Wachtler, "Creating the Perceptions of Consistency and Confidence: A Necessary Condition for Minority Influence," *Sociometry* 37, no. 4 (December 1, 1974): 529–40. https://doi.org/10.2307/2786425.

29 People who have high status: Dawn T. Robinson and Lynn Smith-Lovin, "Getting a Laugh: Gender, Status, and Humor in Task Discussions," *Social Forces* 80, no. 1 (September 1, 2001): 123–58. https://doi.org/10.1353/sof.2001.0085.

29 Individuals who engage in successful humor: T. Bradford Bitterly, Alison Wood Brooks, and Maurice E. Schweitzer, "Risky Business: When Humor Increases and Decreases Status," *Journal of Personality and Social Psychology* 112, no. 3 (January 1, 2017): 431–55. https://doi.org/10.1037/pspi0000079.

29 Why? You can probably guess: Linda E. Francis, "Laughter, the Best Mediation:

	Humor as Emotion Management in Interaction," *Symbolic Interaction* 17, no. 2 (May 1, 1994): 147–63. https://doi.org/10.1525/si.1994.17.2.147.
29	Status also comes from: Francis J. Flynn, Ray Reagans, Emily T. Amanatullah, and Daniel R. Ames, "Helping One's Way to the Top: Self-Monitors Achieve Status by Helping Others and Knowing Who Helps Whom," *Journal of Personality and Social Psychology* 91, no. 6 (January 1, 2006): 1123–37. https://doi.org/10.1037/0022-3514.91.6.1123.
29	As my friend Scott Tillema: Scott Tillema interview with the author, 2022.
30	Years later, one of my research: Jessica Bennett, "I'm Not Mad. That's Just My RBF," *New York Times*, August 1, 2015. www.nytimes.com/2015/08/02/fashion/im-not-mad-thats-just-my-resting-b-face.html.
31	For example, when I asked Stacy: Stacy Brown-Philpot in conversation with the author, November 27, 2023.
31	Aware of the "angry Black woman" stereotype: Daphna Motro, Jonathan B. Evans, Aleksander P. J. Ellis, and Lehman Benson III, "Race and Reactions to Women's Expressions of Anger at Work: Examining the Effects of the 'Angry Black Woman' Stereotype," *Journal of Applied Psychology* 107, no. 1 (January 1, 2022): 142–52. https://doi.org/10.1037/apl0000884.
32	*And* when you're perceived as high status: Alison R. Fragale, Jennifer R. Overbeck, and Margaret A. Neale, "Resources Versus Respect: Social Judgments Based on Targets' Power and Status Positions," *Journal of Experimental Social Psychology* 47, no. 4 (July 1, 2011): 767–75. https://doi.org/10.1016/j.jesp.2011.03.006.
33	These two pieces of information: Ibid.
34	That information alone may be enough: Ibid.
35	Confirmation bias: Raymond S. Nickerson, "Confirmation Bias: A Ubiquitous Phenomenon in Many Guises," *Review of General Psychology* 2, no. 2 (June 1, 1998): 175–220. https://doi.org/10.1037/1089-2680.2.2.175.
36	After her transition: Sharon Begley, "He, Once a She, Offers Own View on Science Spat," *Wall Street Journal*, July 13, 2006. www.wsj.com/articles/SB115274744775305134.
36	As a case in point: Jennifer A. Chatman, Daron L. Sharps, Sonya Mishra, Laura J. Kray, and Michael S. North, "Agentic but Not Warm: Age-Gender Interactions and the Consequences of Stereotype Incongruity Perceptions for Middle-Aged Professional Women," *Organizational Behavior and Human Decision Processes* 173 (November 1, 2022): Article 104190. https://doi.org/10.1016/j.obhdp.2022.104190.
36	People perceived as Assertive and Cold: Lynne M. Andersson and Christine M. Pearson, "Tit for Tat? The Spiraling Effect of Incivility in the Workplace," *Academy of Management Review* 24, no. 3 (1999): 452–71.
37	In 2021, record numbers: LeanIn.Org and McKinsey & Company, "Women in the Workplace 2022," n.d. https://womenintheworkplace.com.
37	For every woman: Ibid.
37	One of the top reasons cited: Ibid.
37	Recipients of incivility: Julie H. Kern and Alicia A. Grandey, "Customer Incivility as a Social Stressor: The Role of Race and Racial Identity for Service Employees," *Journal of Occupational Health Psychology* 14, no. 1 (January 1, 2009): 46–57. https://doi.org/10.1037/a0012684.
37	depression: Sandy Lim and Alexia Lee, "Work and Nonwork Outcomes of Workplace Incivility: Does Family Support Help?" *Journal of Occupational Health Psychology* 16, no. 1 (January 1, 2011): 95–111. https://doi.org/10.1037/a0021726.
37	stress: Lilia M. Cortina, Vicki J. Magley, Jill Hunter Williams, and Regina Day

Langhout, "Incivility in the Workplace: Incidence and Impact," *Journal of Occupational Health Psychology* 6, no. 1 (January 1, 2001): 64–80. https://doi.org/10.1037/1076-8998.6.1.64; Sandy Lim and Lilia M. Cortina, "Interpersonal Mistreatment in the Workplace: The Interface and Impact of General Incivility and Sexual Harassment," *Journal of Applied Psychology* 90, no. 3 (January 1, 2005): 483–96. http://dx.doi.org/10.1037/0021-9010.90.3.483.

37 lower life satisfaction: Sally Lim and Lilia M. Cortina, "Interpersonal Mistreatment in the Workplace: The Interface and Impact of General Incivility and Sexual Harassment," *Journal of Applied Psychology* 90, no. 3 (January 1, 2005): 483–96. http://dx.doi.org/10.1037/0021-9010.90.3.483.

37 At work, those subject: Lisa M. Penney and Paul E. Spector, "Job Stress, Incivility, and Counterproductive Work Behavior (CWB): The Moderating Role of Negative Affectivity," *Journal of Organizational Behavior* 26, no. 7 (January 1, 2005): 777–96. https://doi.org/10.1002/job.336.

37 be less helpful: Kathi Miner-Rubino and Whitney D. Reed, "Testing a Moderated Mediational Model of Workgroup Incivility: The Roles of Organizational Trust and Group Regard," *Journal of Applied Social Psychology* 40, no. 12 (December 1, 2010): 3148–68. https://doi.org/10.1111/j.1559-1816.2010.00695.x.

37 exhibit worse task performance: Christine L. Porath and Amir Erez, "Does Rudeness Really Matter? The Effects of Rudeness on Task Performance and Helpfulness," *Academy of Management Journal* 50, no. 5 (October 1, 2007): 1181–97. https://doi.org/10.2307/20159919; Christine L. Porath and Amir Erez, "Overlooked but Not Untouched: How Rudeness Reduces Onlookers' Performance on Routine and Creative Tasks," *Organizational Behavior and Human Decision Processes* 109, no. 1 (May 1, 2009): 29–44. https://doi.org/10.1016/j.obhdp.2009.01.003.

37 feel less engaged: Sandy Lim, Lilia M. Cortina, and Vicki J. Magley, "Personal and Workgroup Incivility: Impact on Work and Health Outcomes," *Journal of Applied Psychology* 93, no. 1 (January 1, 2008): 95–107. https://doi.org/10.1037/0021-9010.93.1.95; Christine M. Pearson, Lynne Andersson, and Christine L. Porath, "Assessing and Attacking Workplace Incivility," *Organizational Dynamics* 29, no. 2 (November 1, 2000): 123–37. https://doi.org/10.1016/s0090-2616(00)00019-x.

37 experience greater psychological: Pauline Schilpzand, Keith Leavitt, and Sandy Lim, "Incivility Hates Company: Shared Incivility Attenuates Rumination, Stress, and Psychological Withdrawal by Reducing Self-Blame," *Organizational Behavior and Human Decision Processes* 133 (March 1, 2016): 33–44. https://doi.org/10.1016/j.obhdp.2016.02.001.

37 higher turnover: Lilia M. Cortina, Vicki J. Magley, Jill Hunter Williams, and Regina Day Langhout, "Incivility in the Workplace: Incidence and Impact," *Journal of Occupational Health Psychology* 6, no. 1 (January 1, 2001): 64–80. https://doi.org/10.1037/1076-8998.6.1.64.

38 However, when I reached out: Personal communication between Annie Duke and the author, June 8, 2023.

39 Some studies have found: Lilia M. Cortina, Dana Kabat-Farr, Emily A. Leskinen, Marisela Huerta, and Vicki J. Magley, "Selective Incivility as Modern Discrimination in Organizations," *Journal of Management* 39, no. 6 (September 1, 2011): 1579–1605. https://doi.org/10.1177/0149206311418835; Christine L. Porath, Jennifer R. Overbeck, and Christine M. Pearson, "Picking Up the Gauntlet: How Individuals Respond to Status Challenges," *Journal of Applied Social Psychology* 38, no. 7 (July 1, 2008): 1945–80. https://doi.org/10.1111/j.1559-1816.2008.00375.x.

39   others have found that gender: Christine M. Pearson and Christine L. Porath, "On the Nature, Consequences and Remedies of Workplace Incivility: No Time for 'Nice'? Think Again," *Academy of Management Perspectives* 19, no. 1 (February 1, 2005): 7–18. https://doi.org/10.5465/ame.2005.15841946.
40   Participants imagined that they: Deborah Son Holoien and Susan T. Fiske, "Downplaying Positive Impressions: Compensation Between Warmth and Competence in Impression Management," *Journal of Experimental Social Psychology* 49, no. 1 (January 1, 2013): 33–41. https://doi.org/10.1016/j.jesp.2012.09.001.
41   Everyone does this: Bill Thornton, Roberta J. Audesse, Richard M. Ryckman, and Michelle J. Burckle, "Playing Dumb and Knowing It All: Two Sides of an Impression Management Coin," *Individual Differences*, March 1, 2006. https://digitalcommons.usm.maine.edu/psych_students/41.
42   "Being likeable is important": Kate in conversation with the author, April 28, 2023.
43   Her uniqueness, intersectionality: Victoria Pelletier in conversation with the author, May 18, 2023.

3. Get Your Head in the Game

46   Felecia sent me a message: Direct message from Felecia Carty to the author, September 11, 2022; American Negotiation Institute, "The Magic of Similarity: Building Trust for Successful Negotiations with Alison Fragale," Negotiate Anything [Audio podcast episode], Podtail, October 26, 2023. https://podtail.com/podcast/negotiate-anything/the-magic-of-similarity-building-trust-for-success.
47   When I met Felecia virtually: Felecia Carty in conversation with the author, November 8, 2023.
49   Tina Fey: "Tina Fey—From Spoofer to Movie Stardom," *The Independent*, March 19, 2010. www.independent.co.uk/arts-entertainment/films/features/tina-fey-from-spoofer-to-movie-stardom-1923552.html.
49   Justice Sonia Sotomayor: Neil A. Lewis, "Sotomayor, Baseball's Savior, May Be Possibility for High Court," *New York Times*, May 26, 2009. www.nytimes.com/2009/05/15/us/15sotomayor.html.
49   Lupita Nyong'o: Tom Huddleston, "Lupita Nyong'o: 'If I'm Having a Cinderella Moment, Why Not Enjoy the Hell Out of It?,'" *Time Out Worldwide*, September 26, 2016. www.timeout.com/film/lupita-nyongo-if-im-having-a-cinderella-moment-why-not-enjoy-the-hell-out-of-it.
49   Maya Angelou: Maya Angelou, *I Know Why the Caged Bird Sings* (Random House, 1969).
49   Arianna Huffington: Vivian Giang, "8 Female Leaders on How to Overcome What's Holding Women Back," *Fast Company*, September 10, 2014. https://tinyurl.com/bdet3h8d.
49   Amy Schumer: Leah Rose Chernikoff, "Lena Dunham: Amy Schumer Is like Oprah if Oprah Squished Her Boobs Together More," *ELLE*, October 20, 2015. https://tinyurl.com/yrxtdby4.
49   Padma Lakshmi: Padma Lakshmi, "THR Emerging Hollywood: Charlamagne Tha God x Padma Lakshmi," August 12, 2022. https://tinyurl.com/hwjuf8df.
49   Joyce Roché: Phil Simon, "The Empress Has No Clothes: An Interview with Joyce Roché," *HuffPost* (blog), December 6, 2017. https://tinyurl.com/mu2e3xbh.
50   Participants were assigned to play: Adam D. Galinsky, Thomas Mussweiler, and Victoria Husted Medvec, "Disconnecting Outcomes and Evaluations: The Role of

Negotiator Focus," *Journal of Personality and Social Psychology* 83, no. 5 (November 1, 2002): 1131–40. https://doi.org/10.1037/0022-3514.83.5.1131.

50 The more ambitious the goal: Edwin A. Locke and Gary P. Latham, "New Directions in Goal-Setting Theory," *Current Directions in Psychological Science* 15, no. 5 (October 1, 2006): 265–68. https://doi.org/10.1111/j.1467-8721.2006.00449.x.

51 For one, it demonstrates: James Charles Collins and Jerry I. Porras, *Built to Last: Successful Habits of Visionary Companies* (Harper Business, 1997).

51 As Watson reflected: Tavi Gevinson, "I Want It to Be Worth It: An Interview with Emma Watson," *Rookie*, May 27, 2013. www.rookiemag.com/2013/05/emma-watson-interview/2.

52 And Nyong'o expressed: Tom Huddleston, "Lupita Nyong'o: 'If I'm Having a Cinderella Moment, Why Not Enjoy the Hell Out of It?,'" *Time Out Worldwide*, September 26, 2016.

54 There are three types: Robert B. Cialdini, "Of Tricks and Tumors: Some Little-Recognized Costs of Dishonest Use of Effective Social Influence," *Psychology & Marketing* 16, no. 2 (March 1, 1999): 91–98. https://doi.org/10.1002/(sici)1520-6793(199903)16:2.

54 I explained the concept of sleuthing: Felecia Carty in conversation with the author, November 8, 2023.

54 These were colleagues with whom: Robert B. Cialdini, *Influence: Science and Practice*, 4th ed. (Allyn and Bacon, 2001).

57 As sixteenth-century English playwright: AJ, "50 Quotes by Christopher Marlowe," Elevate Society, August 29, 2023. https://elevatesociety.com/quotes-by-christopher-marlowe.

57 For example, *goblin mode*: "Oxford Word of the Year 2022," March 21, 2023. https://languages.oup.com/word-of-the-year/2022.

58 "Stop thinking": Amy Trask and Michael Freeman, *You Negotiate like a Girl: Reflections on a Career in the National Football League* (Triumph Books, 2016).

58 In recognition of her tremendous impact: NFL Enterprises, LLC, "'NFL 100 Greatest' Game Changers: Amy Trask," 2019. www.nfl.com.

58 As she reflected on walking into meetings: John McMullen, "Amy Trask Sees Progress in Promotion of Catherine Raiche; Next Stop Normalcy," *FanNation*, *Sports Illustrated*, June 3, 2021. https://tinyurl.com/bdhpf86a.

58 As a result, confident people: Cameron Anderson, Sebastien Brion, Don A. Moore, and Jessica A. Kennedy, "A Status-Enhancement Account of Overconfidence," *Journal of Personality and Social Psychology* 103, no. 4 (January 1, 2012): 718–35. https://doi.org/10.1037/a0029395; Mark R. Leary, Katrina P. Jongman-Sereno, and Kate J. Diebels, "The Pursuit of Status: A Self-Presentational Perspective on the Quest for Social Value," in J. Cheng, J. Anderson, and C. Anderson (Eds.), *The Psychology of Social Status* (Springer, 2014).

59 "My color": Stacy Brown-Philpot in conversation with the author, November 27, 2023.

59 Similarly, Amy Trask: Amy Trask and Michael Freeman, *You Negotiate like a Girl: Reflections on a Career in the National Football League* (Triumph Books, 2016).

59 Even in fields like academia: Toni Schmader, Jessica Whitehead, and Vicki H. Wysocki, "A Linguistic Comparison of Letters of Recommendation for Male and Female Chemistry and Biochemistry Job Applicants," *Sex Roles* 57, no. 7–8 (August 17, 2007): 509–14. https://doi.org/10.1007/s11199-007-9291-4.

59 In contrast, letters for women: Juan M. Madera, Michelle R. Hebl, Heather Dial,

Randi C. Martin, and Virginia Valian, "Raising Doubt in Letters of Recommendation for Academia: Gender Differences and Their Impact," *Journal of Business and Psychology* 34, no. 3 (April 26, 2018): 287–303. https://doi.org/10.1007/s10869-018-9541-1.

60 In their brilliant book: Linda Babcock, Brenda Peyser, Lise Vesterlund, and Laurie Weingart, *The No Club: Putting a Stop to Women's Dead-End Work* (Simon & Schuster, 2022).

4. Tell Your Story

67 It wasn't until years later: Lori Goler, Janelle Gale, Brynn Harrington, and Adam Grant, "Why People Really Quit Their Jobs," *Harvard Business Review*, January 11, 2018. https://hbr.org/2018/01/why-people-really-quit-their-jobs.

68 A few months into the role: Meghana Dhar in conversation with the author, October 16, 2023.

70 One of my favorite examples: "Stacey Abrams," Wikipedia, accessed July 11, 2023. https://en.wikipedia.org/wiki/Stacey_Abrams.

70 To further complicate matters: Sandy J. Wayne, Jiaqing Sun, Donald H. Kluemper, Gordon Weng-Kit Cheung, and Adaora Ubaka, "The Cost of Managing Impressions for Black Employees: An Expectancy Violation Theory Perspective," *Journal of Applied Psychology* 108, no. 2 (February 1, 2023): 208–24. https://doi.org/10.1037/apl0001030.

70 Without missing a beat: "Stacey Abrams on Writing Herself into the Story—and History," CBS News, May 9, 2021. https://tinyurl.com/m7858sa5.

73 In one survey, more than 80 percent: Annabelle Roberts, Emma Levine, and Ovul Sezer, "Hiding Success," *Journal of Personality and Social Psychology* 120, no. 5 (2021): 1261–86. https://doi.org/10.1037/pspi0000322.

73 Concealing success: Annabelle Roberts, Emma Levine, and Ovul Sezer, "Hiding Success," *Journal of Personality and Social Psychology* 120, no. 5 (2021): 1261–86. https://doi.org/10.1037/pspi0000322.

74 Humblebrags are annoyingly: Ovul Sezer, Francesca Gino, and Michael I. Norton, "Humblebragging: A Distinct—and Ineffective—Self-Presentation Strategy," *Journal of Personality and Social Psychology* 114, no. 1 (2018): 52–74. https://doi.org/10.1037/pspi0000108.

74 Again, the evidence: Ibid.

74 This approach has been shown: Jieun Pai, Eileen Y. Chou, and Nir Halevy, "The Humor Advantage: Humorous Bragging Benefits Job Candidates and Entrepreneurs," *Personality and Social Psychology Bulletin* (December 20, 2023). https://doi.org/10.1177/01461672231214462.

75 Most of us: Chris Littlefield in conversation with the author, February 6, 2023.

75 As Littlefield astutely points out: Christopher Littlefield, "How to Give and Receive Compliments at Work," *Harvard Business Review*, October 12, 2019. https://hbr.org/2019/10/how-to-give-and-receive-compliments-at-work.

76 The dentist replied: Chris Littlefield in conversation with the author, February 6, 2023.

76 One reason we put ourselves down: Cheeky Kid, "100+ Funny Self-Deprecating Quotes and Caption Ideas," *TurboFuture*, February 18, 2023. https://turbofuture.com/internet/Funny-Self-Deprecating-Caption-Ideas.

77 Like other things we say: Michael O'Donnell, Minah Jung, and Clayton R. Critcher,

"The Potential Benefits and Pitfalls of Poking Fun at Yourself:' Self-Deprecating Humor as Impression Management," *ACR North American Advances* 44 (January 1, 2016): 201–6. www.acrwebsite.org/volumes/v44/acr_vol44_1022568.pdf.

77 When "winners": Anne L. Zell and Julie J. Exline, "How Does It Feel to Be Outperformed by a 'Good Winner'? Prize Sharing and Self-Deprecating as Appeasement Strategies," *Basic and Applied Social Psychology* 32, no. 1 (February 23, 2010): 69–85. https://doi.org/10.1080/01973530903540125.

77 It's well publicized: Karina Schumann and Michael Ross, "Why Women Apologize More than Men," *Psychological Science* 21, no. 11 (September 20, 2010): 1649–55. https://doi.org/10.1177/0956797610384150.

78 Specifically, if you commit: Peter H. Kim, Donald L. Ferrin, Cecily D. Cooper, and Kurt T. Dirks, "Removing the Shadow of Suspicion: The Effects of Apology Versus Denial for Repairing Competence- Versus Integrity-Based Trust Violations," *Journal of Applied Psychology* 89, no. 1 (2004): 104–18. https://doi.org/10.1037/0021-9010.89.1.104.

78 We risk damaging: Alison R. Fragale, "The Power of Powerless Speech: The Effects of Speech Style and Task Interdependence on Status Conferral," *Organizational Behavior and Human Decision Processes* 101, no. 2 (November 1, 2006): 243–61. https://doi.org/10.1016/j.obhdp.2006.01.004.

78 This is the rationale behind: Nupur Arya, "Stop Over-Apologizing at Work," *Harvard Business Review*, August 21, 2023. https://hbr.org/2023/08/stop-over-apologizing-at-work.

78 Choosing not to apologize: Tyler G. Okimoto, Michael Wenzel, and Kyli Hedrick, "Refusing to Apologize Can Have Psychological Benefits (and We Issue No Mea Culpa for This Research Finding)," *European Journal of Social Psychology* 43, no. 1 (2013): 22–31. https://doi.org/10.1002/ejsp.1901.

79 Download the Google Chrome extension: Chrome Web Store, "Just Not Sorry—the Chrome Extension," n.d. https://chrome.google.com/webstore/detail/just-not-sorry-the-chrome/fmegmibednnlgojepmidhlhpjbppmlci.

79 And, because it's clear: Alison Wood Brooks, Hengchen Dai, and Maurice E. Schweitzer, "I'm Sorry About the Rain! Superfluous Apologies Demonstrate Empathic Concern and Increase Trust." [Data set], *PsycEXTRA Dataset*, January 1, 2013. https://doi.org/10.1037/e571292013-112.

83 I'm not alone: Rachel Arnett and Jim Sidanius, "Sacrificing Status for Social Harmony: Concealing Relatively High Status Identities from One's Peers," *Organizational Behavior and Human Decision Processes* 147 (July 1, 2018): 108–26. https://doi.org/10.1016/j.obhdp.2018.05.009.

84 *Give and Take*: Adam Grant, *Give and Take: Why Helping Others Drives Our Success* (Penguin Books, 2014).

84 *Think Again*: Adam Grant, *Think Again: The Power of Knowing What You Don't Know* (Viking, 2021).

84 *Hidden Potential*: Adam Grant, *Hidden Potential: The Science of Achieving Greater Things* (Viking, 2023).

85 So we did: Alison R. Fragale and Adam M. Grant, "Busy Brains, Boasters' Gains: Self-Promotion Effectiveness Depends on Audiences' Cognitive Resources," *Journal of Experimental Social Psychology* 58 (May 2015): 63–76.

85 Multiple studies: Alison R. Fragale and Chip Heath, "Evolving Informational Credentials: The (Mis)Attribution of Believable Facts to Credible Sources," *Personality and Social Psychology Bulletin* 30, no. 2 (February 1, 2004): 225–36. https://10.1177/0146167203259933.

87 Her praise of her clients: Rachel Sheerin in conversation with the author, January 18, 2022.
87 For example, Felena: Felena Hanson, *Flight Club—Rebel, Reinvent, and Thrive: How to Launch Your Dream Business* (Felena Hanson, 2016).
89 Although I've been doing this: Eric M. VanEpps, Einav Hart, and Maurice E. Schweitzer, "Dual-Promotion: Bragging Better by Promoting Peers," *Journal of Personality and Social Psychology* (August 10, 2023). https://doi.org/10.1037/pspi0000431.
91 "When you read someone's résumé": Robynn Storey in conversation with the author, February 6, 2023.
91 For example, in 2022: Robynn Storey in conversation with the author, February 6, 2023.
95 Often, though, I would live by: Lou Holtz, "Thought for the day: Don't tell your problems to people. Eighty percent don't care and the other twenty percent are glad you have them," X (formerly Twitter), October 14, 2018. https://twitter.com/CoachLouHoltz88/status/1051638100655525889.

5. Recruit an Army of Other-Promoters

99 "What someone else says": Robynn Storey in conversation with the author, February 6, 2023.
99 However, in this work: Alison R. Fragale and Adam M. Grant, "Busy Brains, Boasters' Gains: Self-Promotion Effectiveness Depends on Audiences' Cognitive Resources," *Journal of Experimental Social Psychology* 58 (May 2015): 63–76.
101 In the early 1990s: Robin Dunbar, "Neocortex Size as a Constraint on Group Size in Primates," *Journal of Human Evolution* 22, no. 6 (1992): 469–93.
101 "Dunbar's number": Robin Dunbar, "Co-Evolution of Neocortex Size, Group Size and Language in Humans," *Behavioral and Brain Sciences* 16, no. 4 (1993): 681–735.
101 Dunbar described: Robin Dunbar, *Grooming, Gossip and the Evolution of Language* (Harvard University Press, 1996).
101 human group size: Patrik Lindenfors, Andreas Wartel, and Johan Lind, "'Dunbar's Number' Deconstructed," *Biology Letters* 17, no. 5 (May 5, 2021): 20210158. https://doi.org/10.1098/rsbl.2021.0158.
101 The 2019 survey: Zoya Gervis, "Why the Average American Hasn't Made a New Friend in Five Years," SWNS Media Group, September 6, 2021. https://swnsdigital.com/us/2019/05/why-the-average-american-hasnt-made-a-new-friend-in-five-years.
102 Within six months: Lars Brandle, "Luis Fonsi and Daddy Yankee's 'Despacito' Sets Global Streaming Record," *Billboard*, July 19, 2017. www.billboard.com/music/music-news/despacito-breaks-record-most-streamed-song-all-time-7873032.
102 The more we're exposed: Robert B. Zajonc, "Attitudinal Effects of Mere Exposure," *Journal of Personality and Social Psychology* 9, no. 2, pt. 2 (January 1, 1968): 1–27. https://doi.org/10.1037/h0025848.
103 Not long after construction: Bertrand Lemoine, "The Artists Who Protested the Eiffel Tower," La Tour Eiffel, June 24, 2019. www.toureiffel.paris/en/news/130-years/artists-who-protested-eiffel-tower.
103 Its physical size: Albert Harrison, "Mere Exposure," *Advances in Experimental Social Psychology* 10 (1977): 39–83.
103 One of the first studies: Susan Saegert, Walter C. Swap, and Robert B. Zajonc, "Exposure, Context, and Interpersonal Attraction," *Journal of Personality and*

Social Psychology 25, no. 2 (February 1, 1973): 234–42. https://doi.org/10.1037/h0033965.

104 Kathy was a brilliant academic: Stacy Cowley, "Katherine W. Phillips, 47, Dies; Taught the Value of Difference," *New York Times,* February 13, 2020. www.nytimes.com/2020/02/13/business/katherine-w-phillips-dead.html.

105 A 1969 study: Albert A. Harrison, "Exposure and Popularity," *Journal of Personality* 37, no. 2 (June 1969): 359–77.

105 Multiple studies have examined: Robert B. Zajonc, "Attitudinal Effects of Mere Exposure," *Journal of Personality and Social Psychology* 9, no. 2, pt. 2 (January 1, 1968): 1–27. https://doi.org/10.1037/h0025848.

105 A later experiment: Norman H. Hamm, Michael R. Baum, and Kenneth W. Nikels, "Effects of Race and Exposure on Judgments of Interpersonal Favorability," *Journal of Experimental Social Psychology* 11, no. 1 (1975): 14–24.

107 She worried: Robin Arzón in conversation with the author, November 9, 2023.

107 "Leverage your differences": "Robin Arzón Teaches Mental Strength," MasterClass, n.d., www.masterclass.com/classes/robin-arzon-teaches-mental-strength.

109 "across offices and functions": Kate in discussion with the author, April 28, 2023.

110 consider the following experiment: Jeannine M. James and Richard Bolstein, "Large Monetary Incentives and Their Effect on Mail Survey Response Rates," *Public Opinion Quarterly* 56, no. 4 (January 1, 1992): 442–53. https://doi.org/10.1086/269336.

111 As part of an experiment: Phillip R. Kunz and Michael Woolcott, "Season's Greetings: From My Status to Yours," *Social Science Research* 5, no. 3 (September 1, 1976): 269–78. https://doi.org/10.1016/0049-089x(76)90003-x.

111 The reciprocity extended: Alix Spiegel, "Give and Take: How the Rule of Reciprocation Binds Us," NPR, November 26, 2012. https://tinyurl.com/5242rjxd.

112 "The guys were working": Meghana Dhar in conversation with the author, October 16, 2023.

113 Talking with Clare: Clare Hart in conversation with the author, June 29, 2022.

114 As an example, a professional: WhatsApp message from Michelle Johnson to the author, May 19, 2022.

117 "Feeling gratitude": William Arthur Ward, "Quotes," Goodreads.com. www.goodreads.com/quotes/189187-feeling-gratitude-and-not-expressing-it-is-like-wrapping-a.

121 I also asked Eden: "Time100 Most Influential Companies 2023: Chief," *Time,* n.d., https://time.com/collection/time100-companies-2023.

6. Get What You Want (and Make Them Love You for It)

127 Kathryn knew these: Kathryn Valentine in conversation with the author, November 30, 2023.

131 Ahead of our time: Larissa Z. Tiedens and Alison R. Fragale, "Power Moves: Complementarity in Dominant and Submissive Nonverbal Behavior," *Journal of Personality and Social Psychology* 84, no. 3 (2003): 558–68.

131 Subsequent research has demonstrated: Erica B. Slotter, Patrick M. Markey, Alexis Audigier, Samantha C. Dashineau, Eli J. Finkel, and Laura B. Luchies, "Love's a Dance You Learn as You Go: Evidence for Interpersonal Complementarity During Romantic Conflict and Its Association with Relationship Outcomes," *European*

Journal of Social Psychology 53, no. 4 (February 21, 2023): 805–22. https://doi.org/10.1002/ejsp.2937.

131 Regardless of how: Larissa Z. Tiedens and Maria C. Jimenez, "Assimilation for Affiliation and Contrast for Control: Complementary Self-Construals," *Journal of Personality and Social Psychology* 85, no. 6 (January 1, 2003): 1049–61. https://doi.org/10.1037/0022-3514.85.6.1049.

133 Women are not penalized: Hannah Riley Bowles and Linda Babcock, "How Can Women Escape the Compensation Negotiation Dilemma? Relational Accounts Are One Answer," *Psychology of Women Quarterly* 37, no. 1 (August 24, 2012): 80–96. https://doi.org/10.1177/0361684312455524.

134 Unlike Assertiveness: Larissa Z. Tiedens and Maria C. Jimenez, "Assimilation for Affiliation and Contrast for Control: Complementary Self-Construals," *Journal of Personality and Social Psychology* 85, no. 6 (January 1, 2003): 1049–61. https://doi.org/10.1037/0022-3514.85.6.1049.

135 Like any form of procrastination: Brian A. Wilson and Tuyen D. Nguyen, "Belonging to Tomorrow: An Overview of Procrastination," *International Journal of Psychological Studies* 4, no. 1 (March 2012): 211–17. https://doi.org/10.5539/ijps.v4n1p211.

136 In one study: Justin Kruger, Nicholas Epley, Jason Parker, and Zhi-Wen Ng, "Egocentrism over E-Mail: Can We Communicate as Well as We Think?," *Journal of Personality and Social Psychology* 89, no. 6 (January 1, 2005): 925–36. https://doi.org/10.1037/0022-3514.89.6.925.

137 Studies have shown: Brett W. Pelham, Mauricio Carvallo, and J. T. Jones, "Implicit Egotism," *Current Directions in Psychological Science* 14, no. 2 (April 1, 2005): 106–10. https://doi.org/10.1111/j.0963-7214.2005.00344.x; Nicolas Guéguen, "The Effects of Incidental Similarity with a Stranger on Mimicry Behavior," *Open Behavioral Science Journal* 6 (2012): 15–22.

140 However, the science shows: Adam D. Galinsky and Thomas Mussweiler, "First Offers as Anchors: The Role of Perspective-Taking and Negotiator Focus," *Journal of Personality and Social Psychology* 81, no. 4 (January 1, 2001): 657–69. https://doi.org/10.1037/0022-3514.81.4.657.

141 Switching to a conversation: Annie Duke in conversation with the author, June 8, 2023.

142 Within a year: Annie Duke in conversation with the author, June 8, 2023.

143 You still make the first move: Geoffrey J. Leonardelli, Jun Gu, Geordie McRuer, Victoria Husted Medvec, and Adam D. Galinsky, "Multiple Equivalent Simultaneous Offers (MESOs) Reduce the Negotiator Dilemma: How a Choice of First Offers Increases Economic and Relational Outcomes," *Organizational Behavior and Human Decision Processes* 152 (May 1, 2019): 64–83. https://doi.org/10.1016/j.obhdp.2019.01.007.

144 When you present multiple choices: Ibid.

144 Notably, three is not: Sheena S. Iyengar and Mark R. Lepper, "When Choice Is Demotivating: Can One Desire Too Much of a Good Thing?," *Journal of Personality and Social Psychology* 79, no. 6 (December 1, 2000): 995–1006. https://doi.org/10.1037/0022-3514.79.6.995.

146 She told Mark Zuckerberg: Sheryl Sandberg, *Lean In: Women, Work, and the Will to Lead* (Alfred A. Knopf, 2013).

147 "People assume": Annie Duke in conversation with the author, June 8, 2023.

149 Studies show that: Xuan Zhao and Nicholas Epley, "Surprisingly Happy to Have

Helped: Underestimating Prosociality Creates a Misplaced Barrier to Asking for Help," *Psychological Science* 33, no. 10 (September 6, 2022): 1708–31. https://doi.org/10.1177/09567976221097615.

149 In the sage words: Jada Pinkett Smith (@jadapsmith), X (formerly Twitter), November 9, 2019, 10:19 p.m. https://twitter.com/jadapsmith/status/1193367559812182016?lang=en.

151 Soon, Kathryn started: Kathryn Valentine in conversation with the author, November 30, 2023.

152 She wrote an article: Kathryn Valentine, "Dear Working Women: Before You Go, Negotiate," *Adweek*, October 27, 2020. www.adweek.com/brand-marketing/dear-working-women-before-you-go-negotiate.

152 Kathryn is a nationally recognized: Kathryn Valentine and Hannah Riley Bowles, "3 Negotiation Myths Still Harming Women's Careers," *Harvard Business Review*, October 4, 2022. hbr.org/2022/10/3-negotiation-myths-still-harming-womens-careers.

152 Kathryn estimates: Kathryn Valentine in conversation with the author, November 30, 2023.

7. Start with the End

154 "But 'when we really need them'": Adam Bryant, "Four Executives on Succeeding in Business as a Woman," *New York Times*, October 12, 2013. www.nytimes.com/newsgraphics/2013/10/13/ipad/women-corner-office.html.

158 The problem with always: Ibid.

159 As psychologist Hal Hershfield: Paul Feinberg, "Q&A: Hal Hershfield on Finding Harmony with Your Future Self," UCLA Newsroom, May 25, 2023. https://newsroom.ucla.edu/stories/hal-hershfield-finding-harmony-with-future-self-book.

159 Hershfield stresses the importance: Hal Hershfield, *Your Future Self: How to Make Tomorrow Better Today* (Little, Brown Spark, 2023).

162 Dekkers quickly advanced: "Marijn Dekkers," Wikipedia, March 2, 2023. https://en.wikipedia.org/wiki/Marijn_Dekkers.

162 Preparing his parting words: *Fortune*, "Bayer CEO: 'This Was the Best Lesson Ever,'" YouTube, January 5, 2016. www.youtube.com/watch?v=-sz8It_wFRo.

164 She started to think: Victoria Pelletier in conversation with the author, May 18, 2023.

165 A woman I know: "Mary" in conversation with the author, May 16, 2023.

165 "psychologically harmful": "Mary" in email communication with the author, March 13, 2023.

165 Victoria knew: Victoria Pelletier in conversation with the author, May 18, 2023.

167 "As much as I love": Mabel Miguel in conversation with the author, December 11, 2023.

168 In one experimental study: Shelley J. Correll, Stephen Benard, and In Paik, "Getting a Job: Is There a Motherhood Penalty?" *American Journal of Sociology* 112, no. 5 (March 1, 2007): 1297–1338. https://doi.org/10.1086/511799.

170 As Amy Schulman points out: Adam Bryant, "Four Executives on Succeeding in Business as a Woman," *New York Times*, October 12, 2013.

8. Teach and Learn

175 But, at over six feet tall: Margaret A. Neale and Thomas Z. Lys, *Getting (More Of) What You Want: How the Secrets of Economics and Psychology Can Help You Negotiate Anything, in Business and in Life* (Basic Books, 2015).

178 In his popular 2017: Atul Gawande, "Want to Get Great at Something? Get a Coach," TED2017, April 2017, 16:37. www.ted.com/talks/atul_gawande_want_to _get_great_at_something_get_a_coach?language=en.

179 "are your external eyes": Gawande, "Want to Get Great at Something?" 9:17.

179 For example, formal mentoring: Frank Dobbin and Alexandra Kalev, "Why Diversity Programs Fail," *Harvard Business Review*, June 12, 2023. https://hbr.org/2016 /07/why-diversity-programs-fail.

179 However, the majority of women: Stephanie Neal, Jazmine Boatman, and Linda Miller, "Mentoring Women in the Workplace: A Global Study," DDI, April 9, 2013. www.ddiworld.com/research/mentoring-women-in-the-workplace.

179 Further, women report: "Now More than Ever, Men Need to Do More to Support Women," LeanIn.org, n.d. https://tinyurl.com/3ykmxbzn; Deepali Bagati, "Women of Color in U.S. Law Firms," Catalyst, 2009. www.catalyst.org.

179 three key development needs: Menttium Corporation, "Menttium 2022 Insights," 2022. https://content.menttium.com/Mktg/2022/Menttium_2022_Insights_White _Paper.pdf.

180 "When people think about": Missy Chicre in conversation with the author, November 3, 2023.

181 This advice went against: Felecia Carty in conversation with the author, November 8, 2023.

182 However, Kathryn might not: Kathryn Valentine in conversation with the author, November 30, 2023.

182 A LinkedIn survey: Emily Jasper and Kristi Hedges, "LinkedIn Report: Women Without a Mentor," *Forbes*, October 25, 2011. https://tinyurl.com/3m6kdza8.

183 "Anyone who knows more": Felecia Carty in conversation with the author, November 8, 2023.

183 For example, *The No Club*: Linda Babcock, Brenda Peyser, Lise Vesterlund, and Laurie Weingart, *The No Club: Putting a Stop to Women's Dead-End Work* (Simon & Schuster, 2022).

184 For that, I'll hop on: Robin Arzón, Peloton HIIT and Hills Ride [Peloton class], October 21, 2022. www.onepeloton.com.

184 As a starting point: Lisa Barrington, "Everyone Needs a Personal Board of Directors," *Forbes*, February 20, 2018. https://tinyurl.com/yvnhzvf5.

185 "One of my biggest mentors": Susannah Hutcheson, "How I Became Peloton's VP of Fitness Programming: Robin Arzón," *USA Today*, February 18, 2020. https:// tinyurl.com/5a6xydy2.

185 "a different lens": Missy Chicre in conversation with the author, November 3, 2023.

187 As *Forbes* reported: Christine Comaford, "76% of People Think Mentors Are Important, but Only 37% Have One," *Forbes*, July 3, 2019. https://tinyurl.com/2p8 tpd5t.

187 "When I was a lawyer": Robin Arzón in conversation with the author, November 9, 2023.

190 As we develop any skill: Frank Anthony De Phillips, William M. Berliner, and James J. Cribbin, *Meaning of Learning and Knowledge* (Richard D. Irwin, 1960).

192 In addition to building: Lauren Eskreis-Winkler, Ayelet Fishbach, and Angela Duckworth, "Dear Abby: Should I Give Advice or Receive It?," *Psychological Science* 29, no. 11 (October 3, 2018): 1797–1806. https://doi.org/10.1177/0956797618795472.

192 "When you're actually": "Robin Arzón Teaches Mental Strength," MasterClass, n.d. www.masterclass.com/classes/robin-arzon-teaches-mental-strength.

193 Over two-thirds of women: Nicole Williams, "INFOGRAPHIC: Women and Mentoring in the U.S.," LinkedIn (blog), October 25, 2011. www.linkedin.com/blog/member/career/mentoring-women.

195 Despite Maggie's extensive scholarly: "Celebrating Margaret Neal's Impact at Stanford GSB," Stanford Graduate School of Business, March 6, 2020. www.gsb.stanford.edu.

195 This form of mentorship: Rosalind Chow, "Don't Just Mentor Women and People of Color. Sponsor Them," *Harvard Business Review,* June 30, 2021. https://hbr.org/2021/06/dont-just-mentor-women-and-people-of-color-sponsor-them.

Conclusion

200 There's a phenomenon: Justin Kruger and David Dunning, "Unskilled and Unaware of It: How Difficulties in Recognizing One's Own Incompetence Lead to Inflated Self-Assessments," *Journal of Personality and Social Psychology* 77, no. 6 (December 1999): 1121–34.

Index

Page numbers in *italics* refer to charts and tables.

Abrahams, Eden, 113, 116–17, 120–25, 196
Abrams, Stacey, 70–72, *71*, 74, 88n, 93–94, 146
Academy Awards, 51–52
Accenture, 165
achievements. *See also* successes (wins)
    aspirations vs., 52
    concealing, 73–74, *82*
    framing, 69
    humblebragging and, 74
    importance of mentioning, 83
    mentoring and, 179
    storytelling and, 71, *71*, 80, 90–93
"Add, don't subtract" rule, 41, 44, 83
adjectives, gender bias and, 59
advice
    acting counter to, 158
    asking for, 188
    giving, 29, 114–15, 126
    putting on paper, 113–15
advocacy, 165. *See also* agent; self-advocacy
Adweek, 152
age, 16, 26
agent, 147–48, 152
airline miles analogy, 154–55, 170

airport, use of time and, 115, 144
Allied Signal, 162
alpha dog, 130–33
ambition, 83, 98. *See also* aspirations; goals
    storytelling and, 69–71, *71*
Angelou, Maya, 49
apologies
    alternatives to, 78–79
    superfluous, 79
    unnecessary, 77–79, *82*, 83–84, 198
Arzón, Robin, 14, 106–8, 184–85, 187–88, 192–93
Asian American, Native Hawaiian, and Pacific Islander (AANHPIs) women, 8n
aspirations. *See also* ambition
    achievements vs., 52
    professional vs. personal, 167
Assertive-Cold quadrant, *24*, 33–34, 36–37
Assertiveness
    adding Warmth to, as likeable badass, 11, 22–25, *23*, *24*, 41, 44, 130, 133–35
    apologies and, 78
    benefits of, 130–31

Assertiveness (cont.)
   choosing seat and, 28
   compensatory impression management and, 39–41
   default reputation and, 35
   defined, 22–23, 23
   dominance vs. task cues and, 26n
   downplaying Warmth to enhance, 40
   eye contact and, 28
   humor and, 29
   initial judgments and, 33
   motherhood penalty and, 168–69
   mutual interactions and, 132
   nonverbal behaviors and, 131
   out-of-office replies and, 88n
   self-advocacy and, 132–33
   self- vs. other-promotion and, 99
   small deposits and, 115, 116
   speech styles and, 27, 42
   Submissiveness as complement to, 131–32, 134
   tradeoff between Warmth and, 129
Assertive-Submissive dimension, 21–25, 23
Assertive-Warm (likeable badass) quadrant, 24, 40
   adding behavior on weaker dimension to enhance, 44
   asking advice from new mentor and, 188
   assessing, and embracing the pain, 200–201
   attending to task cues and, 44
   bragging vs. humblebragging and, 74
   choosing behaviors right for you, 30–32
   choosing your seat and, 28
   compliments and, 74–76
   discretionary activities and, 177
   email introductions and, 125
   eye contact and, 28
   foul language and, 31–32
   giving helpful advice and, 114
   humor and, 29
   humorbragging and, 74
   inferences from job and gender and, 33–34
   introducing yourself and, 105
   mentoring others and, 185, 190
   modeling behavior and, 185
   offering help and, 29
   out-of-office replies and, 88
   praise or other-promotion and, 89
   relationship between high status and, 32
   responses to "How are you?" and, 94–95, 95
   saying no and, 183
   self-advocacy and, 147
   self-deprecation and, 77
   self-promotion and, 85
   small deposits and, 112–14
   smiling and, 30–31
   speech rate, response time, and style and, 26–27
   storytelling and, 69–71
   storytelling audit and, 80
   talking about successes and, 74
   task cues and, 29–30
   value signaled by, 26
   volunteering strategically and, 108
audience
   storytelling and, 80
   understanding, to achieve goal, 199–200
Australia, 9, 154
authenticity
   mere exposure and, 106–7
   strategic, 53–60, 95
awards
   asking for nominations, 53
   status and, 16

Babcock, Linda, 60
Barrington, Lisa, 184
Bayer AG, 162
Bernard, Sheldon, 121–25
Beyond Thank You, 75n
bios, writing, 90–93, 190
Black women, 70, 104, 165
   angry stereotype, 31
   discrimination vs., 59
   equal pay day and, 8n
   microaggressions and, 37
   promotions and, 5
   referrals and, 138
   self-advocacy and, 138–39
   self-promotion and, 70–71
   tech industry and, 13
book club example, 40

boss, incompetent and uncivil, 66
bragging or boasting, 69–71, 74, 99
  brag and thank strategy, 89–90, *90*
  résumé and bios and, 90–92
breast-pumping, 189
Breyer, Stephen, 6n
Brigham Young University, 111
Brody, Lauren Smith, 189n
broken rung, 5
Brown-Philpot, Stacy, 12–14, 31, 58–59
bunglers, 54, 69
burning bridges, 158–59, 180
business cards, 106, 107
business school, 3
  summer internships and, 127–28, 151
business trip, turning down, 158
buyer's remorse, 159

calendar, managing, 143–44
capability, 27, 32
career
  family and, 168–69
  likeability and advancement in, 36–37
  planning, and mentors, 179–81, 183, 185
caring, 27, 32, 71
Carty, Felicia, 46–48, 54, 61, 138, 181, 183
caste, 16
CBS Sunday Morning, 70
characteristics, desired, long-term priorities and, 161–65, 170
charitable contributions, 190
Chatman, Jennifer, 36
cheerleader, 184
cheese board, 115–16, 193
Chicre, Missy, 180, 185
Chief, 121, 121n, 124
Child, Julia, 198
children and family, 185. *See also* motherhood
  as agents, 148
  balancing career and, 196
  building relationships by talking about, 139
  career decisions and, 168–69
  deciding to have, 167
  mentoring by, 185
  return to paid work after having, 189–90
  as tech support team, 193
  three-offer strategy and, 145
chit-chat, 137–39

choices
  giving people multiple, 144
  replacing habits with, 79, 95
  three, as optimal, 144
Christmas card experiment, 111, 117
Cialdini, Bob, 53–54
coaching, 17, 178. *See also* mentors and mentoring
coffee chats, 47
cognitive psychology, 38
Coldness. *See also* Warm-Cold dimension
  Assertiveness and, 24, 33–34, 36–37
  defined, 22, *22*
  kicking behavior that signals, 45
  Submissiveness and, 23–24, *24*
collaborative, strategy to appear, 144
Collecting Nos exercise, 149–50
compensatory impression management, 39–41, 181
competence, 26
  conscious, 191
  conscious excellence as Level 5, 191–93, 200
  humblebragging and, 74
  overestimating, 200
  signaling, 83
  speech rate and, 26
  stages of, 190–93
  storytelling and, 69
  unconscious, 191–93
  underestimating, 200
competence-likeability bind, 12, 32–39, 197–98
  career advancement and, 36–37
  compensatory impression management and, 39–41
  confirmation bias and, 35–36
  incivility and, 36–37
  revered one moment, reviled the next, 38–39
compliments, 42, 137, 170
  rejecting, 74–76, *82*
  responding to, 76
  storytelling and, 80
condescending tone, 37
conferences, 104, 109
confidence, 23, 26, 35
  "I'm just one of the guys" mindset and, 58–59
  mentoring and, 178, 192

confidence (cont.)
 signaling, 83
 speech rate and, 26–27
 storytelling and, 69
 tone of voice and, 104
 "too much" vs. "not enough," 41
confirmation bias, 35, 156
conscious awareness, habits vs. choices and, 79
contacts
 daily connection and, 126
 discretionary activities and finding new, 176–77
 maintaining old, 46–49, 54–55, 126
contributions
 discretionary activities and, 176–77
 long-term priorities and, 161–65, 170–71
control, 6, 35, 78
corporate leadership, 9, 43
 incivility and, 37
courage, 78
cover letter, 85, 99
COVID-19, 112, 141, 152
credentials, 16
credit
 giving others, after compliment, 76
 others taking, 130
cultural biases, 26
cultural fit, 128
curiosity, conveying, 187
customer success, 47

Dartmouth College, 83, 190
daycare, 169, 189
"Dear Working Women" (Valentine), 152
defense, offense vs., 11, 42–44
Dekkers, Marijn, 162–63
Democratic Party, 70
demographics, assumptions based on, 35
depression, 37
"Despacito" strategy, 102–4, 110
Dhar, Meghana, 67–69, 86, 89, 112–14
differences, leveraging, 107
difficult questions, asking, 186–87
disagreeing
 deciding when to engage in, 158–59
 principled, 170
 with purpose, 165–66
disclaimers, 27

discretionary activities, criteria for choosing, 176–77. *See also* volunteering
dominance, 35
 cues and, 26n
doubt raisers, 59
Duke, Annie, 38–39, 141–42, 147
Dunbar, Robin, 101
Dunbar's number, 101
Dunlap, Tori, 188
Dunning-Kruger effect, 200

educational degrees, 5n, 16
effectiveness and enjoyment, maximizing, 200–201
Eiffel Tower, 103
81cents nonprofit, 8
elevator pitch, 47
emails
 carbon copying, 106
 emotions conveyed in, 136
 introductions in, 119–25, 192
 Just Not Sorry extension for, 79
 out-of-office replies and, 86–88, 88, 107, 192
 prospective mentors and, 188–89
 responding quickly to, 45
 self-advocacy and, 136
 self-promotion plus other-promotion and, 89–90
 "shout outs" and, 69, 89
 signature and, 103
 storytelling and, 80–81, 86–88
emotional exhaustion, 37
engagement, 37
entry-level employees, 42–43
equal pay, 7–8
ethics, 54
ethnicity, 5n, 16
Evite, 101
excellence, conscious, 191–93, 200
executive presence, *180*, 183
expectations
 outcomes vs., 51–52
 setting high, 52
eye contact, 28, 30, 45, 105
 hierarchy and, 28

face, mere exposure and, 105
Facebook, 73n, 146

failure
    denying vs. apologizing for, 78n
    feeling like, despite successes, 51
    not advertising, 76–81
    self-deprecation and, 76–77
    storytelling and, 72, 79
    unnecessary apologies and, 77–79
Fast Company, 152
FBI, 29
Fey, Tina, 49
Fifth Trimester, The (Brody), 189n
Financial Times, 13
fireside chats, 141–42, 147
first-mover tactic, 140–42
    multiple equivalents and, 142–44
First Women's Bank, 8
flexible work arrangements, 10, 189
Flickinger, Tara, 201
Flight Club—Rebel, Reinvent, and Thrive (Hanson), 87
Fonsi, Luis, 102
Fortune 50 companies, 127
Fortune "40 Under 40" list, 13
foul language, 31
fractional mentorship, 182–84, 196
French Chef, The (TV show), 198
frequency and familiarity, 102
friendliness, 35
Friendly Strength, 24–25, *24*
Friendly Weakness, 24, *24*, 33, 36, 84
friends and acquaintances, 101–3, *101*
    storytelling and, 80
future self
    making hard decisions and, 159–60
    retirement party exercise and, 161–66
    view from rocking chair exercise and, 166–70

games
    problem-solving and, 15
    unfair, 4, 199
Gawande, Atul, 178–79
gender bias
    negotiation and, 16–17
    not focusing on, 58–59
    recommendation letters and, 59
    removing, as disadvantage, 16
    status and, 26
gender disparities
    adjectives in recommendations and, 59
    asking for raise and, 132
    assumptions about competence and, 36
    business funding, 8
    education and, 5n
    humor and, 29
    incivility and, 39
    interruptions and, 5–6
    MBA salaries and, 9
    mentoring and, 179
    negotiations and, 9–10
    parenthood penalty and, 168n
    pay and, 5
    power and, 4, 9, 11
    promotions and, 5
    self-advocacy and, 132
    self-promotion and, 91
    status and, 4–6, 9–11, 16, 59
    unnecessary apologies and, 77–78
General Electric, 162
Georgia, 70
ghostwriter strategy, *93*
Ginsburg, Ruth Bader, 6
Give and Take (Grant), 84
giving more Assertively, 112–13
Glamour, 189n
glaring, 26n
goals
    Big Hairy Audacious (BHAGs), 51–52, 57, 98
    impression management and, 40–41
    retirement party exercise and, 161–66
    rocking chair exercise and, 166–70
    setting, before negotiations, 135
    thinking like psychologist to achieve, 199–200
goblin mode, 57
golf, 17, 137–38, 201
Google, 12–13, 14, 58–59
Google Chrome, 79
Grandma Marge (maternal grandmother), 155–56, 169–70, 177
Grant, Adam, 84–85, 99, 143–44
gratitude
    expressing, 117, 137
    rejecting, 74–75, *82*
Gugliucci, Nicole, 6n

habits
    changing bad, 45

habits (cont.)
  choices vs., 79, 95
  storytelling and, 80–81
Hamilton (musical), 71
Hanson, Felena, 87–88
hard decisions
  inaction when facing, 158–59
  long-term priorities as guide to, 159–60
Harry Potter films, 51
Hart, Clare, 113–17, 120, 124–25, 196–97
Harvard Business Review, 7, *7*, 152
Harvard Business School, 68, 162
Hays, Nicholas, 11
HBO, 179
"heat level," practice and, 17–18
hedges, 27
help, offering, 20, 29–30, 35, 42
  avoiding incivility and, 37
  identifying type and potential recipients of, 20
  out-of-office replies and, 88
  sharing information and, 113
hepeating, 6
Hera Hub, 87
Hershfield, Hal, 159
Hidden Potential (Grant), 84
Holtz, Lou, 95
hostage negotiators, 29
Hostile Strength, 24, *24*, 33, 36–37, 84
Hostile Weakness, 24, *24*
Howard, Lauren, 6
"How are you?" responses, 94–95, *95*
HP Inc., 13
Huffington, Arianna, 49
humblebragging, 74, 81, *82*
humor, 42, 137
  interrupters and, 29
  out-of-office replies and, 88, *88*
  self-deprecating, 76–77
  storytelling and, 81
humorbragging, 74, 77

ideas
  having yours dismissed, 35
  having yours implemented, 10
"I don't care what other people think of me" mindset, 56–57
"I don't have the time for this" mindset, 60

"I don't want to be a 'status-seeker'" mindset, 53–56
"I'm just one of the guys" mindset, 58–59
imposter syndrome, 49–52, 54, 67, *180*, 184, 192, 194
impression management strategies, 39–41
inaction, playing safe through, 158–60
inadequacy, feelings of, 49, 52. *See also* imposter syndrome
incivility, 36–37, 66
  microaggressions vs., 36n
  psychological effects of, 37
  women leaders subject to, 36–39
incompetence
  conscious, 191
  unconscious, 191, 200
India, 12, 58–59
industry groups, 47
influence, 57
  bunglers and, 54
  mentoring and, *180*
  reciprocity and, 54
  science of, 54
  sleuths and, 54
  smugglers and, 54
Influence Unleashed (Pelletier), 165
information
  requests for, 49
  sharing, about yourself, 68–69
  sharing helpful, 113
  sources of, 85
  withholding, 37
insecurities, 49. *See also* imposter syndrome
Instagram, 57, 68–69, 115
intense, criticized as "too," 41
internal messaging systems, 68–69
interpersonal circumplex, 39–40
  competence-likeability bind and, 32
  defined, 24–25, *24*
  four quadrants of, 24–25, *24*
interruptions, 5–6, 29, 37, 130
interviews, 112–13
intimidation, 26n
In Treatment (TV show), 179
introductions, 29, 107, 170
  emails and, for other-promotion, 119–25
  mentoring and, 194
  requests for, 49

storytelling and, 80
using first and last name and, 105
Iron Maiden, 44, 164

"J" (teammate), 66
Jacobi, Tonja, 5
job searches, 46–48
  cover letter and recommendations, 85
  gender disparity and, 9, 59
  making first move on salary and, 140–41
  mentoring and, 181, 183
  negotiating, 8
  recommendations and referrals and, 46, 49, 55, 59
  signing bonus negotiations and, 50–51, 50
job turnover, 37
joy
  discretionary activities and, 176–77
  volunteering and, 108
Just Not Sorry email extension, 79

Kagan, Elena, 6
"Kate," 19–21, 29–30, 42–43, 65–66, 109, 110, 111, 120–21, 125
Kay, Katty, 6
"Kim," 156–57, 160, 167
Kim, Misong, 102
Kunz, Phillip, 111, 117

Lakshmi, Padma, 49
language, 31, 139
Latinas, 8n
Latinx, 70
layoffs, 43–44
Le Temps (newspaper), 103
letterhead, 106
"L" experiment on status and power and, 33–34
likeability. *See also* competence-likeability bind; likeable badass
  Assertive-Submissive complementarity and, 132
  humblebragging and, 74
  mere exposure and, 102–5
  name and face recognition and, 104–5
  out-of-office replies and, 88
  photo and, 105
  similarity and, 137
  storytelling and, 70–71

likeable badass, 12. *See also* Assertive-Warm (likeable badass) quadrant
  "Add, don't subtract" rule and, 39–42, 44
  alpha dog and, 130–33
  bad habits that weaken story and, 72–79
  collecting nos and, 148–53
  competence-likeability bind and, 32–39
  defined, and interpersonal circumplex, 21–25
  embracing pain of mastering plays and, 200–201
  finding mentors and, 182–90
  future self, as guide to using status and, 159–71
  kicking bad habits and, 45
  making introductions and, 119–25
  mastering the plays and, 14–18
  mentoring and, 175–82
  mentoring others and, 190–98
  mindset and, 46–61
  motivating other-promoters and, 116–19
  picking swing thoughts and, 201
  playing long game and, 201–2
  playing offense, vs. defense and, 42–44
  recruiting other-promoters and, 97–109, 126
  self-advocacy and, dialing up Warmth, 133–48
  self-advocacy and getting "yes" for an answer, 127–53
  small deposits and, 110–16, 125
  as solution to status problems, 19–21, 25–29
  status vs. power and showing up as, 11–14
  storytelling and self-promotion and, 65–96
  storytelling audit and, 79–84
  strategic authenticity and, 29–32
  strategies for telling strong story and, 86–96
  task cues and, 25–32, 44
  understanding needs of others, to desire outcomes, 199–200
  using, not hoarding, status and, 156–59
Lilly Pulitzer, 127, 181, 182
LinkedIn, 6, 47, 126, 165, 182

Littlefield, Chris, 75–76
long game, 201–2
long-term priorities, 201–2
   making hard decisions and, 159–60
   retirement party exercise and, 161–66
   rocking chair exercise and, 166–70

"M," 65–66, 76, 84–85, 130
Macy's, 46
maiden name, 105n
majority-male groups, 58
managers, 67
   promotions to, 5
mansplaining, 6, 11
manspreading, 131, 176
Marlowe, Christopher, 57
"Mary," 165
"Matt," 156–58, 160, 167–68
MBA programs, 9
McKinsey & Company, 65–67, 127, 151
meetings
   setting times for, 143
   speaking up at, 35, 158
men
   as allies, 16–17
   competence assumed for, 36
   getting more credit than women, 35–36
   status and, 16
mentors and mentoring, 14, 109, 176–81, 190–98
   broad vs. deep, 195–96
   eight types of, 184–85
   establishing relationship with new, 187–89
   family and, 185
   filling vacant positions, in fractional, 185–88
   finding your niche as, 196
   fractional, 182–88, 196
   framing self-promotion around, 69
   honesty and, 194
   how to find, 182–90
   importance of, 197–98
   internal vs. external, 185
   levels of competence and, 191–93
   need for continual, 178–79
   peer groups as, 183–84
   people you haven't met as, 185
   putting wisdom on paper as, 196–97
   seeking multiple "imperfect," 182–83, 195
   seeking new, during long career, 189–90
   social media and, 197
   starting to become, 193–94
   taking stock of, 184–85, 190
   women and need for, 179
Menttium, 179–81, 185
mere exposure, 102–10, 125
   name and face and, 105–7
   photos and, 105
   self-advocacy and, 136
   small deposits and, 114
   social media and, 197
   uniqueness and, 107–8
   volunteering strategically and, 108–9, 126
meritocracy, 53
metacognition, 200
meta-competence, 200
microaggressions, 6, 36n, 37
Miguel, Mabel, 166–67
military officers, 139
mindsets, limiting, 49–60
   "I don't care what other people think of me," 56–57
   "I don't have the time for this," 60
   "I don't want to be a 'status-seeker,'" 53–56
   "I'm just one of the guys," 58–59
   imposter, 49–52
   noticing, and replacing with likeable badass mindsets, 61
   plays to practice, 61
   power first, status second, 6–8
"Mitchell, Stacie" example, 98
modesty, 77
Moriarty, Erin, 70, 93
Morrow, Dawn, 124, 125
motherhood. *See also* children and family
   career penalty for, 168, 189
   mentors and, 189
"multiple equivalent offers" strategy, 143–45

name recognition, 180
   mere exposure and, 105–6
name tags, 106

narrative, controlling your own, 69. See
    also storytelling
Neale, Margaret "Maggie," 32, 175–77,
    179–81, 184, 195
needs, fundamental, 6
negotiations, 9, 117, 196
    gender and, 9–10, 16–17
    highlighting benefits for other person
        and, 146–47
    making first move and, 140–42
    not limited to money, 117–18
    other-promotion and, 118
networking, 185. See also contacts;
    mentors and mentoring;
    other-promoters
newsletters, 69
Newsweek, 105n
New York Times, 154
"NFL 100 Greatest" Game Changers,
    58
No Club, The (Babcock, Peyser,
    Vesterlund, and Weingart), 60, 183
nonpromotable tasks, 60, 89, 112, 144
nonverbal behavior, 131, 136
nonwhite women, 15. See also specific
    groups
Noom, 13
Nordstrom, 13
Northcraft, Greg, 137–38
Northwestern University, Kellogg School
    of Management, 104
Nyong'o, Lupita, 49, 51–52

Oakland Raiders, 58
Obama, Michelle, 185
occupation, status and, 16, 35
offense, defense vs., 42–44
office politics, 53
OG (Original Gangster), 13–14
OnePoll, 101
online documents, 106
open-door office hours, 190
organizational psychology, 4, 11, 67,
    176
other-demoter, 168
other-oriented, 26
other-promoters, 97, 116
    becoming, 117, 119
    being uniquely you and, 106–7
    building army of, 125–26, 182

circulating your name and face and,
    104–6
cultivating, 100–101, 117, 119
efficiency and, 100
email introductions and, 119–25
finding, 109
getting mentioned by, 97–98
meeting future, 176–77
mere exposure and, 101–9, 119
motivating, 116–19
negotiating promotions and, 118–19
self-promotion vs., 99–100
small deposits and, 110–16, 119
value of, 98–100
volunteering strategically and, 108–9
outglancing, 28
outsourcing (ghostwriter) strategy, for
    self-promotion, 90–93, *93*
Overbeck, Jennifer, 32
Oxford Languages Word of the Year,
    57

paraverbal signals, 136
paternalistic motive, 73n
pay. See salary
Pecak, Michelle, 121n
peer mentoring, 183–84
Pelletier, Victoria, 43–44, 164–66
Peloton, 14, 106, 152, 184, 185
perceptions
    Assertive-Submissive (badass)
        dimension and, 22–23, *23*
    fundamental dimensions of, 21–25
    task cues and, 30
    Warm-Cold (likeable) dimension and,
        21–22, *22*
performance
    devalued, 37
    review of, 48, 68, 92
perks, 9
persistence, 23, 47
personal board of directors, 184, 184n
personal space, intruding on, 26n
persuasiveness, 26
Peyser, Brenda, 60
Pfizer, 154
Phillips, Katherine "Kathy," 103–4, 195
photos, 105
playful attitude, 15
poker, 38–39, 141, 155

politicians, 70
Porter, Michael, 162
power
  apologies and, 78
  defined, 4
  forms of, 10
  high status and, 33
  importance of status vs., 6–10
  low, 4–5, 33, 34
  low-status and, 8–9, 34, 36–37
  mentoring and, 179
  negotiating to increase, 9
  overfocusing on, while neglecting status, 6–8, *7*
  perceptions of Assertiveness and Warmth and, 33–34
  speech style and, 27
  status as basis, not result of, 8–10
  using, to help others, 10
Power Code, The (Kay and Shipman), 6
powerlessness
  speech style and, 27
  unnecessary apologies and, 78
practice
  being an agent for someone, 152
  daily connection habit and, 126
  desired contributions and characteristics and, 170–71
  finding similarities and, 152
  "heat level" or risk and, 17–18, 49
  kicking bad habits and, 45
  managing mindset and, 61
  managing status and, 17–18
  mentoring and, 198
  narrowing focus of, 201
  signaling Assertiveness and Warmth and, 44–45
  sleuthing, 55–56
  speaking up for others and, 171
  storytelling and, 96
  throwaway question and, for self-promotion, 93–95, *95*
praise, 75. *See also* compliments
  "shout out" emails, 69, 89
preparation, 47, 93
presence, *180*, 181
presentations
  fireside chats vs., 141–42, 147
  helping others with, 20–21
  mentoring and, *180*

  name on slides and, 106
  virtual, 141
problems, telling people yours, 95
problem solving
  developing reputation for, 21, 42–43
  playful attitude and, 15
procrastination, 135, 159
professors, ratings of, 36–37
promotions, 5, 7, 19–20
  mentoring and, *180*
  negotiating, 9–10

qualified, women seen as not, 37, 41
queer women, 15, 43
Quit (Duke), 142

race
  equal pay day and, 8n
  status and, 16, 26
racial bias, 165
raise, asking for, 9, 119, 129, 132, 153
  three-offer strategy and, 142–43
Ralph Lauren, 46
reaction, action vs., and hard decisions, 158–59
reasonableness, 26
reciprocity, 177
  influence and, 54
  mentoring and, 194
  small deposits and, 111, 121
recommendations, 46, 49, 55, 107, 176
  cover letter and, 85, 99
  gender bias and, 59
relationships. *See also* contacts; mentors and mentoring
  building, 28, 155
  concealing success and, 73
  staying in touch and, 54–55
repetition, 98, 198. *See also* mere exposure
reputation
  acting to change unfavorable, 42–44
  confirmation bias and, 35–36
  control over how you use, 10
  default, 33–35
  interpersonal circumplex and, 24, 25
  low- vs. high-status and, 33–35
  men vs. women and, 35
  playing offense not defense to build, 42–44
  status-power assumptions and, 33–34

resources, 8, 10
respect, 6–10. *See also* status
   caring about, 57
   desire for, 7
   impact of lack of, 6
   imposter mindset and, 49–50
   maintaining, 49
   power and, 8
   resources and, 8, 10
response time, 26–27
restaurant recommendations, 29
resting bitch face, 30–31, 186
résumé, 10, 90–93, 99, 190
retirement
   rocking chair exercise and, 166–70, 186
   speech exercise, 161–66, 186
reverse mentoring, 198
Ridgeway, Cecilia, 6, 26n
Roché, Joyce, 49
rocking chair exercise, 166–70, 186
Roughgarden, Joan, 36
rudeness, 36, 45, 134. *See also* incivility

salary negotiation, 48–49
   first-move tactic and, 140–42
   gender disparity and, 9–10
   helping others find value in your ask and, 146
   three equivalent offers and, 142–43
Sale, Jordan, 8
sales tactics, 12, 41
"Samantha," 156–58, 160, 167–68
Samwick, Andrew, 190
Sandberg, Sheryl, 146–47
Santa narratives, 55–56
satisfaction, 6, 37, 51, 133, 148, 158–59, 200
saying no, 183–84
   first-move tactic and, 142
Scalia, Antonin, 6n
school application essays, 90
Schulman, Amy, 154–55, 158, 170–71
Schumer, Amy, 49
Schweers, Dylan, 5
science, 15–16
seat, choosing, 28
self-advocacy, 185, 196
   alpha dog and, 130–33
   backlash and, 127–29, 133
   collecting nos and, 148–51
   face-to-face meetings and, 136
   finding others to help with, 180
   finding similarities and, 137–39
   first-move tactic and, 140–42
   framed around lessons learned, 69
   getting agent for, 147–48
   helping others find value in your ask and, 145–47, 188
   mentoring and, 180
   plays to practice, 152–53
   remaining Assertive, while dialing up Warmth and, 133–35
   starting early, 135–36
   successful, 129–30
   three-offer strategy and, 142–45
self-deprecation, 76–77, 79, 81, *82*, 194
self-esteem, 78
self-promotion
   authentically strategic, 69, 179–80, *180*, 183, 185
   Black women and, 70–71
   boasting and, 69
   brag and thank tactic and, 89–90, *90*
   effectiveness of, 65–67, 84–85, 99–100
   importance of, 67–69
   learning to tell strong stories and, 67–69
   likeability and, 69–71
   need for, even with other-promotion, 98–100
   not as risky as it sounds, 69, 84–85
   other-promoters and, 98–100
   out-of-office replies and, 86–88
   outsourcing strategy for, 90–93, *93*
   practicing, 93–94
   praise and, 89
   source not remembered, 85, 99
sexual orientation, 16
Sheerin, Rachel, 86–88, 107–8, 192
Shipman, Claire, 6
shouting, 26n
shout outs, 69, 89, 117
silencing, 5
similarities, highlighting, 137–39, 152, 181
similarity-attraction effect, 137–38
sleuths, 54–56, 69, 70
small deposits, 110–16, 155
   buying coffee or lunch, 119–20
   developing your own, 115–16
   efficiency, and 116

small deposits (*cont.*)
  email introductions and, 120–25
  getting started on, 116
  giving Assertively and, 112–16
  listing favorite, 116
  mentoring and three rules for, 181–82
smiling, 30–31, 80, 105, 134, 137, 181
Smith, Jada Pinkett, 149–50
smugglers, 54, 55–56
Snap Inc. (formerly Snapchat), 69
social expectations, 57
social functioning, 22
social group sizes, 101–2
social media, 57, 69, 166n
  helping others through, 69
  mentoring and, 190, 195, 197
  name exposure and, 106
  other-promoters and, 107
  posting top tips on, 126
  shout outs and, 117
  small deposits and, 115
  storytelling and, 80, 96
  time efficiency and, 115
  writing profile for, 90–93
Sotomayor, Sonia, 6, 49
sources, self-promotion, 85, 99
speaking
  confidence conveying, 58
  fireside chats vs. formal, 141–42, 147
  quality vs. quantity and, 27n
  speech quantity and, 58
  speech rate and, 26, 30
  speech style and, 27, 42
  standing up while, 130–31
  tone of voice and, 136
speaking up, decisions about, 165–66
sponsors, 196
  mentors vs., 111
Stanford University, 6, 12, 31, 36, *82*, 83, 103, 175
"start with the end" exercises, 159–71, 186
stationery, 106
status. *See also* mentors and mentoring; self-advocacy; self-promotion; *and other specific behaviors and examples*
  Assertiveness and Warmth and, 32
  being likeable badass as key to managing, 11–13, 15–17, 21–22, 25–26, 181
  building, 13–14, 48–60, 99, 171, 175–78

  changing, across different audiences, 38–39
  compensatory impression management and, 40
  competence-likeability tightrope and, 33–34
  deciding when to risk or use, 155–71
  decisions on using, vs. hoarding, 154–59
  defined, 4–5
  demographic characteristics and, 26
  as game that can be won, 14–18
  gender disparity and, 9, 16
  "I don't want to be a 'status-seeker'" mindset, 53–56
  importance of, for women, 5–11, *7*, 36–37
  incivility suffered with lack of, 36–37
  interpersonal circumplex and, 25
  maintaining, as daily habit, 46, 48–49
  power vs., 8, 10–11, 33–39
  practices to improve, 17–18
  task cues linked to, 26–29
  telling strong story to build, 69–73
  variables influencing, 16
Stewart, Martha, 193
StockX, 13
Storey, Robynn, 90–93, 99
Storeyline Resumes, 90, 91
storytelling, 65–96. *See also* self-promotion
  actions after introductions and, 110–11
  advertising failures and, 72, 76–79
  Assertiveness and Warmth and, 67–69
  audit for, 79–84, *82*
  authentic style and, 69
  autopilot and, 79
  avenues for information sharing and, 68–69
  bad habits that weaken, 72–73, 80, *82*
  Black women and, 70–71
  brag and thank and, 89–90, *90*
  building status through, 69
  compliments or gratitude and, 74–76
  hiding successes and, 72–75, 79
  "How are you?" questions and, 94–95, *95*
  humblebragging and, 74
  importance of, 67–68
  importance of how you tell, 70–72

information you disperse and forms
  of, 67–68
low-effort strategies and, 69, 70
mentoring and, 181
"M" example and, 65–67
not as risky as it sounds, 69
noting who is hearing, 80
opportunities for, 80–81
other-promoters and, 98–100
out-of-office replies and, 86–88, *88*
outsourcing, for résumé or bio and,
  90–93, *93*
practicing, to be prepared, 93–96
replacing habits with choices and, 79
science and, 15
self-deprecation and, 76–77
situations that encourage strong vs.
  weak, 80
strategies for telling stronger, 86–96
strong, *82*
stress, 37, 185
stretch assignment, 158
Submissive-Cold quadrant, 23–24, *24*
Submissiveness, 25. *See also* Assertive-
  Submissive dimension
  Assertiveness countered by, 130–34
  default reputation and, 35
  defined, 22–23, *23*
  kicking behavior that signals, 45
  nonverbal behavior, 131
  unnecessary apologies and, 78, 84
Submissive-Warm quadrant, *24*, 33–34
subordinates, giving opportunities to
  shine, 69
successes (wins). *See also* achievements
  advertising, 69, 73–74
  hiding or downplaying, 72–74, 79, 80
  importance of talking about, 68
  imposter syndrome and, 51
  self-deprecation and, 76–77
survey with incentives experiment, 110–12
sweet, 24, 35, 37
swing thoughts, 201
systemic bias, 4

tag questions, 27
talking over people, 45
task cues, 26
  awareness practice for, 44
  dominance cues vs., 26n

powerful speech and, 27
power of, in initial interactions, 29–30
status and, 26–29
task functioning, 22–23
task performance, people subject to
  incivility and, 37
TaskRabbit, 13, 13n, 31, 58
Teach for America, 127
tech industry, 13, 46, 139
TED Talks, 7, *7*, 178, 198
texting, 113–14
thank-you notes, 116, 189, 193, 198
Thermo Electron (later Thermo Fisher
  Scientific), 162
Think Again (Grant), 84
three-offer strategy, 142–45
throwaway question strategy, 93–95, *95*
Tiedens, Larissa "Lara," 131, 176, 186–87
Tillema, Scott, 29
Time, 105n
time efficiency, 115, 144
timid, 23, 35, 45
"to-do list dodgeball," 60
transgender experiences
  assumptions of competence and, 36
  earnings and, 5
Trask, Amy, 58, 59
trustworthiness, 28
Twain, Mark, 10
12 Years a Slave (film), 51
"twenty ways to say no" list, 113, 117, 196

Uber, 152
ultramarathon, 106–7
undervalued person, 6
  standing up for, 158
uniqueness, embracing, 106–7
University of North Carolina, 9, 169
University of Pennsylvania, 12, 31, 38
update meetings, 68, 69
U.S. Supreme Court, 6

Valentine, Kathryn, 127–30, 133, 135–36,
  139, 145–46, 151–52, 181–82
value
  adding, 20–21, 188
  helping others find, in your ask and,
    145–47, 188
  inferences about potential, 25–26
  taking ownership of, 14

values, 165
verbal participation, 27, 29
Vesterlund, Lise, 60
virtual meetings, 112
volunteering, 10. *See also* small deposits
   being strategic about, 108–9, 126
   joy and, 108
   mentoring and, 186
   nonpromotable work and, 112
   as opportunity to meet new people and, 108–9
   three questions to ask before, 108–9
   unique expertise and, 108

Wall Street Journal, 152
"Walt," 68, 112
wants, identifying current, 135
Ward, William Arthur, 117
Warm-Cold (likeable) dimension, 21–25, *22*
Warmth, 30. *See also* Assertive-Warm (likeable badass) quadrant
   apologies and, 78, 84
   Assertiveness and, 11, 24–25, 40
   authenticity and, 42
   begets Warmth, 134, 181
   bragging vs. humblebragging and, 74
   chit-chat and, 137
   cues and, 137
   different ways of conveying, 22–23, *22*
   downplaying Assertiveness to be perceived as, 40
   email and, 136
   expressing disagreement and, 165–66
   eye contact and, 28
   face-to-face meetings and, 136
   first-move tactic and, 140–42
   foul language and, 31–32
   humor and, 29, 31
   initial judgments and, 33
   likeable badass and, 11, 22
   mentoring and, 181
   mimicking, 134
   multiple options strategy and, 144
   offering help and, 29
   out-of-office replies and, 88n
   practicing, 44
   self-advocacy and, 133–38
   self- vs. other-promotion and, 99–100
   similarity and, 137–39
   smiling and, 30–31
   speech style and, 27
   storytelling and, 72–73
   Submissiveness and, 24, 33–34, 36, 78
Watson, Emma, 51–52
Weingart, Laurie, 60
Wharton Business School, 84
WhatsApp, 114
"What's in it for me?," negotiations and, 145–47, 188
white men, default status and, 35
Williams Lea, 113
Winfrey, Oprah, 102
wisdom, offering, 29
withdrawal, 37
women
   being only one in room, 58
   default status and, 35
   men vs. (*see* gender disparities)
   two major disadvantages faced by, 4
women of color, 179, 195. *See also specific groups*
World Series of Poker, 38
Worthmore, 152
written name, 105–6
written notes, 106

Yale Law School, 70
Yankee, Daddy, 102
"You may not remember me, but . . . ," what to say instead of, 48n
Your Future Self (Hershfield), 159

Zuckerberg, Mark, 146

ABOUT THE AUTHOR

ALISON FRAGALE, PHD, is an associate professor and the Mary Farley Ames Lee Distinguished Scholar of Organizational Behavior at the University of North Carolina Kenan-Flagler Business School. Her scholarship has been published in the most prestigious academic journals in her field and featured in prominent media outlets such as *The Wall Street Journal, The Washington Post, Financial Times, Boston Globe,* and *Inc.* A sought-after keynote speaker and trusted advisor, she lives in Chicago with her family.

LET'S STAY FRIENDS!

The end of the book is only the beginning. . .

Visit my website to:

- find Likeable Badass resources
- connect with me on social media
- subscribe to my newsletter
- book me for an event
- and update me on your wins!

Alison
FRAGALE

AlisonFragale.com